Morality's Muddy Waters

Morality's Muddy Waters

Ethical Quandaries in Modern America

George Cotkin

PENN

University of Pennsylvania Press

Philadelphia

Published by
University of Pennsylvania Press
Philadelphia, Pennsylvania 19104-4112

Printed in the United States of America on acid-free paper
10 9 8 7 6 5 4 3 2 1

Library of Congress Cataloging-in-Publication Data
Cotkin, George
Morality's muddy waters : ethical quandaries in modern America / George Cotkin.
p. cm.
Includes bibliographical references and index.
ISBN: 978-0-8122-4227-0 (alk. paper)
1. Ethics—United States—History—20th century—Case studies. 2. Ethics—United States—History—21st century—Case studies. 3. Ethical problems—Case studies. 4. Bombing, Aerial—Moral and ethical aspects. 5. World War, 1939–1945—Moral and ethical aspects—United States. 6. My Lai Massacre, Vietnam, 1968—Moral and ethical aspects. 7. Racism—Moral and ethical aspects—United States. 8. Capital punishment—Moral and ethical aspects—United States. 9. Iraq War, 2003– —Moral and ethical aspects. 10. United States—History—1945–. I. Title.
E839 .C68 2010 *2009041294*

973.91—dc22

For My Father

Contents

Preface

The idea for this book came to me a few years ago, the evening I saw *Hotel Rwanda.* At the time I was writing a book about American cultural criticism since World War II, an engrossing and satisfying project. But the film's depiction of suffering, the moral heroism of Paul Rusesabagina, and the politics of intervention all followed me out into the suddenly uncomfortable night air. I told my wife, Marta, that I needed to write a more relevant book that would grapple with inhumanity—a work that might generate moral clarity and engagement. Marta sagely counseled me to wait a couple of weeks before abandoning my work on cultural criticism. Early the next morning, however, I was at my desk, hunched over the new project.

The book before you took several turns before it gradually attained its present form. At first, I imagined that it would be about scholars and activists—Erich Fromm, Iris Chang, Ben Kiernan, Hannah Arendt, and Robert Jay Lifton—who had devoted themselves to trying to understand and challenge the evil in the world. How could they immerse themselves in the muck of hatred without paying a price? Hadn't Nietzsche famously warned against looking into the abyss of evil, lest it engulf you? What could be learned from these figures of moral authority and their excavations of the landscape of cruelty? While such a book still needs to be written, I ended up on the more familiar ground of postwar American history, starting to wonder if moral questions are indeed answerable with any degree of certitude.

As this work emerged, I came to realize that while we must take moral stands against real evils, such stands—and especially the means we choose to defend them—can be challenged fairly by others. We do well to acknowledge potential truths in other stances, for only out of debate and process can strong moral thinking emerge. Thus, although I remain personally opposed to capital punishment, I have come to respect the position of those in favor of it. While we may never agree on the death penalty, perhaps the volume of our shouting back and forth can be lowered.

Introduction

Americans crave moral clarity. Some ponder how Jesus would act in a particular situation. Others seek guidance elsewhere on how to cultivate a moral character.[1] Even when moral clarity is presumably close at hand, we stumble. Moral strictures—thou shalt not commit adultery, honor thy mother and father, and cherish human life—become matters of testimonial adherence rather than living reality.

Of course, such strictures are invaluable as general landmarks along life's crooked trails. They are inadequate and sometimes dangerous, however, for the tough situations we often confront. Decisions are called for in moral moments when we have to choose between two less than appealing options. Act we must but the manner may be perplexingly paradoxical. Such is the nature of moral moments.[2]

Alas, we often find that even when we begin with the best of moral intentions, things go awry. Rather than questioning the paradoxes of morality or the reign of contingency (moral luck) in situations, we stubbornly ignore complexity and contradictions, determining to soldier on or to condemn a world that does not bend to our moral principles. Beyond parading our moral presumptions, we come to believe that we act more morally the less we think about it. Hence former President George W. Bush proudly proclaimed that he acted from his gut or from his religious feelings. And in the bestselling volume *Blink*, journalist Malcolm Gladwell celebrates how first impressions or inclinations are on target more often than deeper ruminations about a particular problem.[3] Listening to your instinct and acting without careful deliberation appear to be the common responses to present-day moral challenges.

Morality's Muddy Waters: Ethical Quandaries in Modern America rejects such easy certitude and argues that what we need instead is a healthy dose of befuddlement, and even when we are assured that our ends are correct and moral, as in ending a war or supporting democracy, the means to achieve them may be deeply problematic. Acceptance of the difficulty of acting morally starts us on a road toward greater moral enlightenment. It opens up the process that philosopher Hannah Arendt referred to as simply "thinking," which halts us in our tracks, makes us aware of our choices and responsibility, and strikes the chords of tragedy and irony that we need to hear more often.

Like morality itself, the very concepts we employ in discussing and acting on it—empathy, evil, and character—are essential as well as troubling. Without empathy, we fail to inhabit or even appreciate the world of others. With empathy, we sometimes perceive others' experience in a vicarious manner; we prioritize alleviating their suffering over political complexities. "Evil" gets bandied about as a meaningless epithet or rejected as a metaphysical conceit. Yet evil must remain in our moral vocabulary, for it captures much of the horror that happens, both within the world and in our hearts. Moral character, based upon virtue, is, of course, necessary; without it we are blown by the winds of social convention or peer pressure. But how well does moral virtue hold up when confronted with "moral luck," with contingencies that push and pull, that sap our moral stamina? Historical analysis of situations in modern America may help us to reenergize these concepts for moral thinking and acting.

This book is about how Americans have confronted moral issues, sometimes with swagger, sometimes with nonchalance. How have people thought about their actions in moral terms before the dust of history has settled? Were their horizons of moral contemplation cloudy or clear—and why? And how do we, after the fact, consider and debate these actions and events?

Ethics and morality have long graced the disciplines of literature and philosophy. Richard Rorty and Martha Nussbaum, for example, proclaimed that fiction cultivates our ethical or moral sensibilities. This builds upon critic Lionel Trilling's view that literature supports the moral imagination by presenting it with situations teeming with "variousness, possibility, complexity, and difficulty."[4] Nussbaum lauds literature for its ability to evoke the empathy of readers and to place action within a nest of context. True enough. But I part from her conclusion that history engages with moral problems only when it comes more to resemble fiction and thus negates its own methods.[5] To the degree that history is beholden to context, to appreciation for complexity and contingency, to paradox and irony, it partakes vigorously in the conversation about morals our culture desperately needs.[6]

This book hopes to invigorate and expand history's moral compass by pointing it in a somewhat different direction. Historians have, of course, long been devoted to moral concerns and to moral argumentation. They have, for example, charted how and why moral outrage about slavery arose at a particular moment or demonstrated how patriarchy molds moral boundaries. By reading historical analysis and narrative, we can feel empathy with the struggles of slaves, workers, women, and Native Americans against oppression and in attempting to maintain control over their lives. The study of history properly extracts moral lessons and offers us moral guideposts. We begin with these, and must clutch them fervently. The Holocaust was an abomination; the dropping of atomic bombs on Hiroshima and Nagasaki was repellent, racism is wrong, and unfortunately the list goes on. But these bold and valuable statements fail to readily yield sufficient sense of what was done—or what is to be done—in the face of competing moral claims. Too little of traditional history, no matter how compelling its morals and politics have been, has engaged with this moral muddiness. Moreover, traditional historical work has been loath to employ concepts from moral and psychological theory.[7] More needs to be done.

The particular kind of "moral turn" for history that I hope drives the narrative of *Morality's Muddy Waters* is the embrace of moral muddiness and the belief that history and moral philosophy can benefit from explicit dialogue with one another. The best in moral philosophy and ethical theory offers historians invaluable questions and concepts. Moral luck, evil as either radical or banal, empathy, just war, "dirty hands," retribution, and responsibility are a few of the key terms from these fields that inform the analysis within these pages. The pressing concerns of moral philosophy prevent us from resting comfortably on recycled historical claims. As a result, historical narratives are enriched by complexity and productive confusion. Philosophers have increasingly been using history as a preferred method for wondering about abstract concepts in concrete situations. But their work sometimes suffers from inadequate attention to context and historiographical complexity.[8] *Morality's Muddy Waters* attempts to wed history and moral philosophy as a way to consider well-known events and controversies in a new light.

In recent years, a more theoretically informed moral turn has begun in some historical work. Most of these studies focus on wartime situations, often applying the strictures of Just War theory (the claim that civilians are not proper targets, and that if they are struck, it is only when the target's importance is monumental and all efforts are made to avoid civilian casualties) for evaluative purposes. This is a critical endeavor, with nuanced conclusions sometimes advanced as a result. But Just War doctrines, however necessary as moral guidelines, offer too-rigid standards for the modern world: we need ideals; we should strive always to be more humane. In historical studies, however, it is too easy to demonstrate after the fact that the actions of a general during World War II or of soldiers in the Vietnam War were in violation of such rules.[9] History is particularly gifted at showing the shortcomings of easy conclusions and condemnations; historians present explanations for why moral absolutes are more often ignored by historical figures otherwise perceived as conventionally moral beings. The point of history is to muddy the waters of easy moral clarity rather than to confirm our own sense of moral righteousness or political persuasion.

Moral moments flow through history because history is the study of men and women acting and thinking, avoiding or confronting such moments. Of course, unlike historians, these individuals don't have the luxury of hindsight. But the study of history is wonderfully rich in its potential for capturing their moral quandaries. Crucial to this book, then, is allowing moral moments to emerge in their full confusion. We need to learn from historical situations—no less than from present-day ones—that we, like historical actors in the recent past, wander through a fog-enshrouded landscape of perplexing issues. Few targets are as evasive and ever-shifting as a moral dilemma. In this sense, the examination of moral issues, within the frame of historical narrative, helps us see how others have faced up to, or ignored, moral questions.[10]

Morality's Muddy Waters intends to help general readers and historians revisit in a new light momentous moral issues and choices in the postwar history of the United States. It is organized more or less by chronology and divided into sections dealing with wartime situations and home-front concerns. The events and controversies recounted in this book were chosen for their ability to demonstrate how particular moral decisions were made (or avoided) in specific historical moments. Thus we begin with evil as conceptualized by Hannah Arendt following World War II. Her concepts—evil as radical and banal—are tempting ways for us to confront the phenomenon of totalitarianism and to understand how otherwise unremarkable people can undertake horrible actions. As we will see, the tensions within Arendt's perspective complicate matters, albeit in a useful manner.

I move next to the path taken from saturation bombing to atomic bombing in World War II. Given the context of total war, can we with any moral assurance condemn the massive numbers of civilians killed? Does a new custom of war intrude on traditional modes of moral thinking during wartime? How did America's leaders and the public deal with moral issues during this prolonged conflict? I continue with the Vietnam War by proposing the My Lai massacre as a moral mystery, perhaps as an exemplification of evil afoot in the world, in all of its concreteness *and* impenetrability. How did My Lai happen? Do our traditional explanations for it mask a full understanding, leading us away from its radical nature and ultimate incomprehensibility?

I then turn to the home front to examine two of the most challenging moral quandaries faced by American society in the latter half of the twentieth century. The first, racism, is examined through white writer John Howard Griffin's masquerade as a black man in the Jim Crow South. This chapter's topic may seem unrelated to the previous pair of chapters that deal with the killing of civilians in wartime. But the central questions it raises about empathy and moral luck shed some light, however dim, on the potential of empathy to stop the logic of killing, or at least to show us that the faces of its victims are not so different from those of our own. The second moral quandary moves from the perspective on empathy to grapple with capital punishment and the debate over the morality of state-sanctioned killing. In the 1970s, the reinstatement of the death penalty brought the issue to the fore in American society. This chapter contextualizes the problem of capital punishment and accepts that, on a moral level, it cannot be resolved definitively. But in practice, U.S. elected officials, including former Texas governor George W. Bush, predominately failed to embrace careful moral consideration when death penalty cases were decided.

The concluding chapter brings us closer to the present in its examination of those unassociated with the conservatism of the Bush administration and generally beholden to some form of liberal politics and the moral challenge presented to them by the totalitarian dictatorship of Saddam Hussein. Given their heartfelt empathy for the suffering of Iraqis, how could they, or their nation, stand by idly? Was this bloody war in Iraq a moral imperative, a justified humanitarian intervention? Or was such moral clarity on the part of the liberals a sign of their failure to appreciate the muddy waters of the reality of Iraq?

Morality's Muddy Waters claims that the best moral decision-making occurs only after internal struggle and the recognition of bewilderment concerning means and ends. We invariably act with what Jean-Paul Sartre referred to as "dirty hands," choosing less between good and evil than between two degrees of evil, and we must therefore begin to address any moral dilemma with a firm sense of our own limitations on the stage of history.[11]

This book, then, is not about moral oughts; it is about moral ifs, ands, or buts.

In one episode of his 1970s public television series about science and culture, historian of science Jacob Bronowski visited the Nazi death camp at Auschwitz. Many in his family had been incinerated there by Nazis who were armed with the fanaticism of their own moral certitude. Bronowski ran his hands through a muddy puddle that may have contained bone fragments from his murdered relations. He stared into the camera and then pleaded with his audience to reject moral absolutism. True moral thinking, he averred, depended on openness to complexity, willingness to entertain other possibilities, and an imperative to recognize the plurality of the world. Anything less threatens to plunge us into the abyss of fanaticism or nihilism. With this recognition and awareness that moral moments are often muddied and resistant to simple rules and inclinations, we must try to act morally. In the roiling waters of choice and responsibility, our morality needs to be buoyed by humility, self-examination, and a sense of the tragic.

Chapter One
The Problems of Evil

An image in the *New York Times* in the spring of 1945 shows a crate recently discovered by American soldiers near the Nazi extermination camp at Buchenwald.[1] In it are thousands of wedding bands ripped from the fingers of victimized Jews before the Nazis exterminated them by gas, starvation, or overwork. These rings, symbols of commitment and caring, had been reduced by the Nazis to objects for their own aggrandizement. More graphic images from this time refuse to let us rest easily in the face of atrocity. Think here of the oft-reprinted pictures of bodies of dead Jews, stacked as if in woodpiles, or of emaciated Jews, among the living-dead, wondering with hollow-eyed disbelief at the miraculous nature of their own survival. A relative of mine, serving with the United States Army, was among those who liberated one of these death camps. He was shaken to the core of his being by what he had seen. It stained the remainder of his days, and he was always a bit "off," distracted, unable to sink roots.

Should we call what he witnessed evil? If so, how can we explain it? Evil strikes me as the proper term for Nazi totalitarianism, for Stalin's purges, for the genocide of too many ethnic groups since, and even for the use of conventional and atomic bombs against civilian targets during World War II. These events should be understood as evil—as affronts to our moral imagination.[2] Many of the moral moments that will be discussed in this book pivot on the hard ground of evil. But, as we shall see, even when evil is called by name, solutions to it remain clouded by ambiguity. Morality demands that we respond to evil, but it does not tell us exactly what to do. Oftentimes, various forms of evil are forced to duel with one another; we opt for the lesser of two evils, finding ourselves with "dirty hands" rather than with a clear moral victory.

Some readers may chafe at talk of evil as too tinged with religious overtones or weighted by heavy metaphysical baggage. It resists explanation and therefore obfuscates reality or explains away horror—all dangers, to be sure.

But as novelists concerned with the human condition know full well, evil is in the sinews of our existence. In Cormac McCarthy's novels, in the character of the Judge in *Blood Meridian* (1985), evil towers over the landscape, dancing and howling with delight as the rivers run blood-red. In a more contemporary setting in *No Country for Old Men* (2005), Anton Chigurh is a man devoted to his vocation of murder with a strange sense of duty and a total lack of compassion. Think, too, of the well-known character Hannibal Lecter, in Thomas Harris's novel *The Silence of the Lambs* (1988). Lecter delights in murdering and then consuming his victims. The FBI needs his brilliant mind to help them track down a serial killer. Neophyte FBI agent Clarice Starling apparently believes that psychological explanations for human behavior can reveal Lecter's essential motivations. Lecter quickly disabuses her of this notion. "Nothing happened to me, Officer Starling. *I* happened. You can't reduce me to a set of influences. You've given up good and evil for behaviorism, Officer Starling. You've got everybody in moral dignity pants—nothing is ever anybody's fault. Look at me, Officer Starling. Can you stand to say to me I'm evil? Am I evil, Officer Starling?"[3]

Philosopher Hannah Arendt had seen evil actions, and she knew that evil takes various forms. But she wavered over the years about how to conceptualize it. While the embers of the crematoria were still aglow, she set about her grim, near-ten-year task of charting and understanding the evil of her time, in the slim hope that her work might prevent its virulent reappearance. I begin with Arendt because she devoted much of her intellectual and philosophical life to tracking down this scourge, bringing it to judgment in the court of thought, and gauging its complexities.

Arendt in Germany

As a German-born Jew, twenty-six-year-old Arendt witnessed the emergence of Nazi evil. Before she devoted years to thinking about the problem of evil, she had fought it. Her Berlin apartment became a temporary stopping place for anti-Nazi activists fleeing Hitler's terror. She worked in archives to compile a list of anti-Semitic statements to document the spiraling hatred against Jews in Germany, for use at a Zionist congress to be held that summer in Prague. Then Arendt's subversive work came to a quick end. In spring 1933 she was arrested, questioned, and imprisoned for eight days. The arresting officer, however, treated her with fatherly concern: He allowed her to purchase cigarettes prior to her interrogation, and he promised to get her released. Miraculously, he did arrange for her freedom. In an interview thirty years later, Arendt recalled the police officer as a man with an "open, decent face," a "charming fellow!" However benevolent her captor, Arendt could predict her fate in Germany. Along with her mother, she quickly fled, first to Prague, then to Geneva, eventually to Paris, and finally to a permanent home in the United States in 1941.[4]

Americans Facing Evil

Arendt was hardly the only one in America after World War II to contend with the problem of evil. Popular fiction widely vetted the issue. Meyer Levin sought to confront the will to evil and its aftermath. In his bestselling novel *Compulsion* (1956), he examined the notorious case of Nathan Leopold and Richard Loeb. Two brilliant Chicago teens, Leopold and Loeb in 1924 murdered another teenager in cold blood, as a callous expression of their free will. To what degree, Levin wondered, might this will to power, this affinity with evil, be within all of us? As Levin recalled, he had even felt the tantalizing seduction of evil at one point in his life. During World War II, he realized he could rape a defenseless German woman and rationalize it away as revenge for what the Nazis had done.[5] But he chose not to.

In his later work, Levin became obsessed with Anne Frank and the murderous machinery that had condemned the young woman to death. Her purity and talent stood as a beacon, but, he cautioned, she should not become merely a naïve symbol of human goodness. Instead, we must never forget to focus on the evil that was done to her.[6]

Richard Wright, in his 1953 novel *The Outsider,* allows his protagonist, Cross Damon, a chance for a life free from tradition, morality, and commitments to others. Damon's status as a newly minted superman allows him to kill with apparent impunity and lack of regret. Freedom goes to his head, and he fails to realize, until it is too late, that it brings with it responsibilities both to oneself and to others.[7] The concept of unchecked freedom suffuses Wright's novel, but radical evil as a genetic trait comes to define another bestselling work of the period, William March's *The Bad Seed* (1954). Outwardly charming and bright, Rhoda Penmark is a child serial killer, apparently lacking any sense of limits or conscience for her actions. When her caring mother discovers that her own mother was a serial killer, she realizes her child has inherited the "bad seed."[8] This depiction of a serial killer as a sort of genetic development served as yet another explanation for radical evil. Soon after the war, in a similar manner, British historian Hugh Trevor-Roper argued that Hitler's evil was demonic, almost beyond explication, akin to a genetic anomaly, something that simply occurred.[9]

Contemporary theologian Reinhold Niebuhr pondered issues of evil, sin, and free will in almost all of his writing. He viewed human existence as tragic; men and women created evil when they chose to think of themselves as all-knowing, dominating, infinite creatures. Such hubris, such a lack of a sense of limitation, struck Niebuhr as the essence of evil.[10] As he put it in the preface to one of his many books, "Christianity's view of history is tragic insofar as it recognizes evil as an inevitable concomitant of the highest spiritual enterprises."[11] Evil came with the territory of being human, but it had to be fought at each and every turn.

In his journal *politics*, Dwight Macdonald, a free-spirited writer and close friend of Arendt, exploded with moral outrage against the evils revealed by the concentration camps and atomic bombs. Trying to comprehend the Nazi "death factories," Macdonald remarked that "reality has now caught up with Kafka's imagination." This was an apt literary allusion. In Kafka's short story *The Penal Colony*, a modern torture machine etches onto the body of the victim a history of his presumed crimes. Macdonald shivered at how he now lived in Kafka's universe, in a world run "amok."[12] The sum total of insanity and evil afoot was exacerbated by the stunning reality of the atomic bomb: no "good," he wrote, "can be extracted from the Evil" of atomic weapons. Any rationalization for the use of the bomb, Macdonald declared, "reveals how inhuman our normal life has become."[13] Our traditional ways of thinking had, quite simply, been rendered obsolete by the death camps and atomic bombs.

A new world, drenched with evil, confronted Lewis Mumford as well. A well-known urban and architectural critic, Mumford had lost a son in action in Italy during World War II. After the explosion of two atomic bombs in Japan, he became convinced that millions more sons, and perhaps the human race, would soon forfeit their lives to nuclear madness. In a series of impassioned books and essays, Mumford confronted the evil of nuclear weapons: "The end of the world," he announced, was not "apocalyptic hyperbole."[14] Barbarism, disintegration, genocide, irrationality, depravity, and nihilism, for Mumford, became the signposts of a new and frightening evil.[15] Others agreed. In such apocalyptic times, one had to struggle, lest—as Norman Cousins famously wrote in the *Saturday Review of Literature* immediately after the Hiroshima bomb had been dropped—we surrender to the conviction that "modern man is obsolete."[16]

Too often we think of the postwar years in America, when Arendt composed her work on evil, as awash in confidence and consumerism, lulled into mundane conformity by sock hops and madcap television comedy shows. Some historians have argued that the Nazi crimes against the Jews were largely absent from the consciousness of Americans during this period. Yet even in the most optimistic and upbeat books of the postwar years, evil threatens to crash the party. In the bestseller *Peace of Mind* (1948), Rabbi Joshua Loth Liebman admitted at the outset that "we are endowed with explosive energies as ruthless and amoral as the atomic bomb." He noted, too, that ours is an "age of fierce turmoil and harrowing doubts." He desperately wanted, through a combination of psychology and religion, to wean individuals away from anger, anxiety, and hatred, and to deposit them in a safe haven of happiness. Responding to the horrors of the Holocaust, Liebman based his therapeutic ideals on tolerance, love, balance, and forgiveness.[17] But more was needed. Arendt first had to excavate the ruins of Nazi totalitarianism in order to comprehend what had happened.

Writing *Origins of Totalitarianism*

Almost immediately after arriving in the United States in 1941, and for the next eight years, Arendt labored on her study of totalitarianism. In the midst of composition, she learned more about the extent of the Nazi horror. By the time she completed the work, she faced the growing specter of Senator Joseph McCarthy's fanatical anti-communist campaign.[18] Beginning in the 1930s, and continuing into the late 1940s, consideration of the new phenomenon of totalitarianism had become something of an academic cottage industry. Some of these works began when the threat of the Nazi state first appeared on the European continent; the focus of later studies shifted to understanding the nature of the Soviet state and the People's Republic of China. Such worries of course, connected to the realities of the Cold War, which, as historian Leo P. Ribuffo has remarked, "was awash in moral judgments."[19] But the historian Abbott Gleason notes in his bravura study of totalitarianism that Cold War concerns were not central to Arendt's project. She wanted to get to the heart of the matter—to grasp the whys and hows of the rise of the totalitarian state, despite its illogic and fevered madness.[20]

Arendt's *Origins of Totalitarianism* describes how changes beginning in the late nineteenth century set the stage for totalitarianism. The work has a breathtaking structure, proposing to demonstrate how anti-Semitism and imperialism, along with the decline of the nation-state, somehow became an incubus of totalitarianism. At times, the work seemed to escape the bounds of historical analysis and enter into what sociologist Philip Rieff termed a "theology of politics." Rieff recognized that Arendt's book, despite its thick shellac of historical material, was riveted on the spiritual life—the fall of humanity, the appearance of a new form of evil in the world—without a glance at any potential for redemption.

Before focusing on these thorny moral and theological issues, a brief analysis of the argument made by *The Origins of Totalitarianism* is in order. For while Arendt worked hard to present a coherent and wide-ranging historical narrative, her analysis remains confusing. Too often, she lumps together disparate entities or tosses off an ill-considered judgment. No matter how riddled with gaffes, Arendt's text remains a testament to a mind struggling to find moral bearings in a world adrift in evil.[21]

Arendt maintains that the nation-state, whatever its problems in the late nineteenth century, at least offered Jews a modicum of protection. Jews flourished by serving these states as bankers and middlemen, part of an emerging cosmopolitan bourgeoisie. But at the same time, their role in helping bring about the modern social order would paradoxically imperil them.[22] New forces had been unleashed with the development of imperialism. In a narrative that leaves numerous logical gaps, Arendt posits imperialism as having created models of exploitation and criminality that define totalitarian states. Imperialism also fed into racial doctrines that appealed to mobs and elites, especially in new forms of pan-tribalism. Finally, in the wake of the destruction of World War I and the evolution of the mob into the mass (united only by shared feelings of alienation and superfluity), totalitarian movements arose.

The allure of totalitarianism, in Arendt's view, lay in its seductive promises to the masses. By the postwar 1920s, after years of witnessing the declining value of craft skills and in the midst of financial depression, Europe's masses found themselves increasingly cut off from tradition, as well as from their traditional means of economic sustenance. Alienated, they saw in totalitarianism the direction and organic sense of place they had lost. Totalitarianism, in turn, promised to create truth out of fiction, to proclaim itself in step with the laws of History or Nature, and to parade proudly its tribalism and dreams of conquest. The appeal of fascism in part flowed from its aesthetics of power; its rituals and theatricality promoted illusions of solidarity and purpose in an otherwise chaotic world. The irony of this formulation, of course, was that the very impetus that attracted the masses to totalitarianism—their sense of superfluity and longing for order—in time would be the catalyst for its demise. But at the outset, according to Arendt, the deep allegiance demanded from the masses toward the state or leader was sufficient enticement.

Arendt borrowed ideas then current in intellectual discussions of fascism. Sigmund Freud, in much of his work from 1914 on, pondered why people were attracted to totalitarian leaders. He concluded that people yearned to be linked with the certitude and vision that such leaders projected.[23] Emil Lederer also emphasized the ability of modern dictatorships to mobilize alienated masses. He even anticipated Arendt regarding how, under totalitarianism, "independent, spontaneous social forces are destroyed." The course of the state, then, becomes "as unknown and unexpected as the mass-state itself."[24] In addition, Arendt derived part of her understanding of the psychological appeal of fascism to the masses from Erich Fromm, once a member of the Frankfurt School, equally at home with Marxism and Freudianism. In his extremely popular volume, *Escape from Freedom* (1941), Fromm argued that the decline of tradition and religion, attendant on the forces of modernity, had opened up new realms of freedom. But freedom, in his existential view, proved too heady a brew for most individuals. Retreating from the responsibility that came with such freedom, alienated masses of men and women succumbed to fascism's promise of a larger good, a sense of identity, and superiority. Freedom led those psychologically adrift and without economic resources into the hands of the forces that were opposed to true freedom and individuality.[25]

By World War II, totalitarianism had matured into the contemporary quintessence of evil. Concentration camps and grimly efficient secret police organizations maintained control and suppressed freedom, even among followers of the regime. The totalitarian hand slapped its own, as its perverted logic of domination demanded periodic cleansing of loyalists and extermination of all potential threats.[26] For those damned by the ideologues of the totalitarian state—as racial viruses, as inferior races, as political opponents, and worse—an inferno awaited. A new, absolute, and radical evil haunted the world. The appetite of this new evil for destruction and subsequent reconstruction was insatiable. According to Arendt, totalitarianism sought nothing less than "the transformation of human nature itself" (457).

Totalitarianism created "ghastly marionettes," "superfluous" men and women willing to act as either executioners or victims (455). The new totalitarian men and women, in Arendt's description, were stripped of identity and individuality. Spontaneity had been choked out of them by the cruel logic of the state apparatus (453, 455). Auschwitz survivor Primo Levi well captures this insane reality in his description of the *Muselmanner*, the "drowned" person, incarcerated in the Nazi concentration camp: "an anonymous man, continually renewed and always identical, of non-men who march and labor in silence, the divine spark dead within them, already too empty to really suffer. One hesitates to call them living: one hesitates to call their death death, in the face of which they have no fear, as they are too tired to understand."[27]

Seeking to understand and characterize this dark victory of radical evil was at the center of Arendt's theology of totalitarianism. She believed that a rupture had occurred, that traditions and ideals had been shattered by the totalitarian assault. Although she employed the term *evil* sparingly in *Origins*, its presence is felt on nearly every page of the text.

The Problems of Evil

Philosophers and writers have long sought to confront evil. Literary evocations of the Devil and evil over the centuries have included demonic figures of high allure and repugnance no less than figures that are rather slovenly and pathetic. In John Milton's *Paradise Lost* (1667), the Devil appears as the powerful, alternate face of God. Such demonic power, such motivation to destroy, transforms the Devil and evil into both a philosophical conundrum (how does the Devil exist in the face of God's absolute goodness?) and a metaphor for the complexity of the human will. Milton's Devil is more interesting than his God, choosing in the end to exult in his own evil:

> Where Joy for ever dwells: Hail horrors, hail
> Infernal world, and thou profoundest Hell
> Receive thy new Possessor: One who brings
> A mind not to be chang'd by Place or Time.
> The mind is its own place, and in itself
> Can make a Heav'n of Hell, a Hell of Heav'n . . .
> To reign is worth ambition though in Hell:
> Better to reign in Hell, than serve in Heav'n.[28]

Compare the thunderous, calculating Devil of Milton with Dostoevsky's version in *The Brothers Karamazov*. The Devil appears to Ivan Karamazov in a variety of disguises, sometimes handsome and gentlemanly, sometimes shabby, a bit down on his luck. Ivan comes to realize that rather than being all-powerful, the Devil is in part the demonic that resides in his own heart. Ivan also recognizes his own doubleness, his own power to exile the Devil, since Satan is "only one side of me."[29]

As Dostoevsky understood, evil was a thorn in the side of morality, perhaps the ultimate challenge to religious belief. The problem of theodicy posed the question: How could a perfect, beneficent, all-knowing, all-powerful God have created a world where evil is rampant? Answers, of course, conflicted, and they still do. Many philosophers and theologians defended God and faith by proclaiming the gap between man and his understanding of God's plan to be unbridgeable, an abyss never to be spanned, at least in this life. Evil was part of the mystery of creation. Others countered that evil came with God's decision to grant free will to human beings. But problems remained. Should not an all-comprehending God have foreseen the evil that men would commit? And what about problems that went beyond the individual's propensity to do and be responsible for evil—such as the death of an infant after a single breath, or the havoc caused by natural disasters such as an earthquake or hurricane? Following the Lisbon earthquake of 1775—except in the hands of tortured souls such as Dostoevsky—discussions of evil, or God's role as inherent in natural disasters, abated. For some of the more radical Enlightenment thinkers, these disasters simply proved the nonexistence of God or his relative lack of power. Most important, post-Lisbon, while the problem of evil continued to perplex thinkers, its origins were increasingly found within the hearts and mind of human beings.[30]

"The Fundamental Question"

Arendt was aware of these debates about evil, but she also knew that the question had been transformed after Auschwitz. "It was as if an abyss had opened," she later recalled. Arendt realized that she could never bridge the abyss, but she felt that she must attempt to demystify it. In a world where "the fabrication of corpses" in the killing camps had occurred, understanding must intervene to put an end to it.[31] A new form of evil required a new mode of comprehension. Arendt grasped that "the problem of evil will be the fundamental question of the postwar intellectual life."[32] She made this question her own.

A sense of her emerging ideas appears in her response to Frenchman Denis de Rougemont's fascinating book, *The Devil's Snare*, published in

1944. Rougemont's position was existential and religious in its broad outlines. He took to heart Danish philosopher Søren Kierkegaard's criticism of modernity and shared his disdain for the tepid nature of bourgeois life and beliefs. With Kierkegaard, Rougemont feared the rise of the masses as the hallmark of the neurosis and mediocrity of modern politics. Highlighting the boredom of bourgeois life and the deadening nature of reality for the masses, Rougemont described their widespread search for excitement, and how they became easy prey for the purveyors of utopian and violent visions. While Rougemont's analysis lacked Arendt's historical depth, both recognized and feared the existential alienation and loneliness besetting modern men and women. Rougemont also understood, as Arendt would hint nearly twenty years later in *Eichmann in Jerusalem*, that evil is not something external to the individual. It is something ready to emerge "under the cover of wretchedness or fatigue or some temporary disequilibrium," such as an economic depression.[33] As Rougemont phrased it, "I shall tell you where you will be most sure to find [the Devil]: *in the armchair in which you are sitting*."[34]

Arendt criticized Rougemont's theological speculations. She condemned him for a Gnosticism that posited "an eternal fight between God and the Devil" and for permitting undue metaphysical speculation to distance him from reality.[35] Rougemont's characterization of Hitler as a personification of evil made Arendt especially uneasy. While Rougemont refused to view Hitler as "outside of humanity," he saw the dictator as diabolical, acting perhaps as one of Satan's "delegates" in spreading evil in the world.[36]

Arendt, however, avoided confronting Hitler and his Nazi leadership cohort. She was at her best when trying to understand how evil appeared under particular conditions rather than as an abstract or metaphysical presence.[37] But in so doing, Arendt also intentionally missed one piece of the puzzle of evil—the demonic, monstrous expressions of evil in men such as Adolf Hitler or Joseph Stalin.[38]

Arendt readily explained how the labyrinthine bureaucracies of totalitarian states functioned, but she ignored their cult of leadership. Instead of summoning sociologist Max Weber's formulations about charisma, she sought to deflect attention from the leaders of totalitarianism. She mentioned Hitler in passing many times, but without any in-depth analysis of his larger-than-life personality and his mesmerizing appeal. She preferred to situate the success of Hitler and Stalin in their ability to master details and to control palace intrigues within the totalitarian state. In Arendt's analysis, leadership bowed to the imperatives of the totalitarian organization,"which makes it possible for [the totalitarian leader] to assume the total responsibility for all crimes committed by the elite formation of the movement *and* to claim at the same time, the honest, innocent respectability of its most naïve fellow-traveler" (375).

The danger of focusing on Hitler was that it opened up a cult of leadership that verged on the demonic. Arendt worried that viewing Hitler as a demonic presence often served as too simple an explanation for why millions worshipped him. The perils of such reductionism are aptly summed up in two accounts: Hans Frank, the especially brutal ideologue and administrator of Nazi-occupied Poland, excused his crimes by saying, "Hitler was the devil. He seduced us all." And the refugee psychiatrist Fritz Redlich attempted to explain to his wife that Hitler was "mentally ill," suffering from a "delusional paranoid disorder." (After listening to her husband's diagnosis, Redlich's wife replied simply, "Er war ein schlechter Mensch" [he was an evil person]).[39]

Some of Arendt's fellow intellectuals were willing to examine the nature of evil and how larger-than-life figures like Hitler and Stalin put their imprint on history. This was, in part, to refute Marxism's denigration of the individual in history. In their view, repositories of evil, such as Hitler and Stalin, set the agendas for the presumably banal bureaucrats to follow. The mass production, the perfection of the "industrial killing" machine in Nazi Germany, for example, at once required demonic forces (Hitler and Heinrich Himmler with their fanatical ideologies of anti-Semitism) as well as the bureaucracies willing and able to carry out their horrific initiatives.[40] As the historian Yehuda Bauer puts it, "The leadership of Hitler was crucial, because he was undoubtedly the radicalizing factor."[41] Or, as Milton Himmelfarb, editor of *Commentary* magazine, more pithily stated, "No Hitler, No Holocaust."[42]

Depicting Evil in the Camps

Arendt ignored Hitler because she was uncertain about her emerging views on the radical nature of evil. She posited Nazi evil as something strikingly modern, new in both its depth and the extent of its depravity; in many ways, it defied the imagination. While she believed she had captured the phenomenon and implications of totalitarianism, she avoided the motives of its leaders.[43] The problems with her formulation became clear to her through correspondence with German philosopher Karl Jaspers, one of Arendt's mentors and heroes. Jaspers remained in Germany during World War

II but had refused to give any aid or sustenance to the Nazi cause. Arendt wrote Jaspers that Nazi inhumanity had opened up an "abyss" in understanding, "and I don't know how we will ever get out of it." Indeed, Arendt's dilemma went beyond simple problems of morality. She began to realize the difficulty in framing the challenge of evil without falling into mysticism or metaphysics, of making evil into something resembling an aesthetic choice for "satanic greatness." If the Nazis were guilty of perverse crimes against people who were conspicuously innocent, then were traditional moral and legal categories of any value? The guilt of the Nazis "explodes the limits of the law; and that is precisely what constitutes their monstrousness."[44]

Jaspers rejected Arendt's initial tendency to view evil as radical, metaphysical, or beyond comprehension. Instead, he proposed that evil had a "prosaic triviality" rather than any taint of "satanic greatness."[45] Any "hint of myth and legend" fed into a sort of pagan idolatry of Nazi evil. While Arendt agreed with him on this point, as of the mid-1940s she was unprepared to adopt it. The memory of Nazi atrocities against humanity remained too menacing. She clung to the commonsense view that differentiates between a murderer who kills out of passion or self-interest and the Nazi machine of destruction which erects "factories to produce corpses" out of a utopian and illogical fanaticism designed to "eradicate the concept of the human being."[46] This, rather than any sense of "prosaic triviality," constituted evil in its full flowering and was what made it radical. She failed to recognize that the two notions of evil were not contradictory. Indeed, the power of her work on totalitarianism as a phenomenon and on Eichmann as an individual was that evil can be *both* radical and banal in its expression and motivation.

Arendt's discussion of radical evil in *Origins* was deeply informed by her reading of Kant.[47] Kant had set up the categories and language for subsequent considerations of the problem of evil. He viewed evil as not inherent in human nature and rejected any notion of original sin. Evil arises when the individual acts without obedience to moral law. For Kant, the key is the intention of the actor: the desire of the individual to act, or not to act, in accord with practical reason. Hence, evil is the weakness of our selfish nature, our desire to act as if we were God, which undermines our sense of limits and altruism.[48] Radical evil, in Kantian terms, "corrupts the ground of all maxims," representing something wickedly new: a "*perversity* of the heart."[49]

But Arendt's employment of the term *radical evil* differs from Kant's, as the philosopher Richard J. Bernstein explains. For Kant, radical evil constitutes man's break from the moral law; there is no sense in Kant of man choosing with full knowledge to become demonic or evil.[50] Arendt goes well beyond Kant's formulation, in part, because the mass murders in Auschwitz and elsewhere were actions that would have been incomprehensible to Kant's Enlightenment sensibility. Moreover, Arendt's view of radical evil began where Kant's left off. For Kant, evil depended on freedom, contingency, and choice. Totalitarianism had demolished these concepts, along with spontaneity. In this world, evil had assumed a new face.

Making Radical Evil Concrete

Rather than deal with evil as an abstraction, Arendt grounded it in the institutions and ideology of totalitarianism, focusing primarily on German fascism though with minimal discussion of the Holocaust. The few times she refers to firsthand accounts of the concentration camps, it is for background rather than for thick description or emotionally wrenching testimony.[51] While it is essentially true that Arendt's presentation is unsentimental, it also contains powerful metaphors. Notions such as "holes of oblivion" or the "fabrication of corpses" allow Arendt to posit the radical originality of the Holocaust and totalitarianism.[52] Firsthand accounts of concentration camp survivors appear rarely in part because few had been published at the time of her writing, but also because Arendt regarded them as too often untrustworthy, marked by a scripted rather than thoughtful engagement with the experience of evil.[53] Arguably, not one eyewitness account in *Origins* could be described as emotionally compelling.

Arendt composed *Origins* without access to the mountain of survivor and perpetrator testimonies available today or to the subsequent flood of secondary accounts. Yet, as her footnotes indicate, she had sufficient examples of survivor testimony near to hand. For instance, she knew about David Rousset's harrowing account. A fellow philosopher who had before the war taught in a French *lycée*, Rousset found himself deposited in a series of concentration camps for resistance-related activities. His memoir helped her to understand the chaos and illogic of the concentration camp as a world where "everything is possible." His account is an intimate memory of horrors experienced, described, and comprehended. Rousset pulls no punches in portraying a "world like a dead planet laden with corpses" (168).

Evil lurks everywhere in the concentration camps. Rousset describes how the Sonderkommando (special units of Jews charged with herding victims into and then removing bodies from the gas chamber), upon opening the gas chamber doors, confront a "wall of corpses, inextricably intertwined." In another passage, he relates how inmates with "a hideous hunger in their bellies," living in a confined space, "will massacre each other for a half an ounce of bread, for a bit of elbow room" (60–61). In this "monstrous" world, guards are "posted over the dead" and "with orders to kill those [inmates] who eat the scrawny, fetid flesh of the cadavers" (40).

Rousset was the philosopher returned from hell; and he rejected the narrative and conceptual constraints favored by Arendt. In her political philosophy, Arendt always celebrated pluralism ("Plurality is the law of the earth"), the variety of viewpoints engaging one another in a cosmopolitan world of stirring openness.[54] But in her work Arendt never sufficiently confronted the voices of the victims except in an abstract, analytical manner. If she had, she might have been able to join her analysis with a true rendering of the world of the concentration camp. As theorist Elaine Scarry points out, to do this is to hear the screams of the survivors (even if those screams cannot have "referential" content) and, as Susan Sontag came to realize, to put images of hell in context.[55]

Yet Arendt manages to build her own powerful sense of evil. She recognized totalitarian evil as something radically new in history, a manic, self-sustaining attack against humanity. She tellingly borrowed a phrase from Rousset, finding that in the hermetic world of the concentration camp, totalitarian regimes seek to realize their dream that "everything is possible." Here, behind the barbed wire and the crematoria, they aligned and rationalized themselves through the deterministic forces of History and Nature (433). The danger of such identifications, or of revolutionary virtue without limitations, became a key theme of Arendt's *On Revolution* (1963). As she writes there, "The evil of Robespierre's virtue was that it did not accept any limitations."[56] Totalitarianism's fanatical visions of personal, philosophical, and natural necessity made human beings superfluous, as it had the Jews. Its perverted logic applied to the Nazis themselves, hence the *Götterdämmerung* central to their apocalyptic vision. Erasure of the Jews began with minor, often absurd sanctions designed to erode their legal and political rights as individuals, as well as their identities as Germans.[57] Once stripped of their rights and identity, bereft of connection to the nation or polity, the superfluous person is tossed easily into the concentration camp, that "terrible abyss that separates the world of the living from that of the living dead" (441).

Totalitarian evil relentlessly works to obliterate all traces of its victims from history.[58] In the whirlwind of Nazi fanaticism and ideology, Jews were stripped of connection to the familiar objects of everyday life, beginning with jobs, wealth, political rights, and homes. Ultimately, their few connecting threads to the past—photographs, lockets, and rings—were ripped from them on entry into the concentration camp. Arendt compellingly stated, "Like the new type of murderer who kills his victims for no special purpose of self-interest, we may not be aware that anybody has been murdered at all if, for all practical purposes, he did not exist before" (434).

Conditions in the camps—the grinding cruelty and administrative irrationality—eroded the prisoner's essence of being an individual with ties to a group or tradition; all that the individual could think about was survival. "The excremental assault," as Terrence Des Pres has well phrased it, furthers the humiliation and distance between one's former self and the hell in which one suddenly exists. Without access to toilets, forced to soil oneself or to be in close contact with the excrement of others, the prisoner is helpless as the veneer of civilization is stripped away.[59] The past is gone, covered with shit. Like the powers in Orwell's chilling *Nineteen Eighty-Four* (1949), totalitarians seek to control the future, in part, by securing the past. The totalitarian need to rewrite history, especially as evidenced by the Soviet desire for confession on the part of its victims, is central for Arendt. Through confession, the individual—even if innocent—in "reality" accepts the call of the Party "to play the role of the criminal," thus becoming in effect "objectively . . . the enemy of the Party" and confirming the original charges lodged against him or her.[60]

In this totalitarian nightmare the very foundations that make moral judgment and historical truth possible are destroyed. For Arendt believed morality was in short supply in the concentration camps; their machinery ran with a perverse efficiency as a new, abiding rule of order. Her concern was more with the immorality of the perpetrators rather than the morality of its victims. Here Arendt proves more insightful about the camps' overarching logic and less willing to judge the inmates than her fellow survivor and contemporary, Austrian-born psychologist Bruno Bettelheim.[61] As a resolute secularist, Arendt maintains that the notion of a God-given, biblical morality had been banished by the forces of modernity and the horrors recently unleashed. Arendt, when faced with the bloodthirsty and irrational nature of totalitarianism, could neither retreat into a view of history with a happy face of progress nor find the power of the Ten Commandments compelling. No longer could the myths of Judeo-Christianity, in her view, secure authority and obedience. Beyond the decimation of religious ideals, Arendt argued that totalitarianism had sent "three thousand years of Western Civilization" "toppling down over our heads." In its radical lunacy, its fantastical view of the world, its rejection of rationality and of all "implied beliefs, traditions, standards of judgment," the totalitarian machine, in effect, had ended the traditional conversation of philosophy and morality (434). Arendt no doubt agreed with survivor Primo Levi's famous observation, "there is Auschwitz, so there cannot be God."[62]

The Burden of Her Time

In her darkest moments, reflecting on totalitarianism as "the burden of our time," Arendt fell into her own hole of interpretive "oblivion."[63] Accept for the sake of argument her conclusion that totalitarian evil was radical—a form of terror previously unknown and unimagined in human history. The evil of crucifixions, the crusades, slavery, pogroms—the list is endless—pales in the face of modern totalitarian evils, as Arendt realized. At least with past evils, as she understood them, there was logic and self-interest at the core of the crimes. Totalitarian evil upheld an ideal of transformation but was essentially aimless and ineffable in its logic. Totalitarianism's "perverted will" (457–459) had transported it "beyond good and evil," in the least sympathetic reading imaginable of Nietzsche's terms.

Arendt thus painted herself into a narrow corner. If the crimes of totalitarianism were as original and immense as she averred, then could they be anything other than demonic? She never hesitated to describe them throughout *The Origins of Totalitarianism* and elsewhere as "monstrous." But to use the term *demonic* would be to situate evil as mysterious, perhaps outside the realm of rational explication and the march of worldly events. The demonic resisted laws of nature and the wills of men. Even strong structures of representative democracy and public debate, it seemed, were futile against a demonic entity. Such was clearly not Arendt's intent. Arendt was onto something when she remarked on the mysterious nature of evil as something not "humanly understandable." Everything need not be understandable, but it could be interpreted in more or less convincing fashion. And radical evil, despite her best attempts, seemed to slip through her interpretive structure. Arendt's frustrations grew just after publication of the book, when she admitted, "What radical evil is I don't know."[64] Quite an admission from the leading chronicler of the phenomenon of evil.

This doubt became painfully apparent in the conclusions she fashioned, and refashioned, for the various editions of *Origins*. In the first edition, her "Concluding Remarks" emphasized the power of ideologies to harm, the reality of superfluous men, and how the concentration camps, only recently dismantled in Germany but still populating the Soviet Union, remained an affront to the human condition.[65] The stakes were high. "Crimes against humanity have become a kind of specialty of totalitarian regimes" (437). The answer to this deadly, "crushing" challenge was contained in the final three pages of her conclusion. Anticipating the pluralism that would inform her later work, especially *The Human Condition* (1958), Arendt called for human rights predicated not on abstract notions of historical or natural basis, but on her ideal of "human plurality." She urged structures of "human community" that would guarantee human rights.

In the revised edition of *Origins* published in 1958 and reissued in 1966, the "Concluding Remarks" had been replaced by a chapter entitled "Ideology and Terror," hardly a promising starting place for solving the problem of totalitarianism. The best Arendt could do in this new conclusion was to posit a Hegelian movement of history that contained its own dialectic, an overcoming of itself with the possibility of a higher resolution of conflicts. Arendt found hope in that "every end in history necessarily contains a new beginning; this new beginning is the promise, the only 'message' which the end can ever produce" (478–479). The gist of this message was that man possessed a "supreme capacity" for freedom. Such hope seemed paltry in the face of Arendt's demonstration throughout her book that the modern world had demolished communities, created rootless people, and trampled on freedoms. Of course, Arendt was speaking from deep personal experience. She had been a stateless, rootless person for much of the 1930s and 1940s. She knew that a sense of belonging, of feeling part of a community, of participating in the polis were the structures that made for a fulfilling life.[66]

Banality of Evil

The trial of Adolf Eichmann in 1961 for his participation in the murder of millions of Jews afforded Arendt the opportunity to revise her conceptual understanding of evil. In June 1960, Arendt told her friend the writer Mary McCarthy that she was "half toying" with getting a commission to cover the trial.[67] Much to her delight, the *New Yorker* assigned Arendt the story. The Eichmann trial loomed in significance. "The Eichmann trial has us all stirred up," she wrote to Jaspers. "It will, in its totality, become a major symbol of the life of the mind today."[68]

Arendt helped to make Eichmann into a "major symbol" for the conceptualization of "the banality of evil"—which she employed as the subtitle to her controversial and important book, *Eichmann in Jerusalem*. If nothing else, the work helped to usher in an era of Holocaust awareness.[69] Yet many readers felt that she had belittled Eichmann's responsibility as a leading Nazi war criminal and that her "banality of evil" thesis downplayed the monstrous nature of the evil that had been perpetrated on the Jews. Marie Syrkin, a critic and advocate for Jewish causes, denounced Arendt for making the victims of the Nazis look worse than the Nazis themselves.[70] After reading Judge Michael A. Musmanno's unfavorable book review of *Eichmann in Jerusalem*, J. Baron wrote to express revulsion at the visage of Arendt that had appeared in the newspaper—"a face hard as rock and cold as ice in the North Pole." Such ire came because the review had convinced Baron that Arendt's book "desecrated" the Jewish dead. Baron hoped that these dead souls "will swarm around you day and night; they will give you no rest."[71] In slightly less jarring language, critic Norman Podhoretz, a onetime friend of Arendt's, condemned her "manipulation of the evidence" and her "perversity of brilliance."[72]

Why such vituperation? First, in several places in the book Arendt condemned certain Jewish officials for cooperating with the Nazis. From Arendt's perspective, excuses were impermissible; she found these individuals guilty of speeding along the Nazi death machine.[73] Second, Arendt's notion of the "banality of evil" struck many as a rather imprecise term, suggesting that the motivations of some Nazis might not have been quite as horrendous as presumed. Yet, in *Eichmann in Jerusalem*, Arendt had finally achieved her aim of revising her conception of radical evil as it had appeared twelve years earlier in *Origins*. By presenting Eichmann as a relatively innocuous fellow, a dedicated bureaucrat, and a man without independence of mind, she had confronted evil and found it, well, less than demonic. That it could be both demonic and radical, in various manifestations, however, eluded her.

If the problem of evil when radical was that it took on demonic proportions that appeared difficult to counter, then the problem with "the banality of evil" thesis was that evil was now ubiquitous. "Therein lies the horror," wrote Arendt, "and at the same time, the banality of evil."[74] Even if evil did not beat in the heart of every mindless bureaucrat, the upshot of Arendt's analysis for many was that under certain conditions, individuals might well act no differently than had Eichmann. The solution to this new face of evil seemed to be an imperative to think, to live an active life of the mind, so that when the individual confronted momentous moral choices, such a confrontation would include "mature consideration."[75]

Eichmann's Mind as an Open Desk

Arendt's presentation of Eichmann was consistently harsh and ironic. He was a mere functionary, a man without qualities. She found him a startlingly "normal" or "average" man (26). However, when she first contemplated covering the trial, Arendt had described Eichmann as "the most intelligent of the lot" of Nazis.[76] As the trial progressed and she waded through the testimony, she concluded that Eichmann "was a buffoon." It was all she could do to control her laughter as she read the transcript of his interrogation.[77] Most significant, Arendt argued that Eichmann was no fanatic, lacking even a hint of "insane hatred of Jews" or of ideological indoctrination (26, 36). A careerist, comfortable in the womb of the bureaucracy, Eichmann was like the individual Arendt had described in an early essay, "Organized Guilt and Universal Responsibility" (1945): a man concerned with his family, fearful of unemployment, willing to follow orders, and comfortable in self-deception. However Eichmann, Arendt admitted, had some useful qualifications: he was an excellent organizer and negotiator (45).

Arendt imagined how Eichmann had compartmentalized his life, practiced self-deception, and denied playing any role in the killing of Jews. In some ways, Arendt presented Eichmann as the apotheosis of the parvenu, the newcomer to power, the person who wears bourgeois garments in the gaudiest of fashions. Arendt liked to see herself as the natural enemy of the weak *Spiessburger* (the affected, ceremonious bourgeoisie), reviling him and those of his ilk.[78] In addition, and in keeping with his bourgeois nature, Eichmann simply followed orders, efficiently moving along the trains, albeit with their human cargo. He perfectly exemplified the man doing his job, compartmentalized within the bureaucracy, unwilling to peer too closely at what was actually transpiring. After reading Arendt's account, New York intellectual Lionel Abel contended that Eichmann appeared as nothing more than "an utterly replaceable instrument . . . a mere cog in the machine" of the bureaucracy of murder.[79]

Arendt recorded faithfully the times when Eichmann had bumped up directly against the Holocaust. He had often visited Auschwitz, but its eighteen square miles presumably allowed him to avoid seeing the places where the killing occurred. He had, however, witnessed on the eastern front the mobile gas vans that were used to execute Jews. Eichmann protested, however, that "I hardly looked. I could not." It "upset" him too much (89). He retreated back into his sense of duty and loyalty to Hitler, and to the shuffling of papers.

This is not to suggest for a moment that Arendt excused Eichmann of responsibility for crimes against humanity or that she doubted that he deserved to be hanged. He had acted in an evil manner, even if his intention was without evil. The world was a better place for its refusal to exist alongside him. Yet the harrowing point was that Eichmann had been a banal man capable of doing great evil. How could he have done this and lived with himself? At the trial, Eichmann invoked a close-to-the text description of Kant's categorical imperative in his defense, claiming that he was following the moral law (as laid down by the Führer). This seemed sufficient to ease his mind and shrug off his own culpability. Alas, Eichmann missed the essential point. For Arendt, and for Kant, the point was that the individual chose, and could do so only through the act of thinking. In order to act responsibly, one had to think in terms larger than oneself or blind devotion to someone like Hitler, who was clearly not aligned with the moral order (22, 49).

Missing the "Real" Eichmann

The problem with Arendt's depiction of Eichmann is that she greatly misconceived the man and his milieu. The notion that such a mediocre fellow as Eichmann could rise so high in the echelon of the Nazi killing machine strained credulity, as did her seconding of Eichmann's contention that he was ideologically naïve or disinterested. "What is most striking in Miss Arendt's picture of Eichmann," wrote Lionel Abel, "is her omission of any reference to the man's ideology."[80] Thanks to the painstaking research of David Cesarani and Yaacov Lozowick, a different picture of Eichmann emerges. Eichmann joined the evil collusion of Nazi planners early and enthusiastically by finding creative solutions for killing millions of Jews as efficiently and cheaply as possible.[81] As Cesarani phrases it, Eichmann "was a knowing and willing accomplice to genocide." He made choices. He knew what he was doing. And, at the same time, he evolved into a person willing and able to engage in genocide. Nor, of course, was there anything banal about the results of his actions: the deaths of millions.[82]

Arendt also contradicted herself in her understanding of Eichmann as a banal civil servant, someone blindly and loyally following orders. As Albert Breton and Ronald Wintrobe have indicated, the Nazi murder machine was an immense bureaucracy. In order to rise to a central position, as had Eichmann, one had to master a labyrinth of intrigue and compete with other sectors that were always seeking to increase their own power and authority.

In such a competitive environment, Eichmann's emergence meant that he was not only a brilliant player, but also a dedicated one.[83] In *Origins* Arendt had devoted many insightful pages to the bizarre Nazi bureaucracy with its multiplication of offices, vague orders, power struggles, and constantly shifting authority (399–420). She reiterated, albeit more briefly, this same understanding in *Eichmann in Jerusalem*, finding "fierce competition" in the bureaucracy. Clearly, her image of Eichmann as a rather normal, banal individual failed to connect with his rather stunning success in the Nazi killing machine's bureaucracy.

Why, then, did Arendt get so much wrong, and yet so much right, about Eichmann and evil? While she made great strides in adopting the concept of the banality of evil to make it work in this particular situation, she had to shoehorn Eichmann into it. In fact, Eichmann may have been many things, but he was not an ideologically impotent bureaucrat. She was correct, however, in bringing evil down to a concrete level as it might appear in the figure of the typical unthinking bureaucrat. Had Eichmann possessed the capacity of strenuous thought, of confronting moral choices, then he might have been less prone to follow orders. And he certainly proved incapable, or unwilling, to practice empathy.

Evaluating Banality

Arendt correctly identified an important reality of "the banality of evil." The new conception, even if it risked becoming merely a "catchword," as Gershom Scholem averred, did some heavy lifting for Arendt.[84] First, it allowed her to move away from her earlier conception of "radical evil" in its demonic aspects. Second, it did not require that she make a clean break with her earlier thoughts in *Origins*. By the 1960s, it became popularized as a way for opponents of the Vietnam War and other conflicts to explain how bureaucratic logic functioned. Among New Leftists, Arendt's "banality of evil" concept demonstrated how easy it was for normal citizens to contribute to the daily functioning of the war machinery, to lose awareness of how they fit into a logic of destruction.[85]

By underplaying ideology and fanaticism in *Eichmann in Jerusalem*, Arendt was moving toward the then-current view that the age of ideologies had ended. Certainly, such a perception would have placed Arendt and her work within the context of the Cold War, distancing her analysis from economic and ideological issues and tilting toward personality and character studies.[86] In Arendt's understanding of social evolution, we enter into the age of bureaucracy and conformism. Hence, Arendt's Eichmann became a case study of how an unthinking individual exercised power within the womb of bureaucratic normality.

But Arendt's analysis had too many gaps. How, after all, did unthinking, normal individuals get into this situation of becoming unthinking, bureaucratic killers? Or had they always been lacking in thoughtfulness? One response, consistent with Arendt's general views, would have been that anyone might succumb to careerism or become a cog in the machine. Yet Arendt attempted to distance herself from this formulation for the same reason that an emphasis on the demonic was less than useful to her. It excused too much. If everyone was an Eichmann, then the particularity of Eichmann and the usefulness of the concept became worthless by over-application. The furthest Arendt was willing to go was to note that, under certain conditions, most people might act as had Eichmann. If so, then why had Eichmann acted in this manner? For all of the pages Arendt spent examining the man, she did not come to understand him. Perhaps such motives must be ineffable, or banal. But, in the case of Eichmann, they must also bear witness to the force of the demonic, of the specter of evil afoot in the world.

The power of Arendt's analysis of each species of evil is apparent. She did not need to break from radical to banal. They can, and do, coexist. Most important, both conceptualizations of evil are valuable tools for analyzing the horrendous events that pockmark our history.

What Is to Be Done?

In some of her later essays, composed in the mid-1960s and 1970s, Arendt examined how to combat the banality of evil. Conformity and going along with the crowd, blind obedience, and simple amorality were becoming inscribed in modern culture. Eichmann embodied all these tendencies, but he was condemned especially for his rank "thoughtlessness."[87] The antidote for this, according to Arendt, was the ability of mind, engaged in the action of thought. She wondered and hoped about how "the activity of thinking as such" might "be among the conditions that make men abstain from evil-doing or even actually 'condition' them against it."[88]

Little can be done to stem radical evil because it bursts the bonds of precedent, expectation, and often explanation. Certainly, as noted earlier, Arendt avoided confronting Hitler and other individual citadels of radical evil. She eschewed a deep analysis of what Holocaust historian Saul Friedlander has called, "the psychology of the perpetrators."[89] Once such evil manifests itself—in Hitler, Stalin, Pol Pot, and their political movements—then it simply has to be combated. How, of course, remains an open and perplexing problem, as we shall see in subsequent chapters. But at least the beast has been identified and a will arises to bring it to heel, if only for the moment. Given Arendt's tragic sensibility, this was perhaps all she could expect.

With evil as banality, as the unwillingness to think about what one is doing, Arendt's analysis proved both enlightening and frustrating. She makes a convincing case for the power of thinking and of conscience. Once we allow the "wind of thought" to breeze into our minds, action comes to a halt.[90] Thought of this type might stop us from committing acts of evil which, in a certain context, appear to be perfectly reasonable—indeed, even mandated by the power and prestige of the state.

Arendt proposes that banal evil be confronted with serious self-dialogue. The individual must follow the path already laid out by thinkers such as Socrates, Plato, and Nietzsche. When we think, Arendt posited, in agreement with Nietzsche, we shatter idols, topple clichés, and expose moral rationalizations (103). In effect, we lay bare our souls. At the same time, the inner dialogue exceeds its boundaries as we engage others, "invoking and weighing silently the judgments of others" (142). The process of engaging in thought is dangerous, for it forces truths that we might want to ignore to come to the surface. Arendt does not believe that moral truths are innate, something that is repressed in the face of political and personal pressure. Nor does she claim that there is such a thing as human nature that upholds higher values. Rather, thinking seems to open the individual up to a plurality of perspectives, to make the individual aware of how his or her actions affect others. This is a form of empathetic understanding, intellectual as much as it is emotional.[91] And in the act of thinking, we pass judgment not simply on others, but on ourselves. We decide, in essence, whether the person we are becoming is the type of person with whom we want to live. If we come to that realization, then we assume our moral responsibility. Even if we cannot, at a certain point, strenuously oppose the powers that be, we can—as did Arendt's mentor Karl Jaspers—choose to withdraw or refuse to participate in the madness (34).

Yet Arendt's notion of the anodyne of thinking is also frustrating because we are left with the problem of an Eichmann. As for so many of his ilk, Eichmann was simply more comfortable and content in the cocoon of cliché, thoughtlessness, stereotype, avoidance, and compartmentalization. While thinking might have influenced him to desist, how do you get someone like Eichmann or other villains of banality to engage in the process?

For Arendt a rules-based, deep-to-the bone learned system of morality was unproductive, especially for individuals like Eichmann. His problem was that he was such a stickler for rules. Like many others searching for absolutes, pining for guidance and a sense of community, Eichmann easily adapted to what was, in effect, a "complete reversal of legality" as engineered by Hitler and the Nazi system. This meant that Eichmann now "acted under conditions in which every moral act was illegal and every legal act was now a crime" (40–41). Under the old Weimar political order, Eichmann might have flourished as a bureaucrat in charge of coordinating train schedules for the movement of livestock to markets. In Nazi Germany, Eichmann triumphed in arranging for the transport of Jews to their extermination hubs. He simply acceded to the "new order" of moral priorities (41). Genocide, for Eichmann, was a legal commandment. It was no less exacting on his sense of responsibility than the biblical injunction that thou shalt not kill.

Eichmann and others did not jettison the entirety of moral values. Rather they constructed a new view that incorporated values—at least in an abstract sense—from the old system. Eichmann made much of the fact that he avoided involvement in any killing and that he could not tolerate cruelty (42). Rudolf Hoess, commandant at the Auschwitz death camp, proclaimed: "I myself never maltreated a prisoner, far less killed one. Nor have I ever tolerated maltreatment by my subordinates." In such fashion, the reality of commanding an institution dedicated to the extermination of innocent men, women, and children becomes a testament to one's moral fiber and essential humanity.[92] Within such a psychology, where would the act of thinking enter?

Eichmann was hardly alone in his willingness to act in a way that seemed to constitute a transformation of established values. Doctors in Nazi Germany who had sworn to cherish human life soon became destroyers of it. Nazi ideology's transformation of values, entwined with bureaucratic imperatives and the instinct for professional survival, made many doctors willing executioners and nefarious experimenters. Whereas they had once viewed themselves as battling the diseases that afflicted humanity, Nazi doctors now viewed their actions as fighting the virus of Jews. These doctors soon became part of the Nazi killing machine in the concentration camps. They chose who would live and die, and helped to deceive the Red Cross about exterminations in the camp. One inmate in the prison camps noted that the Nazi doctors, whatever initial qualms they might have had about their role, soon settled into their new routines, viewing it as their "normal duty." In Auschwitz, according to one survivor, doctors "felt no compunction about sending people into the gas."[93]

Indeed, the weight of moral considerations was undermined by the very process of extermination. Jews traveled to concentration camps crammed into cattle cars. Ventilation was minimal, sanitary conditions were abominable, starvation and thirst unbearable. By the time they arrived at their destination, after days of sleeplessness, covered by filth and excrement, these Jews seemed to fulfill the Nazi ideological image of their sub-humanity.[94] Such dehumanization made the killing process easier. Franz Stangl, commandant at Treblinka, was a conventionally religious man and not a sadist. He spoke of these Jews as "cargo," resembling cattle being brought to the slaughterhouse.[95] Did Stangl think of what was happening? At times, yes. But at the same time, he compartmentalized these thoughts, worried about his family, demanded of himself that he do his appointed job as best he could, or dulled himself with drink.

In Nazi Germany, as in most totalitarian regimes, there was no premium placed on thinking or wider knowledge of what was going on. Indeed, the point for many was to avoid being aware of the horrors that surrounded them. As one German later put it, there was "danger in knowledge." Hitler crony and armaments minister Albert Speer stated, "I was blind by choice." With other Germans, Speer believed, "we saw only what we wanted to see and knew only what we wanted to know."[96] Nazis practiced a willed ignorance, according to Stangl, as "a matter of survival."[97]

Would Arendt, then, claim that the Nazi doctors, and men such as Stangl, Speer, and even her one-time adviser and soul-mate, philosopher Martin Heidegger, were capable of thinking their way out of the morass of self-deception, avoidance, compartmentalization, and rationalization?[98] Certainly, at moments, they flirted with serious self-examination, but such personal interrogation does not exist in a vacuum. It is caught up in contending ideals and realities, sometimes emotional, sometimes intellectual, and sometimes calculatingly self-aggrandizing. Perhaps if they had engaged in thinking before they were knee-deep in the morass of the killing regime, they might have been able to escape sinking in deeper. Perhaps.

Arendt's concept of thinking as a way to avoid committing banal evil remains valuable. As we shall see in subsequent chapters, the process of thinking in Arendtian terms is often halted or rendered ineffectual by circumstances of the moment. Rather than demeaning the importance of the process, it only highlights how necessary it is that we think about our actions, judge them, and worry that the person we are becoming, through our actions, may not be the person we want to be. Such self-examination is, alas, hard and infrequent. That only makes it more important for us to seize every opportunity we have for it.

PART I

In Times of War

Chapter Two
A Sky That Never Cared Less

Growing Accustomed to the Evils of War

Hannah Arendt prophesied in 1945 that "the problem of evil" would haunt the postwar era. She anticipated that her conceptualization of evil as radical, and later as banal, would help the postwar generation understand and confront totalitarian evil. Arendt was silent, however, on how total wars created a perfect landscape for unhindered evil. She ignored how, in World War II—and earlier, during the Napoleonic conflicts and World War I—the distinction between combatant and civilian became blurred at best and meaningless at worst.[1] Theorists of evil would need to ponder hard about how the widespread bombing of civilians—whether intended to destroy productive capacity, wreak vengeance, or undermine morale, and thereby bring about an earlier end to conflict—represented a new form of evil in the world. Even if the killing of civilians by bombing was an evil, was it sanctioned by its being an increasingly accepted custom of war?

This chapter navigates the muddy waters surrounding the bombing of civilian targets during World War II. It circles back and forth to determine how moral moments are confronted and avoided during wartime. Was the Doolittle bombing raid on Tokyo exemplary of justified bombing of a civilian center? Could the use of poison gas actually be morally humane in a specific, limited wartime situation? Here we will ponder whether the dropping of atomic bombs on Hiroshima and Nagasaki, within the context of the war, was perceived by American leaders as continuous with or as a break from previous bombings. This investigation attempts to get into the minds of American decision makers to gauge how they came to their judgments, to ask if such decisions were made without much consideration of moral implications. Finally, this chapter looks at the issue of moral responsibility on the part of politicians and scientists (especially J. Robert Oppenheimer) regarding the use of atomic weapons. The answers supplied are few; the quandaries are multiple. Such is the nature of moral history examined in this chapter.

For some analysts the morality of killing civilians in wartime is clear. According to Just War theorists, the intentional bombing of civilian targets is immoral. Civilians may be harmed only when a specific target's value for bombing is sufficiently important; civilian deaths in such scenarios must be unintended and proportionate to the target. Other Just War theorists, such as Michael Walzer, accept this definition but use it a bit more flexibly under conditions of "supreme emergency." Such was the case for Britain in the dark, early days of World War II, when the British bombing of German cities as the only available means to pursue war against the Nazis and raise morale at home was an understandable, if still not morally sanctioned, response.[2] But is modern warfare oblivious to such distinctions and concerns?

Would the horrendous bombing of civilians in World War II, while immoral, have been inevitable nonetheless? Might may not make right, but does frequency of a practice make for normality? Will nations use whatever means are available so long as they are convinced these means will hasten the end of the conflict? If so, then is it a chimera to hope for more humane and just warfare? Or are there moral moments, even in modern, total war, when choices are made and paths are not taken that might lead to acts that are immoral? Finally, might the only solution be—as some argued with regard to the dropping of the atomic bomb—that we must prevent wars from happening so that the low standards of civilian immunity in the waging of total war will not be unleashed on future generations?

War Begins

Just before 3 A.M. on 1 September 1939, a ringing telephone jarred President Franklin D. Roosevelt from his sleep. Ambassador William Bullitt was calling from Paris to alert the president that Germany had invaded Poland hours earlier, an act that was certain to initiate World War II. "Well, Bill," said Roosevelt, "it has come at last. God help us all."[3] Although Roosevelt had been, and would continue, working assiduously to aid Britain's war effort, he had to this point not committed America to intervention in the conflict. That came two years later when the Japanese attacked Pearl Harbor on 7 December 1941.

Beginning in the mid-1930s, battles raged in Europe, North Africa, and China that presaged the widespread killing of civilians during World War

II. In the Spanish Civil War, with Japanese abuses in China, and in the Italian bombings in Ethiopia, attacking forces had employed fighter planes and bombers to destroy civilian centers. Guernica, an undefended Basque city, was ravaged on 26 April 1937, when at least thirty-five tons of bombs and incendiary devices were dropped by German Condor planes. An estimated 1,500 civilians died. The destruction of this ancient city quickly came to figure in the minds of many as a frightening emblem of total warfare.[4] Such bombing had, as the poet W. H. Auden expressed it soon after the event, "sprung the trap of Hell."[5] In December 1937, Japanese soldiers unleashed an orgy of destruction in Nanking. Before the horror had ended, approximately 300,000 civilians had been killed; many thousands of women were raped and tortured. Civilians were now, apparently, primary targets.[6]

Willingness to kill civilians quickly emerged as a normal means for waging modern war. Its rationalization developed following World War I, when some military theorists paradoxically praised attacks on unarmed civilians as humanitarian. The Italian military theorist Giulio Douhet posited that, given the horrendous toll of trench-war stalemate during the war, vicious and concentrated attacks on civilian centers might quickly bring a nation to chaos, sap morale, and cause leaders to sue for a speedy peace.[7] The quicker the end of the war, no matter how bloody for civilians, the lower the total of overall casualties. But this soon proved a bloody fantasy of misplaced moral logic. Armed with doctrines of total war, the Axis powers, soon to be emulated by the Allies, pummeled civilian populations.

Anticipating the worst in September 1941, President Roosevelt attempted to return the genie of civilian destruction to its bottle. His message—one he would repeat numerous times in the coming months—implored the warring powers to spare civilians from harm. Roosevelt did not anchor his concerns in a rich legacy of Just War theory, in Kantian ethical demands that people not be treated as a means to an end, or in the numerous peace conventions regarding how wars should be waged. He did consider himself "a Christian and a Democrat," however, and he was sincerely dismayed by high civilian casualties, at least at the outset of the war.[8] He lectured the governments of France, Germany, Italy, Poland, and Britain that the bombing of civilians was a "form of inhuman barbarism." Citing military actions in Guernica and elsewhere, Roosevelt bemoaned how the bombing of civilians "sickened the hearts of every civilized man and woman, and . . . profoundly shocked the conscience of humanity." He wanted his "urgent appeal" to the nations at war to result in their declaring that they would "in no event, and under no circumstances, undertake the bombardment of civilian populations or of unfortified cities." The rigor of this demand, however, was diminished by what followed: "upon the understanding that these same rules of warfare will be scrupulously observed by all of their opponents."[9]

Hitler immediately agreed to the principles, informing Roosevelt that he had instructed German forces to refrain from any attacks on Polish civilians. British Foreign Secretary Lord Halifax replied with perhaps more candor: "All war must of necessity be a brutal bloody business." While previous attempts to restrain attacks on civilians had usually proved futile, Halifax pledged his government to seek "to protect the civilian population."[10] Such promises were wobbly. Hitler and Halifax both seized on Roosevelt's disclaimer that if one belligerent attacked civilians, then the other party had the right to reply in kind.

Despite Hitler's verbal agreement, his warplanes continued strafing cities in Poland and killing civilians. German bombers on 3 September 1939, hit an apartment complex in Warsaw, killing twenty-one and wounding thirty. It was unclear whether the building was an intentional target, but a headline the next day in the *New York Times* decried the attack: "Poles Charge Aerial Gas Attacks on Cities As Germany Agrees to 'Humanize' the War."[11] Hitler proceeded to exact a heavy toll on the Polish resistance. He dismissed the Poles as "animals" deserving "the harshest cruelty." His planes machine-gunned Polish refugees on the roads leading away from Warsaw. As the historian Norman Davies wrote, "Cities were bombed indiscriminately. Fifty thousand died in Warsaw alone."[12]

The destruction soon spiraled as each side returned fire in kind. Tit quickly became tat which, in turn, became terror. Nothing more, nothing less.[13] Hitler was incensed when British bombers hit his cities, and he vowed to "rub out [British] cities from the map." German planes shifted from targeting British airfields and defense systems to blitz-bombing cities. By mid-May 1941, German bombs had killed 40,000 British civilians.[14] The names of the cities hit became etched in the public's mind. In retaliation Britain bombed Berlin, in a hint of the massive bombing of the city to come in 1943 and 1944. British bombers struck Mannheim in December 1940 and Cologne in May 1942. Hamburg suffered severe fire storms after a three-day bombing in late July 1943, with 33,000 civilians killed. The German cities of Hanover, Frankfurt, and Kassel all underwent severe bombing attacks in the fall of 1943. By the final year of the war in Europe, American and British bombers could fly relatively unmolested over German cities, and they killed civilians on a massive scale. As American troops inched closer in 1944 and 1945 to the Japanese homeland, American bombers were able to attack

Japan's urban areas. Almost all major Japanese cities by the summer of 1945 had been bombed, with the most massive desolation visited on Tokyo in March, when close to 100,000 civilians were killed and a quarter of the city was razed.

What can we make of these Baedeker raids against civilian centers? In Europe the bombing of eastern European cities like Warsaw was not part of a systematic attempt to deflate morale and production of war and preparation for invasion; they served, as historian Gerhard Weinberg points out, as early forays in racial cleansing.[15] British bombing of Germany by 1940, and increasingly in 1942, became central to the early British war effort. First, with Britain cocooned on its island after Dunkirk, and with the Soviets by 1941 confronting the Germans on the eastern front, British bombing raids against German cities paid large dividends. They buoyed British morale at a critical moment, forced the Germans to move fighter planes and antiaircraft gun installations from the eastern to the western front, and helped to address Stalin's demands that the British open up a second front in Western Europe. These were all practical rather than moral reasons for the bombing of civilian areas, at least early in the conflict.

Even if the British had been hesitant to strike civilians and preferred to surgically hit critical war production industries and services, the nature of bombing was imprecise, at best. Daylight raids made it easier to drop bombs with greater accuracy, but they also ensured that British bomber losses would be heavier. Even under excellent daytime weather conditions, however, British bombs hit assigned targets only one out of five times; under poorer conditions, the ratio of bombs hitting their targets fell to one out of fifteen times. Indeed, bombs often fell more than five miles from their intended targets.[16]

Despite these troubling statistics, the British established area or carpet bombing as the mainstay of their air campaign. Carpet bombing relied on the assumption that laying bombs over as wide a swath as possible maximized the chances of hitting targets; further, such bombing would cause civilian suffering that would sap morale and productive capacity from the enemy. British bombing policy at the outset of the war was thus, both by necessity and desire, written in blood. It denied Just War demands that civilians be spared or that their deaths be proportionate to the importance of the targets. Total war, in contrast, demanded simply that the enemy be hit hard. Civilian casualties, especially when tied to disruption of industrial and war production, became the modus operandi for the prosecution of modern warfare.

An American Moral Moment: The Doolittle Raid

On the morning of 7 December 1941, Japanese planes torpedo-bombed and strafed the American fleet leisurely anchored at Pearl Harbor. Damage to the ships was stunning, and approximately 2,400 American servicemen were killed. But beyond these losses, the attack shattered a sense of American invulnerability. The sneak attack—undertaken while American and Japanese diplomats were involved in negotiations—seemed especially dastardly. A week after the attack, about half of West Coast residents polled anticipated that they would be bombed at some point in the war.[17]

The situation in the Pacific for the United States immediately following Pearl Harbor was bleak. Japanese forces were claiming more territory, routing British and American troops and basking in their seeming invulnerability to reprisal. As American bombers had to retreat to airbases farther from the Japanese mainland, Japanese confidence grew more assured. Roosevelt pestered military officials to strike at the heart of the Japanese empire.[18] Even if such an attack were militarily insignificant, Roosevelt maintained that it would lift American morale and prick Japanese confidence. The problem was how to achieve such a daring goal.

Within weeks of the attack on Pearl Harbor, American military planners began to hatch an audacious and risky scheme. Since American bombers could not cover the distance to Japan from existing airbases, they planned to specially outfit B-25 bombers to take off from aircraft carrier decks. The initial question was practical: Given the length of the ship's runway, could a loaded bomber attain sufficient speed to take off? Even if it could, the bomber would be unable to return to the carrier; it would have to land on Chinese territory or ditch itself in the sea.

Under the direction of Colonel James H. "Jimmy" Doolittle, the plan rapidly gained ground. While the carrier USS *Hornet* was docked in Sacramento, sixteen specially fitted B-25 bombers were loaded onto its deck for the top-secret mission. Accompanied by destroyers and other ships, the *Hornet* would cruise as close to the Japanese mainland as possible without being detected, preferably to a distance of 400 miles or less. The bombers would take off in late afternoon and arrive at night over their targets. Once the planes had been dispatched, the *Hornet* and its accompanying fleet would quickly retreat back to Pearl Harbor. The American planes were to drop their bombs on industrial and military targets in five Japanese cities—Tokyo, Yokohama, Osaka, Kobe, and Nagoya—and then sprint on extremely limited fuel supplies to emergency landings in China.

In the morning hours of 18 April 1942, while the *Hornet*'s deck was pounded by "rough-house waves" and the ship became a "crazy see-saw," the fleet realized that it had probably been spotted by the Japanese.[19] The B-25s launched immediately, although they now had to travel a distance of 800 miles, effectively sapping their fuel supply and jeopardizing their chances for safe escape after they dropped their payloads. Doolittle's own craft was the first to take off. Each crew had for a month's time carefully studied landmarks and targets for their bomb drops. Once aloft, each plane was to maintain radio silence. In effect, each pilot was responsible for his own bombing and escape.

Crew members reported positive results from the bombing run. They encountered little anti-aircraft fire and minimal resistance—in large part because they had such a strong element of surprise. The planes flew at an extremely low altitude of 1,500 feet, low enough for some of the crewmen to see the faces of Japanese civilians on the ground.

The Doolittle group aimed at valid military targets listed as "military installations," "gasoline refinery and storage works," "aircraft works, an oil storage warehouse, an arsenal and barracks." Captain Ted Lawson, who lost a leg in his crash landing, reported that one of his 500-pound bombs hit "a steel-smelter plant." As he sped past, he noted that "the plant seemed to puff out its walls and then subside and dissolve in a black-and-red cloud." One of his incendiary devices descended "over a flimsy area in the southern part of the city."[20] Doolittle recalled similar success. His plane shook as one of its bombs decimated a factory.[21] One crew member reported that he had "bombed all hell" out of a designated target. Another thought he had scored a direct hit on the Kawasaki Truck and Tank Plant, only to learn later that he had hit "the Tokyo Gas and Electric Engineering Company." Yet incendiary bombs also set fire to the Okasaki Hospital and to some civilian areas, although it was difficult to establish how much damage resulted.[22]

Was this bombing justified? Just War theory demands that civilian lives be spared. The bombing strategy must avoid civilian casualties. Lives may be sacrificed in small numbers and unintentionally, only when bombs go astray after being carefully aimed at significant targets. In one sense, then, the Doolittle Raid failed to meet these strict criteria. The military value of the targets and the damage the sixteen aircraft carrying relatively small loads of bombs could achieve was minimal.

The issue of intention is central to Just War theory. All accounts from those participating in the attack point to Doolittle as being adamant about avoiding civilian and ceremonial targets. He told his men repeatedly to drop their bombs "where they will do the most damage" to military and industrial targets. When queried by a pilot about purposely hitting "residential areas," Doolittle's response was clear: "Definitely not! You are to look for and aim at military targets only, such as war industries, shipbuilding facilities. . . . There is absolutely nothing to be gained by attacking residential areas."[23] Some of his men itched at the opportunity to destroy the emperor's residence, "the Temple of Heaven." They could not imagine a sweeter and more symbolic target for destruction. Overhearing one such discussion among his men, Doolittle intervened. The orders are to "bomb military targets only," he asserted.

Doolittle offered no moral arguments against bombing the palace or civilian areas. Instead, he stated: "There is nothing that would unite the Japanese nation more than to bomb the emperor's home. It is not a military target!" It was, instead, "the home of Japan's venerated spiritual leader." And since Doolittle was in command and responsible for the choice of targets on the raid, his will was carried out. "I unilaterally made the decision that we would not bomb it. I consider this admonition one of the most serious I ever made to bombardment crews throughout the war."[24]

The raid also gained moral justification because of its timing. Morality is often situational rather than absolute. At the particular moment when the raid occurred, American losses in the Pacific were symbolically and numerically significant. Morale at home was lagging. The goal of boosting American morale while delivering a blow to Japanese morale was viewed as sufficient justification for this daring raid early in the prosecution of the war.[25]

The propaganda value of the raid was immense.[26] Civilian casualties were seen as limited and unintended. Revenge for the Japanese attack on Pearl Harbor had been exacted, despite Roosevelt's claim in the Declaration of War against Japan on 9 December 1941, that "we are now in the midst of a war, not for conquest, not for vengeance."[27] Yet the American public's craving for revenge was tinged with racism. In the words of historian John Dower, the chief characterization applied to the Japanese immediately after Pearl Harbor was "treacherous." A U.S. Marine slogan went, "Remember Pearl Harbor—keep 'em dying."[28] The Doolittle Raid allowed for quick revenge, within limits (not that such limits mattered to a majority of the American public).

The response on the American home front was joyous. *Life* magazine gleefully reported that American bombers had "plastered" cities in Japan. While stipulating that targets had been military and industrial, *Life* exulted in the fires the bombs caused, thanks to "the prevailing winds" that "sweep across the city." Americans celebrated the daring of the raid and the youthfulness of the airmen, and urged more raids as soon as feasible. Since the attacks had exposed the vulnerability of Japanese home industry to incendiary bombs, more bombing of civilian and industrial centers, one article concluded, might save thousands of American lives and shorten the war by years.[29]

What can be generalized from the relatively moral boundaries observed in the Doolittle Raid? Its small scale of operation and Doolittle's strict, pragmatic emphasis on bombing restraint made a difference. The symbolic value of the raid far outstripped its actual damage. An intentional attack against civilian targets might have served the tastes of the more bloodthirsty on the American home front, but it would have paid few other dividends. The brilliance of the Doolittle Raid was that it allowed America to respond with alacrity to the attack on Pearl Harbor without ceding the moral high ground. Alas, as we shall see, as the war in both Europe and the Pacific progressed, fewer and fewer climbed to the moral high ground.

A Muddy Moral Moment

A second critical moral moment during World War II concerns the non-use of poison gas. Why, after all, should poison gas have been viewed as an unacceptable weapon compared to the bombs that devastated cities? Was the prohibition on employment of poison gas against either military or civilian targets more a function of fear of retaliation than of moral qualms?

Although poison gas and other chemical and biological weapons were not employed during World War II, each side worried the other might use them. In May 1943, British Prime Minister Winston S. Churchill, relying on secret documents the Soviets had captured from German troops, warned the Germans that if they directed poison gas attacks against the Soviet Union, then Britain would retaliate with gas against Germany. A month later, President Roosevelt issued a similar warning about the "terrible consequences" Germany faced if it were to use poison gas: "Use of such weapons has been outlawed by the general opinion of civilized mankind. This country has not used them. . . . I state categorically that we shall under no circumstances resort to the use of such weapons unless they are first used by our enemies."[30]

Hitler had a deep-seated aversion to the use of poison gas in warfare, no doubt arising from his personal experience at the front during World War I. He gave clear and unyielding orders to his military not to employ poison gas against the enemy. Morality did not enter into his considerations. He was, of course, unconcerned about using gas and other chemical compounds as part of the Final Solution for exterminating Jews and others. But Allied war planners were not privy to Hitler's state of mind, and, especially as Germany's collapse accelerated, apocalyptic scenarios arose that imagined his ordering the use of gas and other chemical weapons.[31]

The United States and Great Britain both seriously contemplated the use of poison gas during the war. Churchill saw no essential difference between bombing enemy cities and using poison gas or chemicals against enemy civilians and soldiers. Angered by the Germans' use of explosive V-1 rockets against Britain in 1944, Churchill sent a memo to General Hastings Ismay, his chief military assistant. He thought the ban on poison gas an "absurd" moral qualm because "everybody used it in the last war without a word of complaint from the moralists or the Church." Churchill's plan was simple: "We could drench the cities of the Ruhr and many other cities" with poison gas. He ordered Ismay to have "the matter studied in cold blood by sensible people and not by that particular set of psalm-singing uniformed defeatists." However, he planned on sanctioning poison gas only if "it could be shown either that (a) it was life or death for us or (b) that it would shorten the war by a year." Churchill acknowledged that British use of poison gas would have to be vetted by "Uncle Joe" (Stalin) "and the President" (Roosevelt).[32]

Roosevelt's opposition to poison gas remained unequivocal. But General George C. Marshall, the army chief of staff, along with other high-ranking military leaders, agreed with Churchill that poison gas was a legitimate weapon, at least against enemy combatants. American commanders knew that the planned invasion of Iwo Jima in early 1945 would be horrific, with an immense number of American casualties. The volcanic island was dense with crags and foliage. Japanese soldiers had constructed an effective tunnel system that made them largely oblivious to softening up by bombing in advance of an invasion by U.S. Marines. The likelihood was that Japanese soldiers would fight until the end. One tactic that began to circulate was the idea of saturating the island with poison gas before invasion. The gas would seep into the Japanese troops' hiding places and kill them. Conquering the island would then be a relative cakewalk.

General Marshall, always cautious and always informed, maintained that poison gas would save American lives, secure the island, and hasten the end of the war. As we shall see, his arguments anticipated those later employed in favor of the use of atomic bombs against Japan. Marshall never swayed. If anything, the heavy loss of American lives in the operation made him more adamant about the propriety of employing poison gas against Japanese resistance, especially on uninhabited islands. We should "drench them and sicken them so that the fight would be taken out of them—saturate an area, possibly with mustard [gas], and just stand off," Marshall advised. Adverse public reactions could be parried. Since all weapons wreak destruction, poison gas, he found, "was no less humane than phosphorus and flame throwers and need not be used against dense populations or civilians."[33]

The invasion of Iwo Jima was bloody beyond belief. The attack began with heavy aerial bombardment and artillery shelling from ships anchored nearby; more than 21,926 shells pummeled entrenched Japanese positions.[34] The island, a little over seven miles long, with the dormant volcano Mount Suribachi dominating the landscape, was acrid with the stench of sulfur. On the day of the invasion, it was overcome by the smell of death. Japanese commander General Tadamichi Kuribayashi reported to his superiors that his well-protected guns had killed more than 2,000 marines attempting to land on the island.[35] Allen R. Matthews, one of the marines stumbling ashore under intense fire, recalled the carnage: "I saw a man sitting on his left hip, his legs sprawling lifelessly sideward." Matthews later reflected: "Death is not merely content to rob of life; it must take dignity, too."[36]

Marines persevered and died. Japanese defenders refused to surrender and were killed. Eventually, the island and its important airstrips were secured by the Americans, but with a heavy toll. Between 4,554 and 6,281 marines died, and perhaps another 20,000 were wounded.[37] Japanese losses were staggering; 18,000 killed out of 21,000 on the island. When alerted to the cost of this battle, President Roosevelt was said to "shudder" and "gasp." According to reporter Jim Bishop, this was the first time Roosevelt had demonstrated such outward emotion to American losses during the long and bloody war.[38]

Perhaps Roosevelt responded emotionally because he had personally overruled Marshall and other military commanders. On the recommendation for the deployment of poison gas, Roosevelt had scribbled, "All prior endorsements denied," and he signed the document definitively, "Franklin D. Roosevelt, Commander in Chief."[39] Of course, Roosevelt acted with full authority and with good reasons behind his decision. Post–World War I conventions, including the 1928 Geneva Accord, had prohibited, under all circumstances, the use of poison gas. Yet the accord had not been ratified by the United States Senate. And, although they constituted an important legal precedent, such edicts hardly proved binding during the war; moreover, such conventions were intended, in spirit if not in word, to outlaw conventional, incendiary, and atomic bombing of urban centers. Roosevelt was enough of a politically independent spirit and power to have crossed the boundary on poison gas, had he so desired.[40]

Marshall pointed out that Roosevelt need not be overly concerned about adverse American public opinion, despite polls to the contrary. The American public was against the use of poison gas, even if it meant an earlier end to the war. In a Gallup poll conducted in September 1944, a remarkable 71 percent said they were against the use of poison gas on Japanese civilian targets, while 76 percent opposed the use of such gas on German civilian targets. But the poll did not ask about the use of poison gas on purely military targets. Public opinion proved to be volatile on the poison gas issue. When asked about the propriety of using poison gas against Japanese cities should the Japanese execute American bomber pilots, 43 percent of respondents gave their assent. In a poll conducted just after the dropping of the atomic bombs, and before the official surrender, 40 percent of respondents said that if poison gas could lower American combat casualties, then it should be employed. Amazingly, in the same poll, 85 percent of those questioned stated they approved of the atomic bombs dropped on Japanese cities. Hence, there is little reason to believe that American public opinion presented any serious obstacle to the president and military over first use of poison gas.[41]

Roosevelt refused to go down in history as the first leader in World War II to approve poison gas in a military operation.[42] But General Marshall, too, had experienced World War I near to hand, and he was more than willing to deploy poison gas under carefully limited conditions.[43] Why?

Moral decisions never occur in a void. Practical reasons also entered into Roosevelt's calculations. The war in Europe by 1945 was winding down. At that moment, even Churchill was wary about using poison gas, out of fear of potential retribution rather than for moral reasons. By using gas even on an isolated island in the Pacific, the United States might grant Hitler the excuse to employ his chemical weapons against allied civilians and soldiers. In theory, he could have loaded it onto V-1 rockets headed for the British Isles, or dispensed it against troops on the European continent.[44]

When confronted with the strategic and limited use of poison gas, and after weighing the loss of American lives against potential military, political, moral, and diplomatic ramifications, Roosevelt acted with authority and determination against his military leaders.[45] In this case, the president used the power of his office to squelch a high-level and perhaps reasonable military request.

A number of points need to be coaxed from this refusal. A cynical conclusion might be that Roosevelt rejected poison gas simply because he feared that Germany and perhaps Japan would unleash their own poisonous arsenals. But is this compromised by Roosevelt and his successor Harry S. Truman's willingness to employ the even greater destructive power of atomic bombs against Germany or Japan? In any case, it is possible that Roosevelt's awareness derived from the fact that poison gas had come to be considered by statute, custom, and public opinion as an unacceptable weapon. As the military commander-in-chief, and as someone who saw himself in a position of moral leadership, he stood firm and vetoed even the limited, and strategically logical, use of poison gas. By so doing, he sacrificed the lives of American soldiers for a principle. Such leadership and thinking proved to be inconsistent. After all, under Roosevelt conventional and incendiary bombing both in Germany and Japan had directly targeted civilians. Is this discrepancy quantitative or qualitative? Simply a case of messy loose ends or conditioned by the morality that emerged with the customs of total war?

Bombing Civilians, by Choice and Chance

By the time the United States entered the war, bombing civilians had been both soundly condemned and widely practiced. American bombing practices generally avoided direct targeting of civilians. Bombing in the European theater of operations was designed to be tactical: to hit German manufacturing, oil facilities, and other installations critical to the war effort. In the Pacific, with the exception of the Doolittle Raid, targets on the Japanese homeland early in the war were exempt from large-scale American bombing runs only because air bases were out of range. As America gained bloody victories and landing strips on various islands, the bombing of Japan became frequent and intense. Although initial bombing practice, as in Europe, claimed to target industrial and military targets, by early 1945 policy had shifted under the leadership of General Curtis E. LeMay. Now the wholesale destruction of justified targets co-existed with maximum destruction of urban areas. The high toll of civilian casualties was celebrated and justified by American leaders and the public.

This shift is often explained by the concept of a moral slide. Small steps—initial mistakes in bombing or small-scale killing of civilians—escalate until the lines blur between aiming at industrial and military targets and the intentional bombing of civilians. Over time, military and civilian officials become hardened to destruction, or it becomes so commonplace that initial qualms are forgotten. Tied to this hypothesis is the view—especially apt for the Pacific theater—that with intensified fighting, the desire to battle according to the rules of Just War diminishes. As individuals are numbed by the horror of warfare, entranced by visions of retribution, and attuned to the harsh realities of total war, their previously rejected means of waging warfare become more appealing and morally untainted. Total war emerges. On 15 May 1940, early in the war, British diplomat Sir Alexander Cadogan wrote in his diary that British bombs that day had hit German industrial cities in the Ruhr Valley area. This would mean, in due time, that German bombers would retaliate against British civilian centers. He sadly observed: "Now the 'Total War' begins!"[46]

Roosevelt quickly arrived at the same conclusion. Of course, he cloaked himself and American fighting practices in moral righteousness (not undeserved). He justified harsh military tactics as necessary means to achieve the moral end of defeating a vicious enemy. He also presumed that it was the enemy who invariably first introduced unsavory tactics: "modern warfare as conducted in the Nazi manner is a dirty business . . . and we're going to fight it with everything we've got."[47]

Thus, in total war a "moral slide" is a less than useful and convincing concept. An unfortunate but more realistic rule of thumb may be that if a warring nation can use weapons against civilian populations in the belief that such destruction will hasten its victory, and if the use of such targeting is perceived not to bring forth equal or worse retribution or political debits, then such bombing will happen. In total war moral moments do happen, as we have seen, but they are few and far between. British and American bombing in Europe was uninformed largely by moral concerns about intentional harm being inflicted on civilians.[48]

Bombing strategy maintained that the best way to win the war was to destroy German industrial and military targets. American strategists believed in the superiority of their technology to deliver precise and powerful destruction. The British, in contrast, found the cost of relatively precise bombing in daytime too heavy for them to absorb; they chose instead to bomb areas at night, with high civilian death tolls inevitably following from the more inexact bombing raids. The American public was untroubled, by and large, by civilian deaths caused by either their own or British bombing. Sometimes, even when Americans acknowledged the loss of civilian lives, the casualties were negated because the raid was deemed to have been in pursuit of valid industrial targets. Sometimes, however, the elation was almost blood-curdling. While the *Atlanta Constitution* admitted that it is "shocking to think of the thousands who must have been burned to death" in the bombing of Tokyo, nonetheless, "with each city thus attacked, we remember the treachery of Pearl Harbor and find calm satisfaction in the knowledge that the Japanese of one more city have learned there is a bill to be paid, which must be paid, for treachery, that retribution for such a deed is implacable."[49]

Civilian death tolls, whether intended or not, stagger the imagination. Although estimates vary, more than 600,000 German civilians died from Allied bombing, and upward of 500,000 Japanese civilians perished from American conventional, incendiary, and atomic bombing. German bombing raids on Great Britain claimed more than 60,000 British lives.[50]

The deaths had been justified early on in the European conflict by dubious claims that such bombing diminished enemy morale, slowed industrial production, and reallocated resources away from the front. By the spring and summer of 1945, America was intent on inflicting the greatest damage on Japanese civilian centers for the same reasons. This was horribly realized in the destruction of Tokyo, a city located—as poet W. H. Stafford might put it, "under a sky that never cared less."[51]

Tokyo in Flames

In the air war against Japan, necessity more than morality dictated military decisions. In taking the war to Japanese cities in the spring of 1945, General LeMay decided that incendiary bombing (which would cause fires over a wide expanse of urban areas) would most effectively paralyze industrial productivity and demoralize the population in Tokyo. He did not frame this mode of attack as an alternative to precision bombing; that was left unsaid. Sometimes the shift from precision to area and incendiary bombing was explained as a response to weather concerns. With Japan often hemmed in by fog, nighttime incendiary attacks against Japanese cities seemingly afforded the best means to punish the enemy.[52] Industrial targets would still be hit, as per official policy, but area bombing with incendiaries would also produce clear proof of destruction, and as civilian casualties mounted, enemy morale would be undermined.[53]

On 10 March 1945, LeMay dispatched more than three hundred B-29 superfortresses to batter Tokyo. Flying low to save fuel and minimize technical difficulties, the planes carried larger than usual amounts of conventional and incendiary bombs. The incendiaries were dropped in a 500-pound bomb that opened up for in-air release of "six pound bombs filled with jellied gasoline." Each of these small devices found kindling aplenty in the wooden buildings that constituted much of Tokyo.[54] A shaken *Boston Globe* reporter, witnessing the conflagration from aboard one of the B-29s, stated that he had "never seen such a display of destruction . . . hundreds of blazes throughout the waterfront area, [the] most densely populated section in the world."[55] Tokyo's fire-break system, designed to contain spreading fires, was quickly rendered ineffective. With close to one hundred of the city's fire engines destroyed and many firefighters killed, the flames burned unhampered.[56] Indeed, the bombing destroyed many industrial targets, including the Ueno railroad station and the Rising Sun Petroleum terminal. In addition, "hundreds of small business establishments directly concerned with the war industry, important administrative buildings and other thousands of home industries were also in the area wiped out."[57] At least a quarter of a million buildings were destroyed. More than 80,000 Japanese civilians were killed.[58]

LeMay was always clear about his purposes. "We were going after military targets. No point in slaughtering civilians for the mere sake of slaughter." But collateral damage obviously figured centrally in the raid. As LeMay later put it, "We knew we were going to kill a lot of women and kids when we burned that town. Had to be done."[59]

Incendiary bombing was becoming something of a dark and exact science. After the war had ended, the Association of Fire Engineers, a trade organization in the United States composed of people with expertise in controlling fires, told of how they had pressured the government to employ them in the war effort. With good reason, they claimed no one was better qualified to plan for the destruction by fire of a city like Tokyo than the individuals most adept at putting out fires. These fire engineers proudly advised the government on the most efficient and brutal use of incendiary devices and on how to get the "best results" in burning buildings and other structures.[60]

A few days after LeMay's raid on Tokyo, the first photographs detailing the destruction appeared in the American press. Taken from high altitude, they showed smoldering clouds of smoke indicating areas that had been decimated by the bombing. Analogy emerged as the best way to communicate the immensity of the destruction. A *New York Times* story, "Tokyo in Flames," noted that fifteen square miles of the city had been destroyed, almost four times the area reduced to rubble by the San Francisco earthquake of 1906.[61] Another story described the swath of annihilation by using a comparison closer to home. If the firebombing had occurred in the New York metropolitan area, Manhattan from Greenwich Village (around 4th Street) to 60th Street, along with areas in northern Brooklyn, parts of Queens, and Staten Island, would have been reduced to smoldering ruins. In Tokyo, it was reported, huge numbers of newly homeless Japanese civilians, as large as the population living in the Bronx or Queens, were sapping the meager resources of the toppled city.[62]

Can Bombing of Civilians Be Justified?

The destruction of Tokyo raised few complaints in America. Such bombing, already common in the European theater of operations, had become a custom of war. Whether the targeting of civilians—either by intention or simply as collateral damage—is morally justifiable remains a compelling question. Justification for the bombing of Tokyo could easily make the atomic bombing of Hiroshima and Nagasaki either a natural progression or a morally fuzzy one.

Most moral philosophers, building upon Just War theory, contend that only under very limited circumstances is it ever justified to attack civilians.[63] Just War theory demands that if the lives of noncombatants are to be sacrificed, then the importance of the target must be staggering. How to determine this? Surely it is disproportionate and immoral for a nation to drop hundreds of tons of bombs on a heavily civilian-populated area around a plant that plays a minor role in war production. But what of more shadowy equations, such as when the destruction of an enemy's capacity to produce atomic weapons at some point in the future might result in thousands of civilian deaths in the present? Moral philosophers A. C. Grayling and Jonathan Glover condemn carpet, area, and incendiary bombing as always "*unnecessary* and *disproportionate*" to the ends to be achieved. Beyond being immoral, such bombing is ineffective. Neither industrial productivity declined nor civilian morale lagged as a result of these unholy terrors. If the acts were wrong according to the laws of war, and also failed as means to achieve a valid military end, then they must be considered as immoral, *tout court*.[64]

Are there exceptions and different ways of examining this issue? Justification for bombing civilians in Germany and Tokyo can readily be offered, no matter how distasteful the reasons may be. The most obvious defense is that the realities of war have evolved over time. In an age of total war, the sanctity of civilians, while an abstract good, is alas a practical nullity. Early in the conflict, civilian lives were deemed to be expendable. As war drags on and as the destruction grows, restraints fizzle. Moral revulsion by this point in conflicts becomes nugatory. The righteousness of bombing civilians is also justified by the belief that if the enemy had the opportunity to bomb your civilian centers, they would. In the trite phrase, "All's fair in love and war."

Historian Robert Newman notes that in the total war of 1939–1945, one marked by tremendous atrocities on the part of the Japanese against civilians and prisoners of war, the point of using weapons against civilians is simple: to inflict the most damage possible and to exact revenge. The goal is to win the war, as quickly as possible. Historians and military analysts may differ over the effectiveness of area bombing (does it hasten an end to hostilities and does it undermine an enemy's ability to wage war?). But from one perspective, the strategic benefits of civilian bombing are less central than the simple fact that they are a means of punishing one's enemy.

General LeMay, with his usual cold bravado, stated that the "whole purpose of strategic warfare is to destroy the enemy's potential to wage war." If such potential resides in urban areas, with high civilian populations, then it would mean the death of "a lot of women and kids when we burned a city. . . . It had to be erased. If we didn't obliterate it, we would dwell subservient to it. Just as simple as that." LeMay mused further that the history of warfare, dating back to ancient times, was about attacking urban centers until "every single soul was murdered." Sad, perhaps, but true, he averred. And if that enemy lacked the strategic capacity to return the favor, then all the better.[65]

Philosopher Robert Nozick has highlighted the pitfalls of subjecting the killing of civilians in wartime to further moral analysis. In an admittedly controversial formulation, Nozick inquired: How does one distinguish between the innocent and the guilty in modern war? What about those civilians who cheered Hitler, who told Nazi authorities about Jews hiding in cellars, or who served efficiently in administrative positions in the Reich? Might all of them as part of the war machine be morally compromised and hence suitable targets? From a different angle, Nozick wondered, why should young men drafted against their wills to fight be viewed as morally acceptable targets? The point of Nozick's moral thought experiment was twofold: first, that there is no firm division between innocent civilians exempt from attack and guilty soldiers warranting attack, and second, that we ask about the range of responsibility. If someone supported Hitler and his nefarious schemes, does he or she become a valid target for wartime retribution if it could be delivered in a surgical manner?[66]

Again, let us head back to Just War theory, which stands as our only viable defense against incursions on civilians. Some of its adherents admit to exceptions to the general rule of civilian immunity in wartime. For example, the philosopher Michael Walzer views the British battle against Nazi totalitarianism as a "supreme emergency" situation. The Nazis stood for everything antagonistic to truth, justice, and humanity. A Nazi victory would have forever deranged European civilization. After the fall of France and the British evacuation from Dunkirk, England was incapable of engaging Germany on the European continent. In this dark moment, it was justifiable for the Royal Air Force to bomb German cities. In Walzer's reading of Just War theory, the righteousness of the cause and the incipient potential for a terrible British defeat are sufficient reasons.

Always hewing to a high moral standard, Walzer remains uncomfortable with this position. He realizes that moral imperatives may conflict. Of course, it is an imperative not to bomb civilians; but at the same time, it is an imperative not to lose a justified war against a horrible enemy such as Nazi Germany. Choosing the second imperative does not deny the first—it simply overrides it. This means that the action is done without self-congratulation. It is undertaken with the grim recognition that in a war, under particular and specific conditions, the guidelines of Just War behavior have been violated. Hence, nearly all participants in a war, however righteous their cause, will have "dirty hands." This is the essential Sartrean dilemma that after "mature consideration," one must choose, one must act. For both Sartre and Walzer, such action is done with a minimum of illusions or pretensions to absolute morality; one acts with an eye open to the taint of actions and the contingency of situations. This is what makes it tragic. Once conditions changed, say after D-Day, when a British and American presence on the continent leveled the field of war against the Germans, the continued bombing of German cities became an abomination, in Walzer's formulation.[67]

The United States was not in a situation of "extreme emergency" during World War II. Does that mean, then, that dropping atomic bombs on Hiroshima and Nagasaki was unnecessary and immoral? There is a compelling logic to such condemnation. Yet it obscures more than it reveals and perhaps brings forth undue and futile acrimony.[68] We must strive to understand rather than to condemn ex post facto. The compelling question is why atomic weapons were never questioned at the time. In part, the answer is that under the emergent customs of total warfare, the thought of abstaining from atomic bombs did not enter into the minds of policymakers. If atomic bombs had to be used, then are claims about moral guilt and freedom of action on the part of key players diminished under the weight of necessity and custom?

"A Smell of Death"

On 6 August 1945, an atomic bomb destroyed the city of Hiroshima; three days later another atomic device pulverized Nagasaki. In mid-September, a month after the Nagasaki blast, a United States naval officer described the city in a letter to his wife. "A smell of death and corruption pervades the place." His "general impression" was succinct and telling: "deadness, the absolute essence of death, in the sense of finality without hope of resurrection."[69]

The scene in Hiroshima was even worse. General Leslie Groves, military administrator for the atomic bomb project, learned from an eyewitness report that "it looked as if the whole town was being torn apart." The blast "was tremendous and awesome."[70] Survivors sometimes envied the dead. Some were instantly vaporized; some had their eyeballs melted by flashing light; others were consumed in the ensuing fires; many died in the crumbling of buildings, or later from starvation, untreated wounds and, in time, from radiation poisoning. While exact estimates of the deaths caused by the atomic bombings are debated, possibly 100,000 to 140,000 perished in Hiroshima by the end of 1945. Another 60,000 more died within five years from radiation poisoning.[71] Of those killed in the initial blast, only 3,243 were soldiers; the rest were civilians.[72]

What makes this morally disquieting is that a compelling case can be made for the inevitability of the dropping of the bombs. Indeed, as historian Barton J. Bernstein puts it, speaking for many who have studied the issue, "At no time did top-level American leaders seek to avoid the use of the A-bomb. They never searched for alternatives, and the so-called alternatives generally looked too risky; therefore, the alternatives were not pursued." General Marshall agreed: "We had to end the war; we had to save American lives. . . . The bomb stopped the war. Therefore, it was justifiable." As Winston Churchill expressed it in his *Triumph and Tragedy* (1953): "The decision whether or not to use [an] atomic bomb to compel the surrender of Japan was never even an issue."[73] In the view of historians and participants, then, the decision to use the atomic bombs was a non-decision, something that was determined in advance, a juggernaut of destruction bound to roll as soon as possible.

This of course does not justify the use of the bombs in moral terms. It could, if one so chose, illustrate the moral infancy of America's civilian and military leadership. Or the muddy waters of morality in a time of war may be sufficient to explain how often thoughtful and moral individuals might view the deliberate bombing of civilians with relatively little moral concern.

Atomic Presumptions

The presumption: An atomic bomb, if available, would be used against Japan (or earlier in the war against Germany). Further, it would be dropped on an urban center. This strikes many of us as unduly cruel and immoral. It was. However, American leadership deemed the dropping of the atomic bomb to be necessary and moral. Necessary, because in a total war one uses the weapons one has, especially when retaliation for their use is minimal; moral, because the bombing of urban centers was, by 1945, common practice. Secretary of War Henry L. Stimson believed that America had "moral superiority" on its side because it had been attacked at Pearl Harbor. How far such "moral superiority" should extend was not clarified. But it was strengthened, in Stimson's view, by his belief that the United States was fighting a war upon whose conclusion civilization rested.[74]

Moreover, the power of the atomic bomb was sometimes seen as simply a more efficient means of destruction than incendiary and conventional forms of bombing. It was viewed as a weapon that would save lives. According to this logic, if the atomic bomb proved as powerful as some anticipated, the Japanese would surrender more quickly, thus ensuring that Japanese lives (those slated to perish from conventional bombing, starvation, and invasion) *and* American lives (prisoners of war, victims of kamikaze attacks, and fatalities from an invasion of the Japanese home islands set to begin on 1 November 1945) would be saved. As some historians have contended, if the atomic bombs had not ended the war quickly, then over a period of six months, perhaps more than a quarter of a million Japanese civilian lives would have been taken during an invasion.[75]

Henry L. Stimson was by all accounts a moral and humane man. In June 1945, while the war still raged, Stimson had expressed concerns about civilian casualties from American bombing of Japanese cities. Some historians find him "suffering increasing anguish" about this.[76] Yet Stimson's concerns went nowhere. In his memoir he claimed he had demanded that Air Force General Henry A. Arnold justify "the apparently indiscriminate bombing of Tokyo." But, Arnold, as Stimson realized from his reports on the bombing of civilian centers in Germany earlier in the war, was usually "exuberantly optimistic" about the accuracy of the bombs and the low civilian death toll.[77] Stimson worried that "now in the conflagration bombings by massed B-29s he was permitting a kind of total war that he had always hated," and thus substantiating or "implicitly confessing that there could be no significant limits to the horror of modern war."[78] Even if Stimson was skeptical of rosy reports on the bombing, he did little. Perhaps, as some historians suggest, he was increasingly in ill health, worn down, and often confused about many matters. Perhaps he simply was unable to pay sufficient attention to details.[79]

But there are two more compelling rationales for his relative inaction. First, like many in power, he avoided looking hard at what was actually happening, preferring to believe what he was told. Thus he wrote in his diary that he was "anxious to hold" American forces in Japan to the same standards for accurate bombing they had demonstrated in Germany. The problem, as he refused to acknowledge, is that such standards were, at best, minimal.[80] Second, Stimson felt his job as secretary of war was not to second-guess the military but to win the war in quick and effective fashion. He invariably held tight to ensure the defeat of totalitarian enemies with the fewest number of American lives lost. When he occasionally attempted to inject his own personal desires or beliefs into military decisions, he did so without moral argument; instead he relied on pragmatic or diplomatic reasoning.[81]

Stimson favored precision bombing against industrial targets. He received regular reports throughout the war on the bombing of Germany and Japan from General Hap Arnold and Secretary of the Air Force Robert Lovett. They celebrated American successes, emphasizing through photographs the accuracy of American precision bombing. Stimson pushed the air force to limit its area bombing, although he acknowledged that the location of Japanese industry scattered in and near cities might demand some tactical shifts. He wanted area and incendiary bombing minimized for pragmatic reasons. He worried that the United States would earn "the reputation of outdoing Hitler in atrocities," and thereby undermine American postwar credibility. He was fully aware, however, that LeMay's bombers had left precious few Japanese cities untouched, and that they had obliterated one quarter of Tokyo.

Stimson did nothing to impose his viewpoint on military leaders. At one point, shortly before the atomic bombs were dropped, Stimson warned Truman that without relatively pristine targets available, it would be difficult to gauge the power of the atomic weapon. The president, according to Stimson's recollection, "laughed and said he understood."[82] Stimson, in turn, did not appear shocked or even dismayed by the "cold joke."[83]

The bombing reached a crescendo only a couple weeks after Stimson's talk with Truman, when LeMay's B-29s scorched Tokyo. The only cities spared from massive bombing besides Kyoto were those penciled in for future atomic attacks. Even after the dropping of the atomic bomb on Hiroshima, incendiary and conventional bombing raids continued against urban targets. On 7 August, for instance, conventional bombing killed 1,408 workers at the Toyokawa naval ammunition plants. On 8 August, American bombers hit Yawata, burning 22 percent of that city.[84]

American political leaders and the public knew about the toll of such bombings on urban centers. Stimson and Harry S. Truman, who became president after Roosevelt died in April 1945, viewed at firsthand the destruction in Germany wrought by almost round-the-clock conventional bombing.

In July 1945, after the surrender of Germany, Truman and Stimson attended the Potsdam Conference, held outside Berlin. The conference was Truman's debut as president on the world stage, where he would negotiate with Stalin and Churchill about war aims and postwar issues. Big decisions and statements needed to be made on subjects ranging from Soviet domination in Poland to when the Soviets would enter the war against Japan. The conference issued a demand that the Japanese surrender unconditionally. Truman also faced the decision of whether to inform Stalin about American progress on the development of an atomic bomb. He only learned about its successful first test in the Alamogordo desert while at the conference.

In the midst of dealing with these momentous issues, accompanied by his new secretary of state, James F. Byrnes, and Admiral William Leahy, Truman went for a car tour of war-torn Berlin on the afternoon of 16 July. The next day, Stimson, also in attendance at the conference but playing only a minor role, took his own tour.

Truman found Berlin still smoldering, "in absolute ruin" from Allied bombing and the Soviet invasion. What he saw goaded him to moral reflection about war and its hideous toll. The "sorrowful sight" of Berlin, he confided in his diary, had occurred because of "Hitler's folly" of world domination. Truman further condemned Hitler as an amoralist. Perhaps most perplexing to Truman was why the German "people backed [Hitler] up" until the bitter end. They had brought devastation on themselves. Truman recognized that the Soviet occupation of Berlin meant acts of revenge would be taken against the Germans—from outright murder, to robbery, to widespread rape—but he understood this abuse. Reflecting more generally about human motivations, he wrote, "It is the Golden Rule in reverse—and it is not an uplifting sight. What a pity that the human animal is not able to put his moral thinking into practice!" He then paused to ruminate about the fate of previous civilizations and ancient cities that had been destroyed, concluding sadly, "that machines are ahead of morals by some centuries."[85] Thus, any personal responsibility on his or Roosevelt's part for the bombing of civilian population cities was allayed. Hitler, with the aid of the German people, had brought the terror down on themselves. History demonstrated that human morality was frail, unable to keep pace with technology. Nothing could be done in wartime, concluded Truman. War was hell.

Stimson wrote few impressions of his tour, perhaps because he had already mused about the morality of destruction that had occurred during his tenure as secretary of war.[86] He confided to his diary simply that he was "distressed at the picture of destruction." Proud buildings had been "gutted." A "dead city" now held "despondent groups of homeless people going from place to place with all their worldly goods" in any type of conveyance they could secure—"little carts, baby carriages, bicycles."[87]

The wages of war were paid in full by the horrendous pain inflicted on innocents, both statesmen concluded. In a total war, the destruction of cities was a sad but natural occurrence. Granted such widely held perceptions, it was hardly surprising that the employment of atomic weapons would raise hardly a peep of protest in governmental and military circles. In part, this was because the precedent for destruction, the custom of war, had been set before the atomic bomb was a reality. Government officials wondered if the atomic bomb was anything more than conventional bombs multiplied and condensed into a single package of destruction. Here the verdict was mixed and often contradictory. This lack of clarity fogged consideration of the deeper moral issues.

Stimson maintained in various presentations before President Truman and the Interim Committee on the Bomb (created in May 1945, with high-level government officials and civilian scientists to examine various issues related to the politics and use of atomic bombs) that the atomic bomb was revolutionary. Even before it had been tested successfully at Alamogordo, Stimson had worried about the bomb's power and potential effect on humanity. In notes he jotted down prior to a crucial 31 May 1945 meeting of the Interim Committee charged with discussing the implications of the bomb, he emphasized, "We don't think it *mere* new *weapon*." Indeed, he referred to it as a "*Revolutionary Discovery*" akin to the Copernican Revolution or the discovery of the theory of gravity. It promised to change the "relation of man to [the] universe," although how was unclear, at this stage. The bomb "may *destroy* or *perfect* International *Civilization*." Or it could be "*Frankenstein or* means for World Peace."[88] Nonetheless, Stimson never wavered about using this revolutionary weapon because he maintained that his first priority as secretary of war was to end the war as quickly as possible and with the minimum number of American lives lost. In the context of war and in the midst of such presumptions, availability of the bomb meant that it would be used.

Many rejected the revolutionary significance of the atomic bomb. The firebombing of Tokyo made atomic destruction appear to be a similarly necessary and justified act of barbarism in wartime. In his usual blunt manner, General LeMay saw "no more depravity in dropping a nuclear weapon" than in having conventional, incendiary, and V-2 weapons hitting civilian centers.[89] Luis W. Alvarez, an atomic physicist who witnessed the atomic bombing of Hiroshima, was of two minds about the singularity of the bomb. In a letter composed to his four-year-old son on the day Hiroshima was destroyed, Alvarez stated that "what regrets I have about being a party to the killing and maiming of thousands of Japanese civilians this morning" were eased by a fervent hope that "this terrible weapon . . . may bring the countries of the world together and prevent future wars." Of course, Alfred Nobel, the inventor of dynamite, had harbored similar dreams that had been crushed. But the atomic bomb, in Alvarez's view, was "so many thousands of times worse that it may realize Nobel's dream."

In terms of the morality of the weapon, Alvarez explained it was simply a more efficient way of killing than the methods that had come before. He contended that "the death and destruction visited" in earlier bombings, such as LeMay's firebombing of Tokyo and other Japanese cities, was more destructive than the atomic bombs dropped on Hiroshima and Nagasaki. While he acknowledged the "spectacular" effect of the atomic bombs, he refused to see them as more morally problematic than other modes of killing to achieve war aims.[90] Alvarez was not alone. Although he viewed the atomic "bomb as an unusually effective means of destruction," the influential scientist Arthur Holly Compton brushed that insight off by declaring that "destruction is destructive."[91]

At the Highest Level of Government

Did President Truman and Secretary of War Stimson, the two men who dealt at the highest level with deploying the atomic bombs, have any choice other than to use these weapons? In the context of the escalating violence of the war and the targeting of noncombatants, they found sufficient justification, if they felt it was needed, in the customs of war already evident. They upheld the logic that atomic bombs would save American lives by hastening the end of the conflict. If pressed, they could further moralize that the bombs would save innocent Japanese lives as well. Was there, as McGeorge Bundy later inquired, "a failure of imagination" on the part of American leaders' thinking about alternatives to the bomb?[92] Serious moral rumination about the bomb was minimal. Truman and Stimson and others were beset by confusions and contradictions about the bomb, its targets, and its impact.[93] All the more reason, then, for thinking about them more seriously and then acting with resolve.

The sole instance Stimson intervened with forcefulness to argue against deploying the atomic bomb came when he insisted that Kyoto be removed from the military's list of cities targeted. His argument was practical rather than moral. He accepted using the atomic bomb on a city and the decimation of its civilian population; he simply felt that the incineration of Kyoto would be a diplomatic blunder. Kyoto had a substantial military presence; it was also the old cultural capital of Japan, full of important objects and associations. Obliterating the city, Stimson believed, would antagonize the Japanese and unite them in a desire for revenge against the uncivilized actions of the United States. General Groves adamantly favored hitting Kyoto. But Stimson put him in his place, demanding the list of targeted cites and then making clear to Groves and air force officials that the city of Kyoto was to be spared. On two separate occasions, as well, in meetings with President Truman, Stimson reiterated his profound opposition to the atomic bombing of Kyoto. Truman agreed that such a target might incite Japanese resentment against the United States and "reconcile" them more readily to the Soviet Union.[94] Neither, apparently, worried overmuch that atomic bombs dropped on two other civilian centers might cause enduring Japanese bitterness, and to a degree, they were right.

As far as scholars can determine, there were no deep moral misgivings about using atomic bombs on Japanese targets until after the fact. Beginning in January 1945, Stimson engaged in many discussions about the bomb and its implications. He regularly talked about atomic issues with his aide,

Harvey Bundy (father of McGeorge Bundy). Almost all discussion, however, focused on strategic issues, on the composition of a press release announcing the dropping of the bomb, and on the implications of the bomb for relations with the Soviets. Sometimes the discussions seemed more convivial than morally wrenching. Stimson noted that "it was very pleasant to sit out there [on his front porch]" the night before, discussing atomic issues with Bundy.[95] Once, after a long day of meetings on the atomic bomb, Stimson stopped by the office of General Marshall for an in-depth talk. But nothing indicates that Stimson, Truman, or Marshall ever considered not using the atomic bomb. There is no indication that they thought at length about the moral dimensions of incinerating a city filled with civilians. Perhaps this is indicative, to a degree, of a hardening of the moral arteries by a long and horrid war, or of how impenetrable to debate the ossified customs of total war had become.

Muddled Thinking

Discussions about atomic bomb targeting reveal muddled thinking on the part of American policymakers. Stimson and other planners emphasized a desire to choose "dual use" potential targets. Targeted areas were to have military and industrial facilities of some import, and facilities could be "surrounded or adjacent to homes or other buildings most susceptible to damage." The phrase "dual use" and the designation of nearby homes as legitimate targets for collateral damage were perhaps clever devices to inhibit moral anxiety, to rationalize away such concerns. Yet the planners also readily accepted the clause, "homes or other buildings" nearby, as formulated by James B. Conant in the 31 May meeting of the Interim Committee. This suggests that the killing of large numbers of civilians had become a minor concern, if it was a concern at all. The custom of total warfare was in place. Precision bombs had a difficult enough time sparing civilians. Stimson and company knew that the atomic bomb would cause immense, indiscriminate destruction. That was, of course, the point: to demonstrate its power, shock the Japanese with fear of additional bombs, and force the end of the war.[96]

After the war had ended, President Truman was often asked about his "decision" to employ the bomb. Truman claimed, "I was always thinking . . . and hoping that the final decision [about the bomb] would be correct."[97] But there was never much of a decision for Truman to make, nor did he try to trouble the issue.[98] It would have taken major determination on the part of the new president, and some heretofore unknown moral heroism or virtue, to have intervened to stop its deployment.[99] In a diary entry on 25 July, Truman expressed his amazement at the destructive power of the bomb that had first been detonated at Alamogordo. He was aware of the power of this new weapon: "We have discovered the most terrible bomb in the history of the world. It may be the fire destruction prophesied in the Euphrates Valley Era, after Noah and his fabulous ark." After these theological asides, Truman stated that it was acceptable to hit military personnel. At the same moment, he also reflected that although "the Japs are savages, ruthless, merciless and fanatic, we as the leader of the world cannot drop this terrible bomb on the old capital or the new." Truman, along with Stimson, was convinced that the bomb's "target will be a purely military one." How one could make such a distinction between a "purely military" or dual target and the civilians who would be incinerated by "the most horrible thing ever discovered" gave Truman little pause.[100]

Ten years later in his *Memoirs*, Truman further complicated our view of the historical record. He wrote that he had been aware of alternatives at the time—such as issuing a specific warning or a demonstration—but he had agreed with his military and scientific advisers that the bomb must be employed as quickly as possible. He cited the Interim Committee's report that it was to be dropped on a target that would increase the chances of convincing the Japanese of the futility of continuing the war. Truman then revealed a still more problematic description of what constituted a proper target for the atomic bomb: "I wanted to make sure that it would be used as a weapon of war in the manner prescribed by the laws of war. That meant that I wanted it dropped on a military target. I had told Stimson that the bomb should be dropped as nearly as possible upon a war production center of prime military importance."[101]

Truman was undoubtedly sincere, but his thinking was muddled. The boundary, in his view, between an urban center and a military target had become nonexistent. After all, only a few weeks earlier, a quarter of Tokyo had been obliterated by incendiary bombs. Surely Truman knew, from reading newspaper reports if nothing else, that civilian fatalities had been immense. Surely he had not hoodwinked himself into believing that these casualties were all military in nature. Could he have been so naïve as to pretend that "the laws of war" did not look askance at the bombing of urban areas teeming with civilians? Or was the taste of final victory, rationalized by the saving of American *and* Japanese lives, too tantalizing? The custom of war, apparently, could be used to rationalize any degree of destruction.[102]

Postwar Justifications

As secretary of war, Henry L. Stimson had been the man most connected with all aspects of the first nuclear bomb's deployment. He felt it necessary to respond to moral and strategic condemnations of the bombing of Hiroshima and Nagasaki that began in the immediate postwar period. The most well-known protest against the inhumanity of the atomic bomb appeared in 1946, when the *New Yorker* magazine devoted an entire issue to John Hersey's gripping account of how the bomb affected a handful of people living in Hiroshima on that fateful day. Within a short time, Hersey's story would appear as a book, *Hiroshima*, which quickly became a bestseller. Hersey's account immediately stirred emotions and public opinion against the bombing. He carefully detailed how the bomb had disfigured everyday civilians in Hiroshima. Although Hersey took no position on the military or strategic necessity of the bomb, and he refused to place the event within any larger historical context, he effectively demonstrated what photographs in the newspapers (that is, those not censored as too explicit) could only hint at: that real people, noncombatants, bore the brunt of the attack and suffered greatly.

Even before Hersey's heartrending account was published as a book, his *New Yorker* article reached a large audience through reprints and by being read and widely discussed on radio programs. Bill Leonard of radio station WABC (New York) urged his listeners to read Hersey's article "again and again" and to realize how "easy and all too possible [it is] to change the Japanese names to American names." In 1946 about 500 radio stations out of 1,000 in the United States carried stories about the article, all but one favorable. Martin Agronsky of WCFL (Chicago) and the ABC network (comprising about 135 radio stations around the nation) called the bombing "a horrible story, . . . full of horror of the monstrous weapon that our country first foisted upon the world." Can you imagine, he asked, such a weapon being dropped on an American city? Agronsky begged his listeners to "Stop the bickering and the fighting and, for humanity's sake, remember the atom!"[103]

In "The Decision to Use the Bomb" (written largely by McGeorge Bundy), which appeared in the popular *Harper's* magazine in February 1947, Stimson gave a straightforward account of the development and employment of atomic weapons. It is so directed in making the case for the use of the bomb that historian Martin Sherwin later referred to Stimson, a bit unfairly, as the "spin doctor" for American atomic destruction during World War II.[104]

Stimson argued that the atomic bomb, no matter how powerful, was similar to "any other of the deadly explosive weapons of modern war," a revision of his earlier perspective.[105] It was tremendously more expensive to produce and immensely more powerful, Stimson admitted, but still basically a military weapon with a single purpose in mind: to inflict damage on the enemy and thus bring the war to a speedy conclusion. The bomb's predominant military value was simple: It promised to save American lives and achieve the unconditional surrender of Japan. Stimson, Truman, and the Interim Committee considered atomic issues in the spring of 1945 without for a moment doubting the legitimacy and necessity of the atomic bomb. Without appending any moral concerns, a scientific panel advising the Interim Committee (made up of leading scientists Oppenheimer, James B. Conant, and Vannevar Bush) had readily concluded that "the bomb should be used against Japan as soon as possible" (13).

Stimson had legitimate worries about flagging American morale after the surrender of Germany. Would Americans be willing to continue the war for unconditional surrender against Japan? The Japanese had, according to most reports, solidified their home defenses and retained an army of perhaps five million. Yet throughout much of World War II, the Roosevelt administration had labored to convince Americans that Germany was the primary threat, hence the greater effort paid to defeating Germany. With Germany eliminated, Stimson worried that the Pacific war would run aground against weakened resolve at home. He felt pressure building at home for a speedy end to the war. And Stimson did not welcome the prospect of a long and bloody invasion of the Japanese homeland, with many thousands of American casualties.[106]

In Stimson's account the proper step was to strike "a dual target—that is, a military installation or war plant surrounded by or adjacent to houses and other buildings most susceptible to damage." In sum, the atomic bomb must achieve maximum effects in terms of psychological shock and destruction of life and property (20). The Japanese fear of more bombs, Stimson argued, would pressure the emperor to side with the peace party and silence the warmongers in his government. The atomic bomb led to surrender.[107]

Had the bombs not been used, Stimson contended, the death toll of Japanese civilians from starvation due to a naval blockade, continued incendiary and conventional bombing, and invasion might have resulted in losses even higher than those sustained in Hiroshima and Nagasaki.[108] Two lessons were clear to Stimson. First, the bombs brought the war to a quick conclusion. Second, war in the twentieth century "has grown steadily more barbarous, more destructive, more debased in all its aspects." Hence the atomic bombs have shown us that "we must never have another war" (21).

Let's assume that this is a fair and accurate accounting of the decision-making process and concerns, even recognizing that Stimson elides certain important issues. Was the decision to use the bomb motivated, at least in part, by "atomic diplomacy," in the well-known formulation of Gar Alperovitz? Certainly American leaders wanted to send a message to the Soviet Union that they had the ultimate military power, and, in turn, that they expected the Soviets to be more amenable to U.S. solutions to thorny post-war problems, especially in Eastern Europe.[109] Such an agenda cannot be divorced from moral questions; indeed, it raises issues about motivation. If the United States used the bomb primarily to intimidate the Soviet Union rather than to hasten the end of the war with Japan, then surely moral turpitude is involved. But the consensus among historians is that atomic diplomacy was tangential, at best, in the decision to use the bomb. There is more validity to the view that dropping the bombs might have been a mistake or at least premature, since Japan was on the ropes and susceptible to inducements to surrender if the United States would agree to allow the emperor to be retained. But this, too, is disputed by some historians who find that Japanese resistance to surrender on any terms was resolute. Others have maintained that the bomb might have been excessive given that conventional bombing, the entry of the Soviet troops into Manchuria, and the naval blockade were pushing Japan toward surrender nonetheless. These are complex issues, to be sure, but along with many historians, I believe the bomb would have been used whether or not the Soviet Union ever existed.

Are Atomic Bombs So Special?

Explicit, in-depth debates over the morality of the bomb were almost as rare in postwar America as they had been during the conflict. One particularly incisive exchange occurred in March 1946, after the *New York Times* had published a draft report from the Federal Council of Churches, signed by theologian Reinhold Niebuhr and others, calling the use of the atomic bomb "morally indefensible." The atomic bombings, along with earlier conventional bombing of Japanese civilian centers, in the view of Protestant leaders, represented an un-Christian war policy of "indiscriminate, excessive violence."[110]

James B. Conant, who had been a member of the Interim Committee and head of the National Civilian Defense Council during the war, responded angrily. How could Niebuhr, who was famous for his tragic sense of life, for his haunted recognition that sometimes in an impure world immoral means are necessary to achieve moral ends, oppose the use of such weapons against a militaristic empire such as Japan? Niebuhr was not a pacifist; he considered himself a resolute realist.[111] Conant argued that the use of the atomic bomb must be viewed in the context of the previous employment of area and firebombing of civilian targets. Should not Niebuhr, the clergy, and the American people be "equally penitent for the destruction of Tokyo" as much as for the destruction of Hiroshima? Why single out the atomic bomb, which had, according to Conant, brought a swift end to the long and horrific war? Only if one were a pacifist would Niebuhr's position make sense. Since Conant knew that Niebuhr was no pacifist, such opposition to atomic weapons in World War II struck him as inconsistent and strained.

Niebuhr admitted that "no absolute distinction could be drawn" between the levels of destructiveness of the various means employed. Indeed, he reverted to one of the key explanations for the use of the bomb, revealing why, in the minds of almost all policy makers, it had always been considered a valid weapon. Niebuhr would have preferred a warning about or a demonstration of the bomb's killing power. If the Japanese did not sue for surrender, then the bomb's use was justified, even, one presumes, against noncombatants, because it would shorten the war and in the process save many American and Japanese lives.[112]

Another reason to go ahead with the bomb was neither moral nor strategic, but practical: not to use it would have been economically wasteful and controversial. The Manhattan Project had been immensely expensive; to have realized in theory and practice an effective weapon and then chosen not to employ it while war raged was an unlikely scenario. Stimson once joked, after learning that the bomb had worked, that he would now avoid going to Leavenworth prison since he had not wasted "two billion dollars on this atomic venture."[113] In addition, as historian Michael Sherry points out, a form of "technological fanaticism" supported dropping the atomic bomb.[114] After so much energy and effort, and so much faith in the power of a single technological innovation to end the war, the chances that it would not be employed were diminished.

Use of the atomic bomb, moreover, was wrapped up in a long-term consequentialist moralism that is common to the customs of total warfare. Policy planners maintained that deployment of the bomb might shock the world into recognition of a new, potentially world-ending weapon. Only from this sobering realization, such reasoning went, would the international community come to its senses and work to outlaw war. While patently utopian, this perspective allowed individuals involved in the production and deployment of the bomb to view their actions in a moral light—one that justified destruction, in part, because it presaged a better world. Thus, claimed Conant, only by using the bomb in combat would the world be alerted to its destructive force and be willing to take "drastic action to control it in the future."[115]

Do Atomic Scientists Know Better?

The only major opposition to the use of atomic bombs during the war came from atomic scientists. Early in the war they had believed with unanimity that the prospect of a Nazi atomic bomb was a nightmare beyond comprehension.[116] Many of them had experienced the iron hand of Nazi totalitarianism, and they were pleased to use their expertise to develop a weapon that might destroy it. American and émigré physicists worked with great haste to produce the bomb. As Leo Szilard later recounted, "Initially we were strongly motivated to produce the bomb because we feared the Germans would get ahead of us and the only way to prevent them from dropping bombs on us was to have bombs in readiness ourselves."[117] J. Robert Oppenheimer wrote to Roosevelt in 1943 to assure him that the scientists "as a group and as individual Americans are profoundly aware of our responsibility." Patriotic responsibility jibed nicely with professional challenges, as the scientists were engaged in a collaborative project that in and of itself was a fascinating and purposeful scientific puzzle.[118]

Moral concerns about the bomb, at least before the surrender of Germany, were rarely voiced. Physicist Hans Bethe later reflected that "during the war—at least—I did not pay much attention" to moral issues about the atomic bomb. "We had a job to do and a very hard one."[119] After all, as Bernard Feld contended, "We were caught up in this activity, which was all consuming," with fifteen- to seventeen-hour workdays and the intense pressure to succeed. Scientists developed "a kind of tunnel vision." In the heat of scientific discovery, one could forget about what effects this work would have on humans. Richard Feynman noted: "What I did immorally was not to remember the reason I was doing it" once Germany had surrendered. Physicist Victor Weiskopf was perhaps most cogent in recalling that while scientists constantly discussed the power of the bomb, the radiation sickness and fires it would cause, they failed "to confront the moral issues" in their work for various reasons, not the least of which was the desire for success and the demands of the war.[120]

Another atomic scientist, R. R. Wilson, recalled that "although I had favored a demonstration of the bomb, I knew that it was not for me to have any say in the decision how or when to use it." He believed then, and continued to maintain, that "use of the bomb really did save American and Japanese lives."[121] Szilard did not think a demonstration on an island would have any effect. He preferred restraint since, in his judgment, Japan was already defeated and surrender was soon to come. He did not, as far as I can tell, worry especially about the round-the-clock conventional and incendiary bombing of Japanese cities that was continuing unabated. In part, this was typical of the moral myopia induced by the customs of war and Szilard's view that the atomic bomb was something especially momentous in the history of the human race.[122] Only Joseph Rotblat, a Polish refugee physicist at Los Alamos, left the project. Like other scientists, his moral scruples about working on the bomb were overcome by imagining Hitler, in his Berlin bunker, ordering the atomic destruction of London as part of his *Götterdämmerung*. But once Rotblat knew in late 1944 that Hitler had no such bomb, he quit the project. He acknowledged that "the morality issue at a time of war" is most crucial. He wondered why other scientists remained committed to the program at this point in the war. He answered that they were driven by curiosity, desire to finish a task, belief that use of the bomb would save lives, or that they had no particular role to play in the politics of the bomb. In any case, most of the scientists, he concluded, "were not bothered by moral scruples."[123]

Scientists were hardly different in this respect from most Americans. Given the developing custom of total war following the massive incineration of civilians from conventional bombing, these scientists accepted that weapons of destruction were built to be employed either against Germany or Japan. Most atomic scientists, unlike their fellow citizens, had more than an inkling of the bomb's qualitative and quantitative difference from "normal" modes of killing. Yet the weapon's value lay in this precise valence—its power promised to end the war more quickly. Aware that atomic weapons represented a threat to humanity overall, these scientists were convinced—or they convinced themselves—that only by having the world view the bombs' destructive power might any hope for future controls be initiated. Even if a demonstration of the atomic bomb could have been set up on a deserted island, atomic physicists Oppenheimer, A. H. Compton, Enrico Fermi, and E. O. Lawrence believed that it would fail to impress sufficiently.[124] Physicist

Philip Morrison argued that "I wanted to drop the bomb to reveal indiscriminate horror; I was sure my fellow men would end war."[125]

Other atomic scientists, however, did come to voice deep concerns, especially after the defeat of Nazi Germany in the spring of 1945. Atomic scientists associated with the Metallurgical Lab (Met Lab) at the University of Chicago had a tradition of feistiness and leftist activism. They believed that science must be an open process, and they wanted their insight into atomic weapons to warrant the attention of military and strategic planners. With Germany out of the picture and Japan on the brink of defeat, they warned against using the bomb. Much of their concern was future-oriented; atomic weapons might destabilize postwar relations between the United States and the Soviet Union, resulting in a disastrous atomic arms race that would threaten to topple the world into a nuclear nightmare.

Under the leadership of James Franck, atomic scientists in Chicago developed two reports, written before the use of the atomic bombs but too late to have significant effect on policy. In the fullest report, drafted in June 1945, Franck and his colleagues warned that how the secret of the bomb was presented to the world was of paramount importance. To use the bombs on Japan threatened to "destroy all our chances" at securing international agreements on the weapons, and it would be sure to shock even our closest allies. Just because we have the weapon, the scientists lectured, does not mean that we have to use it; we had kept poison gas in our arsenals throughout the war. The argument was directed against the "sudden use of atomic bombs," that would undermine "confidence" in the United States and result in "a wave of horror and repulsion sweeping over the rest of the world and perhaps even dividing public opinion at home."[126]

The Chicago scientists urged a demonstration, perhaps in "the desert or a barren island." But it was unclear how such a demonstration of a bomb that had already been described as "of comparatively low efficiency and small size" would ensure Japan's surrender, especially given the immense incendiary bombing damage already inflicted on its cities. If the demonstration, however, failed to convince the Japanese to surrender, then atomic scientists accepted that the bomb "might perhaps be used against Japan." Yet, even here, they wanted the "sanction of the United Nations (and of public opinion at home)," and "a preliminary ultimatum" that might allow Japan to "evacuate certain regions" as a prelude to the dropping of the bomb. The scientists admitted that such a plan was going to "sound fantastic." And beside the point. The Interim Committee had already quickly and effectively dismissed, with Oppenheimer's participation, issues of a warning and demonstration. Nor did the atomic scientists protest that dropping the bomb(s) was inherently immoral. The Franck letter, then, was simply a variation on a minor theme in the non-decision to use the atomic bombs. Although humane in purpose, it lacked any moral argument against the killing of civilians in a situation of total war.[127] Even among the atomic scientists there was a sense of the inevitable, of a force that could not be constrained by the acts of statesmen and soldiers.

Moral Choices

Should we be uncomfortable with this narrative of necessary destruction and moral muddiness? Are we in danger of succumbing to a system of thought—think here of Marxism, or military necessity, or moral nihilism—that diminishes moral choice? In some old-school Marxian formulations, the capitalist who sucks his workers dry is absolved of evil since he is merely doing what he is programmed to do; he has boarded a historical train of development that presumably chugs toward the revolution of the proletariat and ultimately leads to a better world. Such a calculus, of course, bears a strong resemblance to the arguments of Conant and others that the bombing of civilians in World War II was necessary not only to secure the victory for the just, but to prevent future wars. The short-term calculus of suffering overrode the greater suffering that would occur with continued warfare.

Sometimes, as historian Ian Kershaw tells us, choices are fateful.[128] Choice always remains no matter how strongly circumstances intervene. It might be more fully sanctioned if there existed in government circles, especially in times of war, a vigorous moral culture marked by a willingness to engage moral issues before it is too late to do so. Such a culture is necessary but difficult to achieve. When the world tottered on the brink of nuclear war during the Cuban missile crisis of October 1962, the level of discussion and debate was uninspiring. There exists in government circles a culture of consensus. This is marked, as Irving L. Janis and others point out, by an unwillingness to raise sharp questions, to buck certitude, to challenge higher authority. The moral temper of government officials is often marked by loyalty to an already agreed upon policy, lest one appear to be breaking from consensus or not supporting the "team." Policy planners often adopt the most strident options lest they appear weak or hesitant. Moral burdens are seen as problematic rather than as necessary.[129] Intellectuals in government—individuals trained to contemplate various options—have invariably failed to raise the bar of moral discussion. More often than not, they willingly serve the powers that be. Political scientists Richard E. Neustadt and Ernest R. May conclude that historical analogies employed by policy planners, no less than moral questions, have been lacking. Even situations that avert disaster, such as the Cuban missile crisis, seem to attest less to the strategic sagacity or moral depth of political leaders than to pure luck.[130] In the end, nuclear holocaust was avoided only because Khrushchev and, to a degree Kennedy, pulled back.

The custom of war, at least as played out in World War II, presumed that the lives of one's own soldiers were more sacrosanct than those of enemy noncombatants. As General LeMay phrased it with customary gruffness, "We're at war with Japan. We were attacked by Japan. Do you want to kill Japanese, or would you rather have Americans killed?"[131] Is there also some ethical aspect behind Truman and Stimson's repeated conviction that American lives must come first? And, of course, to what degree? The Army Manual states that it is incumbent on commanders to minimize civilian casualties, even at the cost of additional soldiers under their command dying, so long as the losses do not change the eventual outcome of the conflict. But this was not the position voiced by American political leaders.[132] And this is hardly surprising.

Consider this well-worn but useful story. A man is strolling by a wide swimming hole, and he hears the frantic screams of two young children. He rushes to dive in and immediately realizes that he can save the life of only one of the children, and that one of the kids happens to be his own. Surely few of us would condemn his split-second decision to save his own child's life. In an analysis of this exercise, Israeli-born philosopher Avishai Margalit remarks that the ethical, in contradistinction to the moral, presupposes a locality of rules. It is anchored in the "thick" attachments of family, community, ethnicity, religion, and sometimes nation.[133] This contrasts with the universalism at the heart of morals. Truman and Stimson, then, faced an ethical dilemma that consisted of the choice between saving one group (the lives of many thousands of American soldiers certain to be killed in an invasion of the Japanese home islands) and forfeiting the lives of Japanese noncombatants. As noted earlier, estimates of the number of Japanese killed if the war dragged on into the fall was a quarter of a million. Did leaders, then, choose wisely? Did they even consider whether the lives of noncombatants are to be protected over and above the lives of their own soldiers? Or did they uphold the moral calculus that their choice would lessen death overall? These were the alternatives that should have been considered fully.[134]

But this moral tale of necessary and tragic choice also spins on the wobbly axis of how choices are framed. As many historians and moralists argue, the choice to employ atomic bombs was not as simple as Truman and Stimson claimed. Other narratives can easily be developed which muddy this swimming-hole moral tale. Might a demonstration of the power of the atomic bomb (despite all the reasons against it—that it might signal weakness or the lack of available weapons) have been warranted morally? Might a shift in the terms of unconditional surrender have been sufficient for the emperor and those in the Japanese cabinet wanting peace to have prevailed? Might the Soviet invasion of Manchuria, with the continuation of conventional bombing, have been sufficient to force the Japanese to surrender well before the 1 November proposed invasion of the Japanese home islands?[135] The answers to these questions are, of course, resistant to certainty and testing; they are counterfactual and speculative. But they are relevant in moral terms, for they suggest the complexity of the options that were not followed.

Hovering over these moral concerns are questions of virtue and moral luck. Moral luck thrust Truman into the presidency without sufficient training or power. Even if he had the moral character to demand deeper consideration of war department plans for employment of the atomic bomb against a civilian center, he clearly lacked the political will or gravitas in the spring of 1945 to impose any alternatives. Nor was there any inclination, in a time of total war that had been raging for far too long, to question the value of a device that might bring closure quickly, without endangering American lives. In too many ways, then, the complexity of moral decisions, the demands of wartime process, and the logic of sustained destruction mar the potential for "mature consideration." And, as moral psychologists demonstrate, the expression of virtuous acts, the willingness to act in a particular manner, is often less a function of character than of circumstances. If so, then to expect Truman, or even Roosevelt, to have halted the machinery of destruction when it had already been motoring along, is fanciful.

Yet I think the men involved in approving conventional and atomic bombing ceded the highest moral ground by not entering energetically and early into the complexity of moral questions.[136] While Secretary of War Stimson, as his diaries reveal, spent many hours in meetings about the use of the atomic bomb, most of those meetings concerned diplomatic and procedural issues regarding the amount of cooperation with the British and noncooperation with the Soviets. The fullest discussion of options to demonstrate the bomb occurred during a handful of minutes at lunch among some members of the Interim Committee on 31 May 1945. And, as we have seen, the recommendations regarding the target—was it simply to be military or to include civilians, and in what numbers and for what purpose(s)?—lacked clarity. Internal and strenuous discussion was also absent in military and civilian circles concerning the widespread conventional and firebombing of urban areas. Moral questions are often contested and confusing, but they need to be aired. Only by discussion and debate is there any potential for moral action. A failure to rise to "mature consideration" of these issues strikes me as the worm eating at the moral problems confronted by Stimson and Truman. They may have made the correct decision, or they may not have thought any other options reasonable. But they arrived at these conclusions without sufficient anxiety, without sufficient flexing of their moral muscles and minds.

Coda: Oppenheimer's Regret

On a drizzly October day in 1945, physicist J. Robert Oppenheimer strode to a White House meeting with President Harry S. Truman. Two months earlier, in August, thanks in part to Oppenheimer's strenuous and brilliant leadership at the Los Alamos atomic laboratory, the United States had been able to drop two atomic bombs on Japan. Soon thereafter, World War II was over. Rather than bask in his accomplishments, Oppenheimer, as described by Vice President Henry A. Wallace, was tormented by a monumental sense of "guilt consciousness."[137] His anxiety that morning was mirrored by an editorial in the *Washington Post* calling for international controls on atomic weapons and research. While the editorial acknowledged the "promise" of atomic energy for the betterment of humanity, it was alarmed by the "peril" of nuclear madness in the not too distant future.[138]

Such concerns were distant from President Truman's consciousness as he greeted Oppenheimer. Truman was pleased that the atomic bombs had ended the war with minimal loss of American lives and sent a message to the Soviets about American power in the postwar world. Shortly into their discussion at the White House, Truman interrupted Oppenheimer's articulate plea for international control of atomic weapons with a question: When did Oppenheimer think the Soviets would develop their own atomic bombs? Oppenheimer replied that he imagined, along with many of his scientific colleagues, that the Soviets would have such weapons within five years. Truman quickly countered that the Soviets would "never" develop their own atomic bomb.[139] Such bravado stunned Oppenheimer. He blurted out, "Mr. President, I feel I have blood on my hands."[140]

One account has it that Truman barked at Oppenheimer, "Never mind. It'll all come out in the wash."[141] Truman later claimed to have offered Oppenheimer his own handkerchief to help him wash off the blood. Another account suggests that Truman, without a hint of sympathy, said that the blood was on his own hands, and that Oppenheimer should "let me worry about that." After all, Truman was sure of his action; he refused to "waste a minute on regret."[142]

Oppenheimer felt differently. The bomb, he now concluded, had not been necessary to end the war since Japan was already on the brink of surrender. Atomic weapons would soon be produced by the Soviets, and an arms race would only increase the chances for a doomsday scenario. "In some sort of crude sense," he wrote famously in 1948, "physicists have known sin; and this is a knowledge which they cannot lose."[143] At another point, he declared that the bomb had exploded on "an essentially defeated enemy."[144] But these remarks were scattered and left underdeveloped. Indeed, some analysts find that Oppenheimer was purposefully evasive, without real regrets about the use of the bomb on civilian centers. He was, however, deeply worried that atomic bombs and even more powerful weapons in the future threatened humanity's survival.[145]

Immediately following the war, Oppenheimer used the connections and skills he had honed at Los Alamos to nudge atomic weapons policy toward greater openness and control. He remained extremely comfortable among the emerging scientific elite, which was becoming central to the military and industrial complex of the postwar nation. In the words of historian Charles Thorpe, Oppenheimer became a "nodal figure" in the relationship between the state and science.[146] He remained a central figure up to the point he was humiliated publicly at the Atomic Energy Commission hearings in 1949 and stripped of his security clearance. This occurred because he had cultivated some powerful enemies, lied about his connections with known communists, and actively opposed the hydrogen bomb.

However, in the summer months of 1945, Oppenheimer, no less than Truman, had welcomed the use of the bomb. Neither man had shown much anxiety about dropping a weapon of such power on largely civilian centers. Had they acted morally at that time? And might both of them, somehow, have taken morally valid positions in their postwar responses to the bombings? Oppenheimer never had any doubts about what he was doing during the war. Certainly, the fact that the bomb was being prepared to trump any similar device that Germany might be producing was of monumental importance to him. Moreover, as Oppenheimer often remarked, there was an almost "organic necessity" to pursue work on the bomb as a function of scientific curiosity.[147] Pride and ambition also factored into Oppenheimer's desire to succeed. This is hardly surprising or even amoral in the context of total war against a larger-than-life evil enemy.

Perhaps Oppenheimer and other atomic scientists felt guilt over their complicity, but they also tingled with the Promethean power of engaging in a noble cause and the spirit of scientific discovery. While naïve in his expectation that, once the world had seen the horrors visited on Japan by the atomic bombs, it would hasten to control them, Oppenheimer was at least aware of the complexities of his own role.[148] Some consider his postwar explanations as rationalizations covering his ambition, naïveté, or hubris. Others may think that Oppenheimer was, as Truman claimed, a "cry-baby," since his actions had been undertaken with good intentions.[149]

Oppenheimer cannot be said to have shown remorse, although he may have felt shame or regret. Australian philosopher Raimond Gaita defines remorse as the painful realization of the wrong that one has done to someone else.[150] As far as I know, Oppenheimer never issued a public apology for his own role in the "wrong" done to the Japanese noncombatants by "his" bomb.[151] He did, however, clearly experience shame, which Gaita speaks of as less about the wrong that has been done than about what it demonstrates about the agent and his or her own shortcomings. In that sense, Oppenheimer's response to the bombing of Hiroshima and the forces it unleashed was about his shame, perhaps related to his own ambition. But it does not reveal him as feeling especially guilty or remorseful.

Oppenheimer acted within emerging customs of total war, with perfectly reasonable intentions and some moral sanction. His shame, such as it was, should have been directed at his willingness to countenance and support the use of the weapon against noncombatants. His responsibility is most apparent when, during the course of the war, he failed to think deeply about the erasure of the distinction between combatant and noncombatant. At the critical meeting of the Interim Committee on 31 May 1945, Oppenheimer learned that the bomb would be used on a "a vital war plant *employing a large number of workers and closely surrounded by workers' houses*" (emphasis added). He did not protest and, in fact, remarked that "several strikes" at the same time would be "feasible." This was the moment he tasted sin and perhaps trafficked with evil.[152] Or, to put it in Arendt's terms, he had allowed ambition, curiosity, and immediate ends to blunt his moral thinking. The problem was not that Oppenheimer chose wrongly or did anything immoral in working on the bomb and supporting its use against Japan. That will forever remain an open moral issue, one marked by spirited and necessary debate. Oppenheimer failed morally because he did not, during the time, act thoughtfully to question the logic of potential destruction. Such "mature consideration" would at least have indicated that Oppenheimer was living up to the high humanistic ideals he cherished.

Unfortunately, it is in the nature of total war, in its very sinews and customs, to propagate evil. Perhaps we are, as Conant suggested, naïve in thinking that wars can be fought in a moral manner. War is about killing. While distinctions between civilians and military personnel are invaluable and proper, it is important to recognize that they are rarely respected. Wars fought for the most just reasons, according to Hugo Slim, are still infected with the most virulent strains of "anti-civilian ideologies." Wars have always been marked by unjustifiable killing of civilians.[153] Perhaps the only way to prevent such slaughter is to prevent wars from occurring in the first place. Once soldiers are placed in such situations, either from afar or up close, the worst can occur, often for the most mysterious and muddled reasons.

Chapter Three
The Moral Mystery of My Lai

"All Hell Broke Loose"

An artillery barrage around 7 A.M. on 16 March 1968 pierced the calm, clear morning around the Vietnamese hamlets collectively known as My Lai.[1] About twenty minutes later, nine American choppers set down near a rice paddy. Soldiers from three platoons hurried out and tried to form a defensive position around the landing zone. They anticipated a major confrontation with battle-hardened North Vietnamese army regulars and a Vietcong battalion.[2] Instead, they encountered only women, children, and old men. This was surprising, since the soldiers had been told the women and children would be at the market that morning, away from the scene of battle. As the soldiers moved toward the nearest hamlet, a hundred meters or so from the landing zone, they began firing, sometimes into the thick surrounding brush, sometimes at fleeing civilians obscured by the high and lush vegetation of banana trees and corn stalks. They knew that the My Lai villagers supported the Vietcong, and they believed that many in the area were dangerous enemies. The soldiers, mainly from Charlie Company under the command of Lieutenant William Calley, had received their orders from Captain Ernest Medina. They were on a "search and destroy" mission. That much was certain. But within that designation, interpretations varied—from general agreement that all structures were to be burned and all animals and foodstuffs destroyed, to the conviction that all inhabitants should be killed, no matter what their age or gender.

The soldiers moved forward in zigzag formation. As platoons intermingled, soldiers became separated from their normal combat buddies. Many soldiers later claimed they had not seen any killing of civilians. Yet by the end of that day, at least five hundred Vietnamese civilians, most of them women, children, and elderly, had been slain at close range by American soldiers. Once the assault began, no shots were directed at nor was any incident of resistance reported against the advancing Americans. "There was no enemy resistance," stated machine gunner James Bergthold.[3]

On entering the village area, tunnel rat Herbert Carter remembered that "all hell broke loose." Soldiers "went in the village and started killing and burning."[4] One of the first to kill, according to Grenadier Harry Stanley, was rifleman Allen Boyce. "He grabbed an old man" and "threw him" into a well, before dropping a hand grenade down inside it.[5] Some killed reluctantly. Squad leader Kenneth Schiel initially resisted his orders to kill. "I don't want to do it, but I have to because we were ordered to do it," said Schiel, according to one witness. Once Schiel began firing into a group of eight or nine civilians, none of whom offered any resistance or had any weapons, his comrades joined him.[6]

Some killed with glee. Fred Widmer borrowed a .45-caliber handgun, then walked toward a two-year-old child and shot him in the neck, at point-blank range. Widmer laughed and then said, "Did you see that fucker die?"[7] Some raped with abandon. "Sergeant [Kenneth] Hodges took one girl . . . and drug her into a compartment, like in a hootch there, you know, and hootches don't have doors or nothing, and you could see, and he raped one girl inside there. And then there was three other guys and one girl all at one time."[8]

As the outrages continued and civilian casualties mounted, some soldiers would later claim they killed for humanitarian reasons. While resting and eating lunch, soldiers Richard Pendleton, Bill Doherty, and Mike Terry heard moans coming from a nearby gulley. There they found a score of bodies; a few were still alive, including a woman who had been shot four times in the back with small arms fire. Terry—a devoutly religious Mormon—then shot her, to put her out of her misery.[9]

Those in command that day actively participated in the slaughter. Sergeant David Mitchell and Corporal Paul Meadlo rounded up forty to forty-five civilians in the center of the town. Meadlo presumed he was to guard them. Lieutenant Calley came by soon after and asked Meadlo, "You ain't killed them yet?" According to Meadlo, Calley started shooting at the Vietnamese, and Meadlo, Dennis Conti, and Mitchell joined in. Meadlo fired four clips of ammo, or about sixty-seven bullets from his M16. After dispatching this group, Calley and Meadlo went to another, larger group of about seventy-five, and they proceeded to kill them as well.[10] Captain Medina also got into the bloodshed. According to some observers, Medina shot at point-blank range a crying boy of about three to four years old. Medina's bullet made "pieces" as the boy's "head flew off."[11]

By noon, the villages of My Lai could be described as looking like "the devil's butcher shop."[12]

A Moral Moment

Arendt taught us that evil shows two faces—the radical and the banal. Her formulations seem to apply with equal vigor to the events of that day in March 1968. As we will see, the young men who killed that day were normal; they carried standard moral values. Yet they killed without provocation. Banal and radical evil strode along together into My Lai. Explanations aplenty—all of them predictable and reasonable—capture the "absurdity and moral inversion" of the massacre, in all its horror.[13] Obedience to authority, the ambiguity of orders, desire for revenge, and dehumanization all enter into the natural universe of explanation.[14]

Psychologists Stanley Milgram and Philip Zimbardo tell us that institutions shape our responses, that we readily obey authority, that even when our moral inclinations point in one direction, they are easily overridden by circumstance and situation. All this is without doubt true. We know that Calley killed and ordered others under his command to kill at My Lai. He is someone who can be blamed and made the focus of our warranted disgust for what happened that day. Moreover, given the testimony of the soldiers that in the army one follows orders and that they were unaware or insufficiently capable of following the rules of law given to them on wallet cards, they killed usually without questioning.[15]

But these explanations ultimately fail to allow for understanding the radical nature of evil at My Lai. Radical evil was part of these men's mien that day, and it defies, in part, our expectations and explanations. Such wanton murder is irreducible to antecedent conditions. In many of its aspects, the massacre will forever remain a moral mystery, a moment that challenges all our ideals about how people act. I agree with novelist and Vietnam veteran Tim O'Brien's view of My Lai. In addressing how this could have happened, O'Brien simply contends that his unit and most others in Vietnam faced similar hardships and carried many of the same attitudes with them to Vietnam. The My Lai massacre, O'Brien concludes, is "going to remain a mystery."[16] But that does not mean we should avoid trying to enter into its heart, to comprehend in our limited fashion what happened. The moral challenges it presents demand more, and we must wonder about whether such radical evil could have been contained.

Why do the murders at My Lai shock our moral sensibilities perhaps more than the saturation and atomic bombings we discussed in the chapter on World War II? Some draw a direct line from Hiroshima to Vietnam. Walter H. Capps found that an unwillingness to respect civilians and the reliance on technology in World War II paved the way for Vietnam. The technologies of long-distance killing and the devastation of Vietnam were something to which Americans had long ago become inured.[17] The bloodshed during the earlier war was monumental in comparison with the five hundred killed at My Lai. While hundreds of thousands of civilians were slaughtered at long distance by bombing in World War II, the moral issues and circumstances were complex and confusing. One may condemn such bombings and question their necessity after the fact, but one can also understand the logic that led to those attacks. The bombings occurred in the context of a Just War, and a utilitarian calculus kicked in that allowed those in power to maintain that civilian deaths would hasten the end of the war and minimize the sum total of civilian and military deaths. However problematic this means-toward-an-end logic may have been, it is hardly absurd to many of us.

What makes My Lai morally abhorrent and fascinating is that the killing was done at close range and without apparent necessity. The names and faces of the men who pulled the triggers are known to us; indeed, they went unpunished by courts of law—with the exception of Calley, and his punishment was minimal—and live among us now, sometimes with their demons at bay, other times with them exploding to the surface. Ron Haeberle's photographs from the site render obvious not only the scale of the slaughter but the "identities" of its victims—small thin women, infants, and the elderly. As Arthur Koestler and others have remarked, "statistics don't bleed."[18]

My Lai is compelling also because we can imagine ourselves deposited into the ranks of Charlie Company. For those of us old enough to have been eligible for the Vietnam conflict but who did not participate—saved by the moral luck of a student deferment or a safe number in the draft lottery—we wonder how we might have acted in that moral moment. Would we have killed—grimly, methodically, or gleefully? Would we have shrunk from the bloodletting by keeping a low profile, wandering away from the main action? Or would we prefer to believe that we, unlike anyone that day, might have been able to stanch the killing, to alleviate the suffering?[19] Yes, it is easier to imagine ourselves in the uniforms of the members of the three platoons in My Lai that day than as civilians in Dresden or Tokyo, being rained down on with destruction. As Fred E. Katz puts it bluntly, "in their makeup" the men at My Lai "are us. They are ourselves. . . . In them we are obliged to confront a side of our own human nature that really exists."[20]

Did the soldiers at My Lai surrender totally to the army's demand for obedience to authority—their training to the army's imperative that soldiers follow orders? Did the slaughter occur because orders were ambiguous? Are we faced here with a simple but common case of competing ethical imperatives: the demand to follow orders and the injunction against harming civilians without justification? Did the circumstances of a vicious, guerilla war douse the flames of virtue in the characters of these young men? Or might the mystery of My Lai—its close-up killing and ineffability—be the stuff that constitutes radical evil? Certainly, these soldiers had less time and mental inclination to question their orders than did Oppenheimer, Truman, and Stimson. Is it reasonable to inquire if they might have been able to exercise a more "mature consideration" in response to the moment? Some did, some did not. Is there any moral resource these men might have drawn on to avoid the murder spree?

I can imagine a chorus of protest about focusing on the men who killed at close range that day. After all, why should they be singled out for moral analysis—and perhaps implicit condemnation—when they were mere pawns in a larger, evil game? Here we deal with a hierarchy of sin and degrees of punishment. The men at the top, from Presidents Lyndon Johnson and Richard Nixon to Secretaries of Defense Robert M. McNamara and Melvin Laird, were the true architects and perpetrators of the policy of body counts, search and destroy missions, the use of Agent Orange, political assassinations, forced removals of citizens, and many more dark policies. Yet they remained, all too often, unscathed, shielded from moral evaluation and condemnation. Armed forces personnel at the highest ranks issued orders and directed the machinery of destruction on the population of Vietnam. Why are the moral failings of the men at My Lai a consideration when, in contrast, pilots dropping bombs from thousands of feet above villages destroyed thousands more lives? Artillery captains giving the order to shell a village also killed many more, without any sense of moral responsibility, shame, or horror.[21]

These are valid complaints, and I do not intend for my narrow focus on the grunts at My Lai to limit the blame. The civilian officials and military brass who wantonly pursued this war, who devised the policies and who lied about it, all deserve moral condemnation. Even the perceived need to uphold American honor, to stem the tide of revolutionary nationalism, to meet treaty obligations, and to adapt to the realities of fighting a guerilla war all fail to justify the problematic nature of this war. Moreover, while moral issues are often muddy, sometimes they are relatively clear. What happened in My Lai and during much of the war in Vietnam was wrong, pure and simple, from my perspective.

I focus attention on those young men because of the moral complexities with which they struggled. We also often find ourselves confronting situations marked by a conflict between beliefs, a relationship with authority, a sense of pressure from one's peers—albeit with far lower stakes. The Americans at My Lai were in a sense representative of us all. They retain responsibility for their actions even if every option involved compromise of conscience or responsibility. The massacre was a moral moment of immense proportions in terms of its challenges and larger meaning. It was a moral moment our nation only slowly realized and, in the end, refused to confront.

Crimes Without Punishment

Ron Ridenhour knew some of the soldiers at My Lai, and although he had not been there himself, he had heard tales about it that shocked his sense of morality. By chance, he ran into Michael Bernhardt, one of the men in the staging area that day. Bernhardt confirmed for Ridenhour all of his darkest fears about what had happened. Upon returning to the States, Ridenhour resumed his journalism studies at Arizona State University. He decided that something had to be done. His matter-of-fact letter, dated 29 March 1969, describing what he believed had happened at My Lai, was sent to various governmental offices and to senators and congressmen. In the next-to-last paragraph, Ridenhour admitted that "I do not know for *certain*" what happened that day in My Lai, "but I am convinced that it was something very black indeed." Slowly, the letter moved up the governmental hierarchy and finally received attention.[22]

In November 1969, the massacre became a public sensation when the *Cleveland Plain Dealer* published photographs of the scene taken by army photographer Ron Haeberle. Investigative journalist Seymour Hersh, prodded by Ridenhour's letter, began interviewing My Lai servicemen and published a detailed account of the atrocity. Calley, with only a short time remaining on his enlistment, was charged with killing more than one hundred Vietnamese in My Lai. That same month, General William C. Westmoreland, commander of American forces in Vietnam, appointed General

William Peers to conduct a high-level investigation into what happened in My Lai and to explain why it had not been properly handled as a massacre by higher-ups in Vietnam.

General Peers went about his work quickly and methodically. He built up a team of investigators and office staff to interview participants in the alleged massacre. He went up the chain of command to see what orders had been given and, importantly, how army officials had failed or refused to investigate the atrocity. Peers was soon convinced that a massacre of immense proportions had occurred at My Lai: "a large number of women, children, and old men possibly in excess of four hundred, had been ruthlessly killed." He also recognized that the army had covered up the massacre from the start. As in the Watergate scandal, Peers later noted, officials deceived and lied in order to protect themselves and put their own interests above those of the common good.[23]

Over the next five years, efforts to punish those guilty for the massacre became increasingly less viable. A couple of early cases against soldiers were brought before juries that found the perpetrators innocent, either on the grounds that they were following orders or that Vietnamese civilians had sufficient potential to cause harm. Many of those involved in the killing escaped prosecution because by the time the government was ready to move with charges, they were out of the army, vulnerable only to the highly unlikely prospect of a civil suit. While the Peers report demonstrated that many officers above the rank of captain were negligent at best and deceitful at worst, none was convicted of crimes, although some were forced out of the service.[24]

Before the books had closed on the My Lai prosecutions, twenty-five individuals were charged with various crimes, both as participants in the murder and for aiding the coverup. Six soldiers were court-martialed, but only Calley was convicted. Two generals, Major General Samuel W. Koster and Brigadier General George H. Young, Jr., were charged with having committed between them forty-three "acts of misconduct or omission." It was revealed that Koster knew from the first day that at least twenty civilians had been killed. But he chose not to investigate those deaths with any ardor, and as a result, he may not even have known the extent of the killings at My Lai. Having served as superintendent of the United States Military Academy at West Point after leaving Vietnam, Koster was subsequently stripped of his Distinguished Service Medal and soon mustered out of the service.[25]

Only Lieutenant Calley was brought to trial. His defense was simple: He had followed orders from Captain Medina. Moreover, he claimed justification for killing more than one hundred civilians because "they were all the enemy, they were all to be destroyed."[26] Convicted by a military jury for the premeditated killing of twenty-two people at My Lai, Calley was sentenced to life imprisonment at hard labor. The appeals process dragged on for five years, becoming a political football and national cause célèbre. A few days after Calley's conviction at the end of March 1971, President Richard M. Nixon intervened in the case. Well aware that many in the nation viewed Calley as an unfortunate victim, Nixon declared that pending appeal, Calley would be confined to house arrest. By the end of August, Calley's sentence had been reduced to twenty years' imprisonment. A month later, Medina was acquitted of ordering Calley and his platoon to kill civilians. In 1974, although the Supreme Court had upheld his conviction, Calley was a free man. His punishment was further reduced to ten years by Secretary of the Army Howard H. Callaway. Overall, Calley served only a third of that sentence, under house arrest, before he was paroled.[27] He admitted that he had killed some civilians, but he maintained that he had been made into a useful "scapegoat" for the army, a mere "fly in the ointment" because of his refusal to lie and cover up.[28] Yet he and a good number of men in the three platoons at My Lai that day had gotten away with murder.

Some sages have remarked that the cost of My Lai can be calculated in how it fatally wounded America's ideal of national innocence. Theologian Reinhold Niebuhr, who had long addressed the nature of sin, contended after Calley's conviction that America would cast off its false and innocent image as a Redeemer Nation, a city upon a hill, and come to a more realistic understanding of its actions in the world. The My Lai massacre had "shattered" illusions of national innocence. "This is a moment of truth when we realize that we are not a virtuous nation." Since Niebuhr's utterance in 1971, the notion of American innocence has refused to die; it is the political and diplomatic equivalent of a virginity that is constantly lost and somehow mysteriously reclaimed.[29]

Moral Baggage

For all intents and purposes, the young men at My Lai exemplified American innocence, naïveté, and bad luck. What moral madness or amorality could allow them to gun down unarmed civilians, to shoot the brains out of infants? Michael Bernhardt was there that day, and he estimated that 90 percent of the men were involved in the killing spree.[30] This estimate seems too high, given that some men killed fleeing civilians; others killed civilians accidentally by dropping grenades into shelters or tunnels that might have been booby-trapped. And some men, we know, refused to fire on civilians or wandered away from where the murders were occurring. But whatever the number of killers, many were engaged both actively and passively in the killing spree.[31]

Circumstance often trumps character during such violent eruptions. The soldiers had been frustrated prior to the My Lai encounter. They had lost a favorite sergeant just days before, and some men had been wounded or killed by minefields, snipers, or booby-traps. The enemy for the men of Charlie Company had been invisible. Charging into the village of My Lai, at least, gave the soldiers some tangible targets for revenge. Poor leadership may also account for the massacre; the anxiety of these young men, in an initial combat situation, contributed as well. All of the men, even after a short term in Vietnam, spoke about how they had come to disrespect the Vietnamese, to believe that they were overtly antagonistic to Americans and their war aims. Some later stated that they considered all Vietnamese civilians, even children, the enemy, since a child could grow up to be a Vietcong soldier. Within this context, the My Lai massacre comes to make some sense, although analysts differ about whether it was an unusual occurrence or rather just a larger example of the business-as-usual approach to killing civilians in Vietnam. Things are more complicated than this, in both a hopeful and a bleak sense.

The best way to approach what happened, and the ambiguities of its ethical aspects, is to look at the young men involved in the killing. We need to unpack what they carried with them, and what they lost, in the war zone.[32] Even if Sergeant Bernhardt's estimate of those involved in the killing errs by half, many managed to kill that morning, without apparent self-recrimination. None returned from combat and hurried to confess to a chaplain or to complain to higher military or civilian authorities.

The soldiers were normal young men, with an average age of about twenty-one. They were mostly members of the baby boom generation, although mainly from working-class and impoverished backgrounds. They were to become part of the most studied generational cohort in American history. By force of circumstance and desire, these men went to Vietnam and into the armed forces rather than into university classrooms, hippie communes, or Canada to avoid the draft. Some of the soldiers—Calley, Bernhardt, Ridenhour—briefly attended college, but like so many young people, they were underprepared intellectually or emotionally to continue.

They dropped out and were swept up in the web of the draft, or they joined the army because they knew they were about to be drafted. Some of the soldiers in the platoons had grown up poor, in the barrios and ghettos. For them the army was either an escape or a prison that was unavoidable.[33]

We now think of this generational cohort, coming of age in the 1960s, as committed to rebellion. But the constituent parts of that rebellious spirit—alienation, despair, distrust, anger—often led to noncommitment and drift. The soldiers in the First Platoon, from Calley on down, were of this generation, and they all exhibited what scholar Kenneth Keniston referred to as "inner confusion, disunity, and fragmentation" in their moral sensibilities. No less than others of their generation, they were searching for meaning, "*yearning for absolutes*." They would not find them in the big muddy of Vietnam, however.[34]

Many of these young men were from solid religious backgrounds. Staff Sergeant David Mitchell's father was minister of the Raspberry Baptist Church in St. Francisville, Louisiana. Mitchell attended segregated schools and joined the army in 1960, finding there a sense of community and direction. A high school graduate, twenty-six years old at the time of the massacre, Mitchell was charged with the murder of thirty Vietnamese civilians at My Lai.[35] Another soldier, Michael Terry, was a devoted Mormon. According to Ron Ridenhour, Terry "was, I thought, one of the finest people I had ever met. He was the all-American boy: wrestler in college, all-state champion, had respect for everybody around him, didn't swear, didn't speak badly of women, and wasn't into a lot of the sort of macho bragging that was going on by a lot of people. He was just a very fine human being."[36] Although Terry dispatched wounded civilians, he did not beseech his commanders or implore medics to get medical aid for the wounded. He simply shot them.

Nothing stood out in particular about Paul Meadlo. He was from an industrial area of Indiana, and he was as normal as they come. He worked hard in a factory and expected little to come easily to him. But his basic training and experiences in Vietnam changed him. As his mother put it, "I gave them a good boy and they made him a murderer."[37]

Most attention has, of course, been focused on Calley, his values and character. Some described him as "an average American." Yet one commentator called him a "child of the new South, déclassé, amoral, ill-educated, uncertain, anxious, even over-anxious to please"—and without any firm moral grounding.[38] These deficiencies became apparent after the massacre, but there is little indication prior to it that Calley was particularly amoral or hard-hearted. He was, quite simply, typical of his time and place. Twenty-four years old and in command of the first platoon, Calley came from a conventionally middle-class, religious home. An aunt referred to Calley's family as "good Christians," "a loving church-going family" at the 1,500-member Rader Memorial United Methodist Church in El Porta, near Miami. His father made a good living selling heavy equipment when Calley was a youth. The family lived in a nice house, owned a boat, and had a cabin in North Carolina. Calley was reasonably popular at school, even if an undistinguished student. Although he would, as the family's fortunes declined, drift around and drop any outward religious commitment, there was nothing in his background to indicate a lack of moral training. He simply appears as a middling young man, unclear about what to do with his life. At one point in his drifting, he got a job working on the railroad, helping to break a strike. He apparently felt no anxiety or guilt about this. The job simply was a new opportunity for him to make large amounts of money, albeit with a backbreaking schedule and minimum of training.[39]

American religion in the 1950s and 1960s, the formative years in the lives of Calley and his soldiers, was somewhat tepid. Religion rested less on the individual struggling with salvation, monitoring carefully his or her own spiritual progress and sins, than with the church as a place for fellowship that resounded with moral platitudes. While children grew up with a host of moral imperatives, those strictures were rather flimsy, hardly open to the depth of understanding that might make them meaningful. Hence, for a generation that felt alienated for many reasons, there was a nagging sense that while morals were valuable, in practice they were malleable. Virtues were celebrated and good character was upheld, but the parents of this generation seemed to lack moral backbone and an inner sense of certitude. The relation of their parents to the world of authority was "other-directed," in sociologist David Riesman's famous phrase. Here the imperative was to avoid strong judgments and solid moralism in order to get along, to be part of a team. The moralist was something of an outcast in the 1950s, as most religions stressed comfortable salvation and sociability above moral introspection and anxiety. Gone were the days of an inner-directed search for moral lapses; present was the other-directed character, a person without any firm moral structure or values.[40]

Calley, Mitchell, and others in the platoon experienced various difficulties in their late teens. Typical of their generation, they either lacked a sense of direction or were denied outlets for maturation. Some, like Calley or Haeberle, were not cut out for college (which would have carried a deferment from military service). Others worked in dead-end jobs, waiting for their draft notices. Some, like Mitchell, were handicapped by racism. These young men looked to the army for direction as well as a community and value system. As one of Calley's high school friends remarked, Calley "had always been sort of searching for his niche. He liked the Army. I think it kind of gave him a spot . . . gave him a home."[41]

These young men, then, brought traditional morality and character with them to Vietnam. It proved insubstantial, unable to weather the moral challenges of the war. None of them had shown an earlier propensity for evil. But radical evil was a presence at My Lai that day, even if not anticipated by these young men. None of them, I suspect, entered My Lai that day with the intention of slaughtering babies and raping women. Their journey to My Lai was no doubt made possible by the losses they had previously experienced, a desire for revenge, the dehumanization of the enemy at the heart of the war, and an opportunity for reveling in destruction. All of them were, as far as we can tell, banal individuals, without boiling hatred in their hearts and without time or willingness to think too deeply about their sad situations. Calley's killing that day was aberrant. Since his release from confinement in 1974, for many years he lived a mundane, middle-class existence as a family man, without any criminality, in Columbus, Georgia. While many others involved in the massacre had rough postwar lives—chased by demons real and imagined—they were not as a group particularly prone to acts of violence or horror. The young men at My Lai that day were normal Americans. So, what happened?

The Comforts of Authority

A host of psychological studies, some begun even before My Lai, help to explain what happened. All were carried out under the shadow of Arendt's thesis that given particular circumstances, the most banal of individuals can perpetrate the most horrendous of evils. The main currents behind these studies, most famously conducted by Stanley Milgram at Yale University and Philip Zimbardo at Stanford University, fit nicely into the presumption that modern men and women, no matter their religious, class, or educational backgrounds, have a respect for and follow authority. Moreover, circumstances—the looming presence of authority or the rituals of institutions and the pain of deprivation—are sufficient to undermine moral virtue and character. Summing up a host of studies, Kwame Anthony Appiah concludes that we tend to do the "right" thing most often when circumstances are favorable for our doing it. Even the barely noticed scent of flowers near a beggar can influence us to give money more readily than we would to another beggar standing in range of a smelly garbage can.[42] Hence, it has become a given that what happened at My Lai was an indictment of the power of institutional culture, a dehumanizing war, and incompetent authority. It almost seemed that in the face of these forces, the young men could do little more than to kill.

Milgram had read Arendt on the banality of evil. He wanted to set up an experiment that would examine, under controlled circumstances, whether individuals from all backgrounds would commit acts that, under different circumstances, they would find morally abhorrent. Over a period of three years, beginning in 1960, Milgram and his team carried out a series of demonstrations to determine why people commit actions that are distasteful at best, immoral at worst. Upward of 60 percent of those tested—unpaid and without any commitment to the experiment—were willing to administer what they believed to be shocks that could be physically harmful, even lethal, to a subject. When torn between the admonition of the authority figure to continue with the administration of shocks and the harrowing cries of the subject, more than a majority of individuals continued to pull the lever at a level that read "Danger, Severe Shock."[43]

Following the experiments, some of the shock-administering subjects were questioned at length or participated in discussion groups. Many of them stated that they were able to continue administering the shocks, no matter how much anxiety it caused them and how much apparent pain in the victim, because they had been assured by an authority figure that the experiment was necessary and that the pain was transient. Pressure to obey authority indicated to Milgram that we are programmed to function within institutions and in the face of authority in a manner that diminishes our own sense of choice and erodes our sense of responsibility. As the wife of one subject put it, after learning that her husband had been willing to administer high-level shocks, "You can call yourself Eichmann."[44] More widely in American culture, discussions of the My Lai massacre often resulted in analogies being drawn between an Eichmann-like willingness to kill on orders and the actions of soldiers in Vietnam.[45]

Zimbardo's experiment at Stanford in 1971 also acknowledged the power of authority and obedience, but it focused more on how institutional circumstances and role-playing warp moral responsibility. Zimbardo recruited a bunch of young men, weeded out any with personality disorders, and then assigned them roles to play. Some of the subjects were to be prison guards, others were to be prisoners. In short order, the prisonlike environment had hardened the guards. They began to embellish their power in a sometimes cruel manner. As one "guard" put it, "My enjoyment in harassing and punishing prisoners was quite unnatural for me because I tend to think of myself as being sympathetic to the injured, especially animals. I think that it was an outgrowth of my total freedom to rule the prisoners, I began to abuse my authority."[46] Those playing the role of prisoner, despite their ability to exit from the prison if they requested it, sank into states of dehumanization and hopelessness. And all this occurred over a period of less than two weeks. The conclusions were clear: The system can corrupt individuals, no matter what character and virtue they carry into it. Zimbardo concluded, "Good people can be induced, seduced, initiated into behaving in evil ways. They can also be led to act in irrational, stupid, self-destructive, antisocial and mindless ways when they are immersed in 'total situations' that impact human nature in ways that challenge our sense of the stability and consistency of individual personality, of character, and of morality."[47]

Between a Rock and a Hard Place

Certainly the Milgram and Zimbardo experiments go a long way toward explaining how, in the situation of My Lai, a bunch of young men with conventional moral baggage could act the way they did. After all, they had been following orders and had been given tacit permission to seek revenge for fallen comrades. They had been living up to the institutional demands of killing the enemy, however defined.

The army brass of the Peers Commission investigating My Lai, men who had seen combat duty in other wars, were stunned at how the soldiers had acted, especially how they had violated clear army regulations. Military tradition, if nothing else, should have negated such outrages. Had not the army issued authoritative directives about how the soldiers were to act toward civilians? Why was that tradition and authority countermanded or ignored? Army officials, in a sense, were good Kantians, functioning in a moral universe where moral imperatives were obvious and easily followed. In the view of military officials, enlisted men and officers should have known that the killings in My Lai were unsanctioned and immoral, according to the Geneva convention and the army's own procedures. During the Peers Commission hearings on the My Lai massacre and subsequent coverup, witness after witness was queried by the panel: "Were you aware of the Geneva Convention's rules for the treatment of prisoners?" "What is the proper procedure for stopping a fleeing, unarmed civilian?" "Were you issued, and did you read, the wallet card, 'Nine Rules for Personnel of the U.S. Military Assistance Command, Vietnam,' or the flyer, 'The Enemy in Your Hands'?"[48]

The army brass naïvely asked the My Lai killers and bystanders if they were familiar with these rules. They presumed that prescriptive moral rules, if understood by the individual, would guide action under trying circumstances. They failed to appreciate how difficult it is for anyone—especially a soldier in a combat situation—to navigate between contending moral imperatives. Finally, they underestimated the extent to which the army's mantra of "follow orders without question," drilled into recruits during basic training, served as the guiding moral imperative for almost all soldiers. Most of those appearing before the commission admitted that they had learned the lesson too well. Even if given an obviously illegal order, Bergthold told the commission he would obey it. That was simply the moral imperative in the army.[49]

Yet the rules are clear regarding what constituted an illegal order, and that soldiers must not follow orders that deviate from the rules. The "Nine Rules" deal with how soldiers in a foreign country should comport themselves. Soldiers are to treat the Vietnamese with respect, attempt to make friends with them, avoid behavior they might find offensive, and realize that "we are guests here: We make no demands and seek no special treatment." As far as they go, these are wonderful suggestions for conduct. As soldier after soldier testified at the Peers Commission hearings, the problem was that these cards were distributed without comment. Soldiers either stuffed them into their wallets or lost them. Few read the rules and even fewer took them to heart. No effort was expended on the part of the army to instill these rules with the discipline and courage required to countermand another imperative: obey orders.

The soldiers were also issued cards that dealt with "the enemy in your hands." Again, the rules are clear and helpful, designed to comport with the Geneva Convention. Soldiers should treat prisoners "firmly" as well as "humanely." They were admonished to care as much as possible for wounded enemy, to protect them, and to abstain from any actions that would be harmful to the prisoner. Indeed, if the soldier violated any of these rules, he would be committing a "criminal offense." The soldier "is personally responsible for the enemy in his hands." When questioned about these rules, however, soldiers admitted that while they were aware of them in principle, in practice officers and enlisted men violated them with impunity on a regular basis. Even if the rules had in general been followed, an order circumventing the rules from a superior officer would take precedence. A captain trumped a Kant.

Sergeant Thomas Kinch had gone through basic training at Fort Dix, New Jersey, and he planned on a career in the armed forces. He believed that revenge motivated the killings at My Lai, and that the troops had been under the impression that they were to destroy everything, including civilians (36). Kinch himself had not harmed any civilians, and he demonstrated that he was a thoughtful witness to the Peers Commission officers. At one point they asked "if you thought that an order to shoot women and children is a lawful order?" With General Peers in attendance, Kinch responded that while he had been told in basic training that "there is such a thing" as an unlawful order, the point of his training boiled down to "in the Army an order is an order."[50]

Roy Trevino, a private at My Lai, was assigned to the Second Platoon. He was clear about the situation: The Vietcong controlled My Lai, and the civilians there sympathized with the enemy. The mission was to "search and destroy," which meant that "everything that is in" the village was to be destroyed. Whether that included civilians was less than certain. He was charged with no crimes, and he stated that during the mission, "I kept pretty well to myself. I didn't pay much attention to what was going on."[51] The only shooting he had done that day, he related, was an unsuccessful attempt to kill a duck. Trevino had been trained in how to handle prisoners, stating proudly that he knew the "seven S's": "search them, to separate them, to keep them silent," although he could not bring forth the remaining rules.

Trevino comes across in his testimony as a character. He admitted that he preferred to shoot only at those who first shot at him. He was wounded by a mine a couple days after My Lai. "I'm lucky I'm not dead," he told the commission.[52] After recuperating in Colorado, Trevino went AWOL; he was later arrested and returned for another tour of duty in Vietnam. He was someone who had learned the hard way, albeit without philosophical erudition, the problems a soldier faces when presented with orders in conflict with moral imperatives.

Admitting that his questioners "will think I'm crazy," he demanded to know how they could sit there and fail to appreciate the problems he faced in Vietnam. Trevino asked the commission if he might make a statement. Although marred by problematic syntax, Trevino effectively communicated his anguished point:

> We got the orders to go into that village and search and destroy, what else could we do? We go and disobey an order and you do it, I mean you disobey an order, you get a court-martial for disobeying an order. Now you do something like that and they are going to try to hang you just because you killed somebody, that is what I don't understand. That is why I can't wait to get out of the Army, not because I have anything against it, but the Army is not my type of life. I'd much rather be a civilian or a hippy or something and if they say search and destroy you go in there and destroy and search and destroy and if you don't do something they tell you to do it and they try to hang you for it.

A few minutes later, after one of the non-uniformed members of the Peers Commission lectured Trevino about the rules of war and the responsibility of soldiers to report war crimes, Trevino asked if it was okay for him to ask the commissioner a question. The exchange is worth quoting verbatim, for it illustrates the gulf between high-ranking officials and the grunts at the front:

Trevino: "Have you been in the Army?"
Official: "Oh, yes."
Trevino: "Okay, I'm sorry. If you were like me—I was a PFC when I was there—and the CO says if they shot at you in a village burn it, and you get one shot from the village, would you flatten it?"
Official: "Your CO says if you get one shot from the village to flatten it?"
Trevino: "I'm not saying my CO, but say you have a CO that tells you, 'Okay you go into this village and if they take one shot at you flatten it, to kill everything,' would you do it?"
Official: "You're talking about a village where there were civilians living, men, women, and children?"
Trevino: "Yes. And they took a sniper fire at you and then took off?"
Official: "No, I wouldn't."
Trevino: "Even if you were given orders?"
Official: "Knowing what I know, I wouldn't. But I can understand somebody thinking these were orders and they had to obey them."

A bit later:

Official: "There are certain—I well understand the need, you know, for soldiers to obey their orders and you appreciate that, as a soldier too, you have to obey your orders or things won't work. It's a fact there are certain things that a soldier must not do and this is the law of the country. One is—even if you are incompetent—one is not to mistreat noncombatant civilians, women and children that took no part in the action. This we are obligated by the treaties and laws to refrain from. So, it's illegal to kill noncombatant civilians."

Trevino: "Whether they are ordered to or not?"

Official: "That's right."

Trevino: "They should teach you that when they come in basic training, it should be more than 8 weeks. They should have it maybe for 16 weeks, where they can teach you what you can do and what you can't do—"

Official (Interposing): "Do you think it would be practical if they laid this down and told people there are certain things you've got to obey and there are certain things that are illegal?"

Trevino: "Right, and if they get you in a court-martial they say, we are going to court-martial you for disobeying an order and we say, you look up Article 16 or such and such. And that is how a private like me can protect himself if he does any wrong and he has his article right there."[53]

Trevino craved a simple, rules-based morality. Some may argue that if one had been driven into him and his fellow recruits during basic training, different conduct might have resulted. But this was unlikely for a variety of reasons. First, he was operating under ambiguous orders, perhaps purposely so. This put much of the burden of interpretation on the backs of grunts. Second, the actions of Medina and Calley at the scene certainly indicated that the killing of civilians was sanctioned and acceptable. Third, in order for moral rules to work, they must be capable of avoiding conflict with one another. They must be part of a system of morality, where the individual is pushed to think things through for himself. Finally, the My Lai situation raises challenges to our need for moral clarity: Can a system of ethics, even one that is ingrained in the individual at home, survive the jarring experiences of war in a faraway land?

Orders and Authority

Soldiers operated that day under orders that were ambiguous at best.[54] In the early evening of 15 March 1968, Captain Ernest Medina, almost universally respected by his men, described the assault that would occur in the morning. Medina stated that he expected the 48th Vietcong Battalion, composed of between 250 and 280 men, to be in the vicinity, ready for a major confrontation. Americans would be outnumbered and should anticipate, at the point of landing, heavy fire from the enemy. The three platoons were to "search and clear" the village after the enemy troops had been routed for "bunker complexes, the tunnels, the houses, for weapons, equipment and whatnot in the village."[55] Medina further noted that the villages would be empty of women and children; they would be at the market that morning. He did not, according to his recollection, tell the platoons that they were to kill civilians or destroy wantonly.

Of course, Medina's account cannot be taken at face value. While almost all his troops had difficulty trying to recreate the tone and content of the talk two years after the event, there seemed to be consensus on some aspects. Many characterized the briefing as "like a college pep talk" before a football game.[56] Medina noted that they had lost men in recent outings into enemy territory and that this was a chance for them to even the score. He claimed that civilians would not be in the villages, either because they had been warned away by pamphlets detailing the impending attack (on the face of it, a rather absurd notion) or because they would be at the market. To a man, each soldier recalled that Medina had said they would be confronting a major contingent of enemy troops.

Beyond this, things get murky. Recollections had become tainted by the intervening years and by retrospective knowledge. Since some of the men were accused of murder, they would fare better if they, or their comrades, could pin the blame on Medina and his orders. They would then be seen less as free agents than as misguided or uninformed soldiers simply following orders from a respected, superior officer. In any case, some of the soldiers testifying before the Peers Commission were quite precise in their memories of what Medina had stated and intended: Kill everyone because they were all Vietcong or Vietcong sympathizers. According to Dennis Bunning, it was "sort of a revenge thing," a "search and destroy mission." Medina "just said we're to kill everything in these villages."[57] In Sergeant Kinch's recollection, Medina said, "As far as I'm concerned anyone there is a VC suspect or a VC sympathizer . . . I want everything burned to the ground, and killed tomorrow."[58] The term "everything" recurs in the accounts: "Medina said 'get everything,' " which to Thomas Flynn meant, "women, children, cows, and pigs and anything that was out there. . . . We were supposed to kill them."[59] Indeed, one soldier not accused of crimes related that Medina "told us everything there was VC, children would grow up to be VC, and women were VC sympathizers."[60]

Others found "everything" less inclusive. Medina, according to Sergeant Leo Maroney, was not talking about killing kids: he simply meant that the men should be careful, search for weapons, and destroy tunnels and homes.[61] Anyone fleeing the Americans should be presumed to be an enemy and shot.[62] While search and destroy missions were normally intended to deny returning enemy shelter and food, some of the soldiers claimed that on this mission they were told by Medina not to kill livestock or burn houses. Yet Bernhardt thought Medina "would just as soon kill" a Vietnamese person as look at him or her. He found his orders clear: "destroy this area and this [enemy] unit."[63] If the soldiers "killed a bunch of civilians" in the process, "it wouldn't make any difference." Medina, however, does not appear to have explicitly told the soldiers that they were to have a free hand in killing women and children—perhaps because he sincerely believed the villages would be vacated at the time of the attack.

We will never know the intent or content of Medina's ambiguous orders. The moral point they raise about the nature of the war in Vietnam goes far beyond anything Medina might have said or implied that day. As soldier Henry Pedrick summed it up, "The orders could have been interpreted in different ways to different persons according to their emotional structure. One person might interpret it to kill if he wanted to."[64]

Vietnam was a war of attrition. Victory was measured less by land claimed than by the number of enemy killed. The pressure on military officers was to kill the enemy and pump up a "body count," which psychologist and antiwar activist Robert Jay Lifton called "the perfect symbol of America's descent into evil."[65] A high or low body count might decide the future career potential of an officer. The pressure was on to inflate body counts and to be imprecise about who counted as an enemy. Hence, when unarmed civilians were killed at My Lai, many of them were reported as enemy killed to commanders. The logic of search and destroy fell more heavily on the third word in the equation, and it polluted distinctions between enemy and civilians. A common saying among the military was, "If it's dead and Vietnamese, it's VC."[66]

In such an ambiguous situation, of course, more precise limits on the meaning of search and destroy would have been useful. Without a doubt, Calley took Medina's words to mean that anyone found in the village—no matter what age or gender—was to be eliminated.[67] Calley always maintained that his orders were simple: "annihilate every living thing in My Lai."[68] Here we come upon a crucial reality: Did Calley's authority extend so far that he could impose his will on the men who served under him? Or was

My Lai more complicated on the issue of authority and circumstance? Was Calley a loose cannon, or did things go awry from the start, and, if so, why?

Calley's Killings

I want to complicate this all-too-predictable scenario of authority, institution, and individual responsibility. Calley's killings probably did arise from his problematic interpretation—perhaps overinterpretation—of Medina's orders. But Calley's authority to order his men to kill was, at best, limited. Many of the men did not obey his orders, sometimes by wandering away from the center of action, other times by refusing a command point-blank. And if Calley cannot be pinned down as the instigator of the bloodletting, then what explains the event? To be sure, revenge, ambiguous orders, and dehumanization of the Vietnamese all played a role. Something is missing when the massacre at My Lai is framed as a logical outcome of American policy and problems, which then locates the issue of the massacre as an exercise in the banality of evil. Evil showed its face in My Lai, but it was radical in nature. We should not ignore how circumstances helped it to explode.

Look at Calley's pictures from the time of the massacre and trial. He is a young man without much presence, just shy of twenty-five at the time of the massacre, boyish-looking, not imposing physically or mentally. Yet after the massacre some referred to him as "hard-faced," a killer awaiting his chance.[69] There are no indications of his having any sadistic tendencies, and he was never in any real trouble with the law before his service in Vietnam. He was a young man without direction and purpose, certainly, but hardly atypical in that regard. By and large, many remembered him as a conventional, polite, and kind young man. As one of his civilian acquaintances put it, Rusty Calley "had compassion for other people. He was concerned about other people's lives." She could not imagine him capable of murdering anyone.[70] Others referred to him, in contrast, as having a "robot-like personality," as someone easily programmed to kill.[71]

A failure at most things, Calley was an eager-beaver soldier, described by a friend as a "gung-ho Army man," enthusiastic almost to a fault.[72] Calley found in the service the direction he craved. He adored Medina as a leader and father figure. Calley was, as some of his men stated, an "apple-polisher," an officer who wanted to do well, to be respected by his men, and who was ready to volunteer for dangerous assignments. But he was barely competent, having difficulties reading a map, and thus placing his men in dangerous situations. He had some authority by dint of his lieutenant's rank rather than from his presence and competence. But he was forced to admonish his men to remember, "I'm the boss."[73] This indicates he was aware of his lack of authority; and he avoided issuing orders his men would not follow.[74]

Rather than being particularly unintelligent or dull, Calley was swept into the situation, plucked for officer candidate school at a time when officers were desperately needed for service in Vietnam. Calley did, however, make it through the training, circumscribed though it might have been by the school's pressure to graduate more officers.[75] For all his failings—and they should not be ignored—many of the men in his platoon looked at Calley without disdain, even after the massacre. Calley was simply trying hard to be an effective officer; he wanted to do well, he wanted to win the respect of his men. Few of the men interrogated at the Peers Commission hearings blamed Calley for what had happened at My Lai. At the same time, Calley was often viewed as a short man trying to act big, to prove himself to his men and to Medina.[76] Jay Buchanon, an experienced sergeant, summed up his overall view of Calley as a "typical second Lieutenant" marred by his unwillingness to take advice and by a lack of maturity.[77]

The killing began at My Lai because the men were fired up, expecting a major clash with veteran North Vietnamese soldiers. They also carried with them a desire for revenge, and they operated, as noted earlier, under orders that were at best ambiguous. Of course, they had to have sufficiently hardened themselves and dehumanized the Vietnamese in order to fit small children and others under the rubric of the enemy. Indeed, this theme of the "mutual dehumanization," to use a phrase coined by Vietnam expert Bernard B. Fall, of the Americans and the Vietnamese is commonly employed to explain the massacre.[78] As the Americans did to the Japanese during the World War II, and vice versa, they came to see the enemy as less than human, reducing them to epithets such as "gook, dink, and slope." The testimony of many of the My Lai killers and bystanders bears this out. In addition to rejecting "the humanity of the victims," Americans became dehumanized in their own fashion.[79] No one would argue that dehumanization crept like a vine in the dark jungles of Vietnam, but it is simply inadequate to explain the extent of the killing that day. It is as much an effect as it is a cause.

The killing began at the periphery, perhaps even in a way that comported with military procedure. Fearful of the incoming troops, some Vietnamese civilians might have attempted to run away to the relative safety of the bushes; perhaps, too, either they failed to understand Americans' commands to stop or the soldiers shot first without any warning given. This early killing definitely set the stage for the massive destruction and murder that continued throughout the day.

Let us return to Lieutenant Calley and his role. Calley believed that everyone in the village that day was marked for execution because they were members of the enemy or potential members of the enemy. If we can believe Calley's later testimony at the trial, he was unable or unwilling to distinguish among potential enemy combatants, real combatants, and innocents. Consider his interrogation at his trial by Captain Aubrey Daniel about the moment when Calley was opening fire on people in a ditch.

Daniel: "Did you see women?"
Calley: "I don't know, sir."
Daniel: "What do you mean you weren't discriminating?"
Calley: "I didn't discriminate between individuals in the village, sir. They were all the enemy, they were all to be destroyed, sir."[80]

There is something palpably Eichmann-like in such statements from Calley. He comes across as someone without passion or hatred, only as a man who had been given orders and decided that he would follow them explicitly, without any thought about their legality, logic, or necessity. Even if an order was illegal—and there is no indication that Calley felt this way about Medina's presumed directive to kill all civilians—he was duty-bound to carry it out, lest he be punished by personal humiliation, jail time, or execution. He did, however, maintain that after carrying out an illegal order, a soldier could choose to go through channels and file a complaint.[81]

At least twice that day, with the help of Sergeant Mitchell and other soldiers, Calley brought Vietnamese civilians to ditches. According to Paul Meadlo, Calley's orders were unclear about what was to be done with these people. Meadlo believed that he was simply to guard them as prisoners, according to normal procedure. But when Calley returned a few minutes later, he apparently berated Meadlo for not doing his job, which was to "waste" them. If so, then Meadlo failed to meet the challenge. According to Meadlo's account, Calley in disgust opened fire on the people in the ditch. Then Meadlo, along with a few other soldiers, began firing as well. His weapon was turned on automatic fire; he quickly expended four clips of ammunition, more than sixty-seven shots, from his M16 weapon. He figured that he may have killed ten to fifteen of the noncombatant men, women, children, and babies in the ditch. After that group was butchered, Calley and his men moved to another area, where about seventy-five Vietnamese had been rounded up for execution. As Calley put it to Meadlo, "we got another job to do." They began pushing the civilians into a ravine "and we started shooting them, so together we just pushed them all off, and just started using automatics on them. . . . somebody told us to switch off to single shot so that we could save ammo." When asked by reporter Mike Wallace during a famous television interview about the My Lai massacre how he had felt during the killing of the babies in particular, Meadlo replied, "I don't know, it's just one of those things."[82]

The story of Meadlo's participation and willingness to follow orders is complicated. Charles Sledge, Calley's radio telephone operator, claimed that it was Meadlo, rather than Calley, who opened fire on the civilians in the ditch that morning.[83] Other accounts differ. According to Dennis Conti, who was accused of murder and rape at My Lai, upon Calley's direct order, Meadlo began shooting. But then, Meadlo "started to cry." He gave Conti his weapon, and removed himself from the killing, although there were still civilians, mostly children, in the ditch.[84] Another soldier, Joseph Konwinski, stated he had heard Meadlo being berated by Calley to shoot. Meadlo apparently "was in tears" about the order to kill the civilians. It was not, then, simply "just one of those things;" it was, rather, one of those things he may have been forced to do at the behest of his commanding officer.[85]

Lieutenant Calley ordered the civilians killed because he believed that orders from Captain Medina demanded that all Vietnamese in the village were to be considered Vietcong or Vietcong sympathizers, and hence killed. We can blame Calley for his rather literal understanding of Medina's orders; we can blame Medina, too, for the ambiguity of the orders, for his willingness to stay on the periphery of the action at My Lai, and for his failure to call a halt to the bloodbath.

Soldier after soldier testified at the Peers Commission hearing that they had been trained to follow orders. When Lieutenant Calley, along with sergeants Mitchell and Hodges, began executing civilians, they felt they could only follow orders. They acted as if they were trained automatons. As Milgram and Zimbardo would confidently explain, they were part of an institution that put a bounty on unquestioned obedience to authority. They had been dehumanized by the violence they had previously encountered; they did not see the Vietnamese as fellow human beings but rather as objects of derision—gooks or slope-heads, all of them either actively engaged, tacitly supporting, or one day capable of becoming a killer of American soldiers.

Like Eichmann, anxious to move up the bureaucratic hierarchy, some killed because not to kill would put a blemish on their army records. Squad leader Schiel was ordered to kill civilians. He did not want to lose his position, according to one witness, so "he finally did start doing it . . . shoot into a bunch of people."[86]

Making Moral Choices

Still, these interpretations come up short. We must remember that even in Milgram's experiments, one third of those engaged refused to administer shocks at the highest levels. The same was true, in a manner of speaking, at My Lai.

Authority was not always able to trump individual conscience or virtue. In fact, the chaotic nature of the movement of American forces through My Lai meant that many of the soldiers were split off from their platoon, often intermixed with soldiers from a different platoon. They were beyond the sight of their commanding officers. Some of these men wandered away, thus avoiding involvement in the killing. Even when confronted by a superior officer such as Calley, they ignored his order to kill civilians.

A few soldiers in My Lai that day recall that Sergeant Michael Bernhardt refused to kill and made it clear to others that he thought it unnecessary. According to Thomas Partsch, a grenade launcher with the Second Platoon, Bernhardt complained to fellow sergeant Jay Buchanon and to Lieutenant Calley, but they ignored him.[87] Buchanon admitted as much. Bernhardt stated, "'This is not my cup of tea, I don't get kicks doing this,' or something like that."[88] Another sergeant present, Dennis Bunning, refused to kill civilians without cause.[89] A big man, not easily intimidated, Bunning saw up close much of the violence at My Lai, from the raping to the murdering. Since he considered such actions to be wrong, and since he was not a lifer in the service, he was able to say to himself, "I'm not going to do it." What is revealing and sad about the moral virtue exhibited by sergeants Bernhardt and Bunning was that they were unable or unwilling to halt the process of destruction and abuse on the part of others. Bunning reported that when he intervened to stop a rape during an earlier attack on another village, he had been warned to butt out or face being shot by his fellow soldiers.[90]

Other soldiers, at least according to their own testimony a year or two after the trial, related that they had managed by a variety of means to avoid killing civilians in My Lai. Sometimes they did this by simply staying away from scenes of execution. Private Roy Trevino claimed that he "kept pretty well to myself."[91] While Second Platoon medic George Garza willingly shot at cattle and pigs in the hamlet, he refused to aim at people: "I couldn't do it."[92] Robert Maples rejected orders to kill: "I'm not going to kill those people."[93] Another soldier rifleman, Fred Dustin, would not kill the civilians he rounded up and guarded.[94] When PFC Herbert Carter asked PFC James Dursi if Calley really intended to kill civilians in a ditch, Dursi answered in the affirmative. Yet he refused to participate. According to Dursi, Meadlo asked him, "Why aren't you firing? Shoot." Dursi replied, "I can't." He claimed that he told Calley as much: "Send me to jail, but I'm not going to shoot."[95] Thomas Partsch also stated that a soldier could refuse such an order. Calley's authority, especially in chaotic circumstances, was less than overwhelming. Other soldiers avoided the killing by falling sick at the sight of it.[96]

Situations are never absolute. Obviously, some soldiers summoned up their sense of humanity, called on their moral values, and refused to kill. Nothing in the backgrounds of these men suggests they were better educated or more religious than those who killed. They were the 30 percent minority Milgram found in most of his experiments. But these soldiers were not in an experimental situation, they were in combat: they had suffered blows themselves and had seen their friends blown up by booby-traps and landmines. They had, as psychologist Robert Jay Lifton put it, undergone a process of "psychic numbing," making them more prone to abuses. They often shared a hatred for the civilians in Vietnam, and they knew that refusal to follow an order could result in disciplinary actions or the disdain of their fellow soldiers. But refuse they did.

It is important to keep in mind that in similar situations, as author Tim O'Brien emphasizes, other soldiers managed not to kill, despite all sorts of provocations, if not direct orders. "Although I experienced exactly what those people experienced in the same place," stated O'Brien, "we didn't cross the line. Why did those people cross the line? Why didn't we cross the line? That's the abiding mystery."[97]

Blood Meridian

There can be pleasure in killing, a touching of hands with the devil, a feeling of absolute power over a cringing human being about to be reduced to nothingness. This desire to do radical evil must also be counted as part of the moral challenge of the massacre. Some of the soldiers killed with excitement, knowing full well that there would be no retribution, only praise for their adding to a higher kill count of "enemy." As one Vietnam veteran exulted after killing some Vietnamese, it was "the biggest rush you ever had in your life."[98] This was a once-in-a-lifetime opportunity, and some embraced it.

The literature on the attraction of killing supports this, by and large.[99] Psychologist Lifton notes the "*machismo of slaughter*" in his work on Vietnam veterans, but he narrowly defines it as arising out of fear, as a response to the potential of any Vietnamese civilian being the enemy.[100] Joanna Bourke, in her study of men at war in the twentieth century, details how soldiers were urged to be bloodthirsty and how easily they adjusted to that role. Acts of kindness, honor, and compassion, no doubt, occur during wars. We must never forget, however, that war is about killing. It is a sort of semi-controlled primitivism; men are expected to kill under orders.[101] Killing is not a faucet that can be turned on and off at will. Nor is it one that some men necessarily want to stop. Philosopher J. Glenn Gray's reflections about men during World War II are appropriate here. Men, he writes, can take "a delight in destruction." Indeed, as a close reader of Arendt, Gray noted that in war "radical evil" appears "which makes the medieval images of hell and the thousand devils of that imagination believable." There is a "mad excitement of destroying." He locates this "delight in destruction slumbering in most of us."[102] If you still think men don't take joy in killing, recall the cheers at Folsom Prison that greeted the lines in the Johnny Cash song: "I shot a man in Reno. / Just to watch him die."

Nothing, however, indicates that Calley killed with any glee. He did kill with intent of purpose. As his prosecutor, Aubrey Daniel, put it at the trial, Calley was sane; he knew what he was doing, and he chose to follow what he should have known were illegal orders. His execution of civilians "just can't be justified."[103] Like that banal man, Adolf Eichmann, in Arendt's rendering, Calley killed out of a sense of duty and obedience, out of a desire to follow the logic of his superiors and their war. He did so unemotionally, in a way described by two of his men as "cold-blooded." A two- or three-year-old child "crawled out of the ditch" full of dead bodies, and in Charles Sledge's memory, "someone hollered: 'There goes the kid, or something like that.'" Calley ran after the child, "threw him back in the ditch and shot it." Moments later, Calley "interrogated" a priest by slamming a rifle into his face and then shooting him in the head.[104]

Others killed because they could. Sergeant Gary Roschevitz was one of those who killed with relish. According to one of his men, Roschevitz raped a number of Vietnamese women and then killed them.[105] He ordered one soldier, Varnado Simpson, to kill a small group of detainees. When Simpson hesitated, Roschevitz "grabbed my M-16 away from me, put it on automatic fire, and killed all of the Vietnamese who had been standing there." Later, Simpson would enter into the action on his own, killing perhaps another twenty civilians. Years later he would recall: "I just started killing any kind of way I could kill." His violence exploded "from shooting them to cutting their throats to scalping them, to cutting their hands and cutting out their tongues. I did that."[106] Soldiers began systematically burning a group of thatched huts, as the twenty or so inhabitants were huddled into a group, under guard. Roschevitz decided that he would fire an M-79 grenade launcher into them. To gain better range and maximum blast effect for his weapon, he clambered up a small hill. He then blasted the group out of existence.[107] Fred Widmer also killed that day and with elation. After dispatching one of his victims, he was reported as exclaiming, "did you see that fucker die?"[108] After the killing spree, Widmer apparently took snapshots of bodies in the area: "Widmer enjoyed that mess . . . Widmer was a blood-thirsty little ol' joker."[109] Thomas Partsch said that some of the men were "having a ball" doing the killing.[110] The soldiers, as Konwinski remembered, were gleeful: Daniel Simone "dug" the killing.[111] Others tortured their victims, stabbing them repeatedly with their bayonets.[112]

Men raped. One soldier described three men forcing a woman to perform sexual acts on all of them at the same time. Clearly, this was not a situation where the men felt even remotely at risk from the enemy. A famous photograph by Ron Haeberle appearing in *Life* magazine showed a young woman holding a child, buttoning up her blouse after soldiers had tried to rape her. They had been forced off by an older woman; she is shown in the picture being restrained by another family member. The older woman is angry and weeping. A young girl in a white blouse has fear on her face. With good reason. A moment later all these unarmed Vietnamese were executed at close range by American soldiers.[113]

Perhaps the massacre was the result of a powerful combination of forces, and at that moment moral values were discarded in an orgy of violence. Desires for revenge, ambiguous orders, anxiety about battle, and opportunity combined that day. Orders to search and destroy everything living warranted some men's killing. They encountered a "tipping point," to use Malcolm Gladwell's apt phrase, an opportunity for killing, and they took it.[114] As historian Christopher Browning has made clear in his important work on the German Reserve Police Battalion 101 during World War II, even when soldiers have an option to exempt themselves from something they should perceive as immoral, or at the very least distasteful, they choose to participate.[115] Peer pressure, the desire to be one of the group, to avoid being seen as a wimp all create the situation for the type of massacre that filled the ditches with blood in My Lai.

The massacre did not assault all of the soldiers with equal force. Even a year or two after My Lai, some of the men involved showed no sense of grief, dishonor, or regret. Sergeant Martin Fagan said of the massacre, "I know it doesn't seem legal with little kids, but they just did it." Perhaps it was because there were three or four "cold-blooded people in that company." While some in the company felt bad about the events that day, others took the attitude: "Tough shit. War is hell, and they [the civilians] shouldn't have been there."[116] Others wrote it off as "the misfortune of war."[117] Some rationalized the killing of children as necessary: after all, these kids would grow up in a few years to be Vietcong and thus dangerous. Better to kill them early.[118] For many of the men, "killing a Vietnamese was just killing an old dog or something."[119] According to Sergeant Kenneth Hodges, interviewed more than twenty years later, the kids and women at My Lai "were soldiers. They were trained that way." He felt no regrets: "I feel that we carried out the orders in a moral fashion and the orders of, of destroying the village, of killing the people in the village. I feel that we carried out our orders, and I feel that we did not violate any moral standards."[120]

Character, Circumstance, Conclusions

The reality of My Lai will forever elude us, although we can pin down relevant causes that begin to explain the evil. Certainly, as various psychologists contend, these normally sane, conventionally moral young men were corrupted by the dehumanization on display daily in Vietnam; they were placed in what Robert Jay Lifton has characterized as "an atrocity-producing situation." This began with the rigors of basic training, as the army attempted to reduce the soldiers to automatons poised to follow orders, no matter how outrageous, and programmed to kill. Some soldiers in Vietnam felt that they had, in the words of historian Christian G. Appy, "a godlike license to destroy."[121]

The very context of the war, with its language and assumptions—body counts, search and destroy, free-fire zones—and the psychological damage caused by the deaths of one's comrades, led to a hardening of hearts. When combined with a mounting hatred for an often invisible and elusive enemy, soldiers sought revenge and catharsis under the banner of official approval against anyone they could find in My Lai.[122] In Lifton's judgment, GIs in Vietnam were both victims of these circumstances and executioners. While Lifton has always maintained that the soldiers were responsible for their actions and deserving of punishment, the logic of his presentation, and the overwhelming list of conditions that explained their willingness to kill, diminishes the force of his conclusion.[123]

But the mystery of My Lai continues to elude us. As journalist Myra MacPherson observed, it is impossible to explain "why some behave one way and others not."[124] Some reported that the men were under control of their superiors on the ground; others claimed that a breakdown of control occurred rapidly. We are uncertain that the officers in charge that day, including Captain Medina and the higher-ups circling in helicopters above the scene of the massacre, had any intention or desire to stem the destruction.

Historian Michael Belknap, himself a Vietnam veteran, reflects that "there was a moral vacuum in Charlie Company. The whole unit was drifting into a culture of violence in which anything seemed permissible."[125] While attributing their actions to a breakdown in authority or a breakdown in the mental health of the soldiers or the development of "a culture of violence" is psychologically insightful, it is inadequate to the task. Remember, men from the other two companies joined with Charlie Company in the mania of destruction. As Tim O'Brien constantly reminds us, in similar situations, under similar circumstances, soldiers did not kill civilians or execute babies at point-blank range.[126]

We just know that radical evil was unleashed that day. The faces of some of the soldiers beamed as they murdered and raped. Indeed, Michael Bernhardt stated thirty years after the massacre that he did not hold conditions in Vietnam responsible, nor did he think that things happened because they were ordered. Rather, he claims that the My Lai killers "were lost *before* we got there. Everybody was in character that day. They didn't need an enemy to fine-tune them. They didn't need Vietnam to set them off. They were already that violent. . . . We didn't need Vietnam to create a My Lai. We had social problems *here* that created that."[127] This is a very sobering interpretation, and it gets right to the heart of the problems of moral philosophy when it comes to character and circumstance.

The army brass were clearly operating with a moral system that was full of content and empty of meaning. They believed that rules and orders would be sufficient to uphold moral values. They failed to see that no matter how correct the moral rules they distributed to the men, they would conflict with the imperative that was drilled into the soldiers daily during basic training and backed up by the threat of severe punishment: Follow orders without question. Calley could not remember what he had been told in classes about the rules of war: "Nothing stands out in my mind what was covered in those classes." He was crystal clear about another set of rules: "all orders were assumed to be legal, that the soldier's job was to carry out any order given him to the best of his ability."[128] Others recognized the clash between abstract moral rights imprinted on wallet-sized cards and the intent of basic training to make the men obey orders: "An important ingredient in the cauldron of evil we call My Lai," wrote lawyer and army veteran Robert Rivkin, "is the Army's glorification of obedience and its contempt for conscience."[129]

The rules-based moral ideals about how to treat prisoners, about how to present oneself to civilians, and about respecting and adhering to the Geneva Convention were reasonable. Moral ideals and prescriptions are imperative. Alas, in some situations, they are irrelevant. Moral systems that are predicated on men living up to moral strictures often fail, for many reasons. As Arendt so pointedly remarked about Eichmann, when at his trial he was asked to give a summary of Kant's moral imperative—to be obedient to universal rules of conduct—he did an acceptable job, hitting on the general outlines, but miserably failing to recognize that his actions were corrupt to the core.[130]

Aristotle had a different idea about morality. He maintained that morality does not come from on high, and it is certainly not contained in a set of rules. Rather, morality is in cultivation and education of the virtues, a striving for excellence in qualities such as courage. But he recognized that courage, for example, could be rash, as when one person decides to oppose an entire army. Aristotle thus viewed character as a clinging to a mean, a sense of moderation in the virtues. The virtues were inherent within men, entities that blossomed as a result of education, training, and most important, exercise. One becomes courageous or compassionate by acting in that manner. Over time, it becomes part of one's character structure. In Aristotle the ends of moderation, courage, or compassion are not debatable; they are givens. However, the means we employ to achieve these ends are always in question and a matter of deliberation.[131]

A case can certainly be made that the young men in My Lai were lacking in their cultivation of virtues. We can bemoan how, by the 1960s in American society, individuals had by and large lost inner-directedness, marked by a willingness to follow his or her own interior moral gyroscope. And we can agree with political scientist Wilson Carey McWilliams that a "conscious morality" might forestall the killing of innocents.[132] We must remember, as historian Loren Baritz tells us, that these soldiers were young: "It was thus a teenage war led by amateurs."[133] Although the soldiers had conventional religious training, the army had sought effectively to break down any sense of deliberation on their part, to blur their attention to ends. The army wanted only obedient followers of orders.[134] They succeeded well with someone like Calley, and they failed with someone like Bernhardt. But the army also understood, I suspect, that peer pressure, the desire to fit in, as well as the disciplinary function of obedience to authority and the threat of punishment were sufficient to override ethical protests. Bernhardt and the others were able to be courageous by not killing innocents, but they were stymied when it came to stopping the killing. Their comrades-in-arms may not have all wanted to participate in the killing, but they did—perhaps out of a weakness of the will, perhaps out of a desire to be part of the orgy of destruction, perhaps because this was a once in a lifetime opportunity to be God and the Devil all at once.

The question arises as to whether Aristotelian virtues as part of one's character remain relevant in a wartime situation. Did the daily grind of being shot at by an elusive enemy, of seeing close friends die from landmines and booby-traps, of being picked apart by mosquitoes and fear on a daily basis, contribute to the destruction of character? As Tim O'Brien writes, the soldiers carried much of their previous lives with them to Vietnam, but how much of it, especially their compassion, survived in these conditions? Of course, the whole point of virtue, in the Aristotelian sense, is that, if properly cultivated, it is capable of surmounting unfavorable conditions. To expect virtue to reign under perfect conditions is like expecting the sun to warm on a cool day. It is no choice, no challenge.

Studies of those interned in Nazi concentration camps give a mixed view on the ability of virtue to survive under conditions of radical evil. In some of the depictions of these camps, starvation and fear led to an animal-like thirst for survival. Men and women whose characters were of the highest caliber in normal life became machines bent on survival, willing to steal a crust of bread from a weaker inmate in order to keep themselves going. Yet according to other analysts, examples aplenty exist of virtues such as compassion and friendship surviving the harshest of conditions in the concentration camps.[135] Indeed, without them, survival would have been impossible.

It seems too easy to suggest that in My Lai these men had been stripped of their own humanity, that their character had failed them. While I am convinced that these young men often were lacking firmly developed characters and that they were faced with competing ethical imperatives—obey your orders and do not kill innocents—they still retained their ability to make choices. They did not suffer a complete breakdown of their cultural values, although their values had come under severe attack. But they suffered nothing resembling a case of "ontological vulnerability," a sense that the world as they knew it had come to an end.[136] They continued to write letters home, to pray to their God, to eat their normal foods, and to hope that the nightmare of Vietnam would end when their hitch was completed.

Nor was their situation in My Lai that horrendous. Yes, there may have been a couple of shots fired at them on landing. But it was clear that they were not under any sustained attack. They moved through the hamlets with relatively little fear for their lives. While under wartime conditions one is often thrust into situations where one responds on instinct for survival, such was not the case at My Lai. They were presented with the choice to kill or not to kill. Some chose the former, others chose the latter. We can never predict how one is going to act in such circumstances with any certitude. Yet we can still contend that in the case of My Lai, the actions undertaken by these men were wrong, no matter how complex and difficult the war. And still that does not pull us out of the muddy waters of evil.

This is not to say that these men intended to do evil that day. They did not. Nor am I seeking to pin the ultimate blame on some metaphysical demon of radical evil whispering in their ears. But we will never understand My Lai if we seek to frame it only with pat explanations. Something always eludes us in these situations, for in similar circumstances different outcomes resulted. We can look at the My Lai massacre from various perspectives. It can be viewed as what happens when competing moral imperatives are placed on the slim shoulders and unformed characters of soldiers. We can then presume that given a license to kill and under orders, most will kill. The My Lai massacre can also be comprehended as showing what happens when freedom without constraints presents itself to young men. The opportunity to exert absolute power of life and death will be embraced, invariably with horrible results. Finally, we can see that some of the men chose—perhaps because of their characters, perhaps because they feared retribution, perhaps for reasons that will forever remain unfathomable—not to kill, not to rape, and not to lose their sense of humanity. The mystery of My Lai evades lists of reasons. It is to be found in the complexity of the human condition. However deep the ultimate mystery, it remains important to remember the words of Robert Jay Lifton, who has spent many hours with Vietnam veterans and pondering My Lai: "We cannot avoid the abyss; that is our history. We repeat it, if we are ignorant of it and if we cannot confront it. . . . Like other people, we are capable under certain circumstances of taking plunges into evil."[137]

PART II

In Times of Peace

Chapter Four
The Hate Stare: Empathy and Moral Luck

A Hanging in Mansfield

That it happened on 2 April 1960 is both significant and chilling. An effigy with a half-white, half-black face hanged from the stoplight and confronted commuters traveling along the main street running through Mansfield, Texas. Everyone in town knew the effigy was meant to represent and to intimidate local resident John Howard Griffin. A few days earlier, residents learned from a story in *Time* magazine that Griffin had darkened his skin and traveled through parts of the South as a black man. During his journey, he had been subjected to a host of abuses. But what haunted him most was the "hate stare" from whites—the look that communicated disdain for the existence of black people. Griffin had been blind for nearly ten years following injuries suffered during his service in World War II. This probably made him more attentive to the "visual dynamics" of seeing racism once his sight miraculously returned in the late 1950s. Griffin's pain from the icy hate stare thus became a rhetorically powerful and biographically anchored device in his account.[1]

The *Time* article ignited a campaign of intimidation against Griffin. According to a young white preacher, everyone in Mansfield "considers Griffin just like a nigger. The decent folks don't have any respect for him at all. . . . They figger he should just live out there with the niggers."[2] Threats referred to him as a "half-nigger bastard," and warned him that "YOUR TIME IS UP. YOU ARE MARKED." Griffin wrote in the isolation of a barn/study on his parents' farm, listening to Bach and "waiting to be slaughtered" by white supremacists. "Is tonight the night the shotgun blasts through the window. . . . Is tonight the night they . . . come and drag me out and castrate me, as they have promised?"[3]

In a chilling, undated, handwritten account of uncertain provenance, someone writing under the name Noel Thomas Cash related, in mock-heroic form, how he and a group of other teenagers had carried off the hanging of the effigy. The writer describes how they constructed the effigy using old newspapers and hangers, and how they outfitted it in bow tie, sport jacket, jeans, and Griffin's trademark dark glasses. The letter includes a diagram detailing the logistics of getting the effigy high up on the traffic signal. Cash's account barely hints at any deep-seated hatred; he claims his actions were nothing more than a prank, a "fun" "adventure" that resulted in "many hours of laughter" for him and his friends.[4]

Evil, as Hannah Arendt made clear in the early 1960s, has various faces. The hanging of the Griffin effigy is evil in perhaps its most banal light: hateful without so intending.[5] While these young men disapproved of Griffin's racial masquerade, and they no doubt opposed his recent attempts to integrate schools in Mansfield, they showed no concern that hanging an effigy might be perceived as a serious threat to Griffin and his family. By mid-morning, after young men had alerted the *Fort Worth Star-Telegram* about the story, the effigy was taken down, transported to the town dump, and photographed there with a sign behind the effigy that stated, "$25 Fine for Dumping Dead Animals."[6] As a grim coda to this prank, within a week of the effigy hanging, a cross was burned in front of a black school, not far from Griffin's residence.[7] By August 1960, he and his family had fled to Mexico so that he could continue working on an account of his life as a black man in the segregated Jim Crow South.

In the previous chapters we have looked evil in the face with the help of Hannah Arendt. We have seen evil and moral muddiness in World War II bombings and a slaughter in Vietnam. The fires of fanaticism and the customs of war conspire to blunt moral feelings and to topple structures of virtue. Perhaps it is invaluable, at this point then, to examine one man's ingenious attempt to do something morally responsible and shocking. However clumsy and lacking in finesse his attempt might be—especially to our more racially aware eyes—his exercise in experience and empathy has much to recommend itself as anodyne to the horrors that dominate the preceding chapters.

In confronting racism in the Jim Crow South and trying to understand the pain of its African American citizens, Griffin was acting in a virtuous and moral sense. Nothing was muddy about his intentions or about the results of his escapade. If he opened the eyes of some whites to racism, thereby challenging tired traditions, entrenched authority, and moral ignorance, then he was acting in an exemplary moral fashion. Alas, even in the realm of moral virtue, things are never quite so stark. Empathy, while a moral virtue of the highest order, is an insufficient guide to action. It has its own problems, as we shall see later, when we examine the empathy felt by liberal war hawks over the suffering of Iraqi citizens under the regime of Saddam Hussein. Empathy allows us to identify problems, to widen our circle of humanity, as it did for Griffin. It opens us up, as philosopher Charles Taylor puts it, recognition of the authentic of other's being.[8] Empathy does not, however, necessarily resolve what is to be done about a problem. But it does help us to recognize problems, and that is a starting point for moral "mature consideration."

A Journey into Fear

In the early fall of 1961, Griffin's book *Black Like Me* exploded into print.[9] It was a bestseller and remains in print today. Publication of the volume was, no doubt, a nightmare come true for Cash and others like him. Griffin was, in effect, a race traitor—someone who had, albeit temporarily, willingly cast off his whiteness for another identity.[10] By testifying about his experiences as a black man, Griffin earned the empathy of many white readers for the suffering he had faced. The contingent nature of Griffin's fate—obvious to his readers who knew that he was "really" a white man—sealed the bond of empathy between Griffin and his readers. White readers, especially, felt Griffin's pain as a black man all the more because they knew he was white.

Griffin's odyssey began rather melodramatically, on a New Orleans evening in early November. After taking the drug Oxsoralen under a doctor's direction, exposing himself for long hours under a sunlamp, and covering parts of his body with a vegetable dye, Griffin achieved a transformation. Griffin described how his "nerves simmered with dread" as he glanced in the mirror.[11] He finds "a stranger—a fierce, bald, very dark Negro." Within moments, he is convinced that "all traces of the John Griffin I had been were wiped from existence"; in their place "was a newly created Negro" (12). As the clock dramatically tolls midnight, Griffin takes to the streets, entering into his temporary life as a black man.

What moved Griffin to undertake "the oddest project of my life," as he phrased it in his journal?[12] His claim that he wanted to examine the high incidence of suicides among African Americans in the South rings hollow. His journals are extremely revealing about his inner emotional and intellectual concerns. Griffin at the time had faced both practical and spiritual challenges, adjusting to life as a blind man following the war, and later converting to Catholicism. And yet the journals remain silent on the issue of what prompted him to take on the persona of a black man.

In the mid-1950s, Griffin had become deeply concerned about civil rights after interviewing people for a study assessing the potential effects of school desegregation in Mansfield. He found whites engulfed in fears about everything. They sought to escape their fears by asserting racial pride, acting as bullies, and displaying pure hatred against blacks. In 1956, one Mansfield "woman of perfect character" reportedly reacted to the hanged effigy of a black person by wishing whites had hung a "real nigger." This incident "curdled" Griffin's blood, he wrote, and perhaps impelled him to try to better understand black suffering and white perceptions.[13]

This could have been easily accomplished by interviews and traditional research. Griffin's racial masquerade, however, partly grew out of the Catholic tradition of social activism. As Dorothy Day lived in poverty to minister to and identify with the needs of the poor, Griffin would live as a black man to testify to blacks' suffering and to reveal to whites the extent and irrationality of their racial hatred.[14] His work would combine "Action and Contemplation," as one of his favorite Catholic philosophers phrased it, by witnessing the horrors in the outside world while peering deeply into the white soul.[15]

Whatever his motivations, Griffin found his identity as a black man both too visible and too hidden at times. He is invisible in the sense that whites cannot see him as a real person, with his own desires, intellect, and individuality. He is rendered invisible because of white stereotypes, clichés, and blindness toward blacks. But *Black Like Me* is more about seeing, about how whites in the South view and treat blacks in inhumane fashion. Griffin is recognized immediately as a black person whenever he searches for a bathroom and is told to walk a mile or more to find one reserved for blacks. He is recognized immediately when he sits on a park bench and is warned to vacate it because it is for whites only. He is recognized immediately as a black person when threatened by white hoodlums, or when a driver decides to prevent him from disembarking from a public bus. And he is recognized immediately by the "hate stare" that greets him because he is black.

After his initial time in New Orleans, learning how blacks are expected to act around whites and scrounging for work with little success, Griffin heads to Hattiesburg, Mississippi. He asks the white ticket-taker at the bus station when the next bus leaves for Hattiesburg. She gives him a look of pure "disapproval," a stare that was "so exaggeratedly hateful" (51). Stunned to be treated in such a degrading manner, Griffin politely inquires: "Pardon me, but have I done something to offend you?" He soon realizes that it is his color alone that offends the woman. When he tries a second time to buy a ticket and get change by presenting a ten-dollar bill, the ticket person's "face flushed," and she "fairly shouted: 'I *told* you—I can't change that big a bill.'" When Griffin persists, even to the point of suggesting that she summon the manager, the ticket-taker then "jerked the bill furiously" from Griffin and dumped the ticket and change on the counter with great force. "I was truly dumbfounded by this deep fury," Griffin observed. "Her performance was so venomous." But Griffin feels pity for her, which he imagines shows in his face. It only makes her angrier that she should be viewed in such a "condescending" manner by a black man (51–52).

Griffin claimed to have begun his journey with an interest in answering the sociological question of why Southern blacks had such a high incidence of suicide. The answer quickly becomes clear as his existence as a "black man" in the South becomes "burdensome" (118). He longs to return to the privileges of whiteness: to being able to sit at any open seat on a bus, to be treated with respect, to have options about where he lives. As a temporary black, he is indignant about having to go "searching for those things that all whites take for granted" (100).

Griffin's life spirals downward as he moves on to the black section of Hattiesburg. He describes his blacks-only hotel room as "decrepit" and complains of the noise of the jazz music that "blared through the street with a monstrous high-strutting rhythm that pulled at my viscera" (67). Again, he turns to the mirror and comes to feel "lonely and hopeless . . . agonizingly estranged from the world of order and harmony" he had enjoyed as a white man (67). In one of his more melodramatic moments, he feels "the momentary flash of blind hatred against the whites who were somehow responsible" for the horrendous indignities he has suffered (69). Griffin imagines an outbreak of violence and escapes to the home of his friend, the pro–civil rights newspaper editor P. D. East. At the sedate East home, Griffin finds temporary relief from his terror before summoning up his courage to resume his life as a black man (73).

His "journey into fear" takes him next to Mobile, Alabama. In his journal, Griffin recalled visiting Mobile with his parents as a youngster, remembering it as having had "an aura of calm and graciousness." Now, disguised as a black man, "I found none of those whites I had once loved."[16] Instead, he uncovers only bigotry and hatred. The beaches are reserved for whites only, although he learns that the funds to pay for the whites-only beaches come from gasoline taxes paid by blacks as well as whites (84). Needing to use a bathroom, he is told by the white proprietor of a custard stand that there is one fourteen or fifteen blocks away. Attempting to make a human connection with the proprietor, Griffin asks if he might dart into the "dilapidated outhouse" in the back, a structure he imagines as so horrible that "certainly no human could degrade [it] any more than time and the elements had." His request is denied. Griffin trudges on, finding the weight of his blackness an increasingly heavy burden (85–86).

By the end of his six-week journey, Griffin returns home for Christmas with his family a changed man. He is humbled by the "isolating effects" of the "totality of . . . Negro-ness" (111). He never felt safe in his adopted skin, always having to mind his etiquette around whites, always fearing violence, and always encumbered by his status as a second-class, or lower, citizen. Although he claimed to have undertaken the journey without having any "brief for the Negro," the conclusions he draws are simple and apparent to anyone: Southern blacks are treated horribly through no fault of their own. And this must change.

Griffin's Moral Moment

Griffin's act of racial transgression helps us understand a particular moral moment when whites in the South systematically denied blacks their civil rights and treated them as second-class citizens and human beings. This was a moral affront because racism refused the particularity of black individuals, and fit them within a rigid stereotype that limited their possibilities. Griffin wrote what is essentially a moral text designed to increase empathy among whites for the plight of African Americans. He anticipated well philosopher Lawrence Blum's view of racism as "a Moral Evil" that required a "moral conversion" on the part of his white readership.[17] Griffin also enacts during his journey central issues of empathy, moral luck, and identity. Instead of fixating on the social and institutional structures of racism, Griffin reported what it meant to feel racism. *Black Like Me*, then, can be viewed as a key text in what historian Daniel Wickberg has called "the History of the Sensibilities."[18] Griffin's entry into the realm of empathy is an odd staging, a dramatic presentation of what it means to suffer from the perspective of a white man who has never had to suffer for his color.

Griffin embodies "no-fault suffering" in the sense that he is an educated, family-oriented, sober, and religious *white* man. On one level, his change is superficial—nothing more than darkened skin pigmentation. Yet the implications of this change resound, allowing white readers to imagine the pain African Americans face on a daily basis as being without cause or necessity. At the time of his masquerade, Griffin's work was viewed positively by African Americans. Even Malcolm X remarked that Griffin's book helped whites to understand better the horrendous realities black people faced daily. Of course, as Malcolm X and others recognized, while "it was a frightening experience for him . . . a make-believe Negro," it was "what *real* Negroes in America have gone through for four hundred years."[19]

Despite the book's positive initial reception among African Americans, despite the book's sales of more than twelve million copies in various languages, and despite the generations of white readers who have attested to the book's power in shaping their consciousness of race, Griffin's racial masquerade has been consigned to the dustbin of history and today is seen as embarrassing and problematic.[20] Scholars of the civil rights movement almost never mention *Black Like Me*.[21] Those who have looked at *Black Like Me* in some detail usually come from the fields of American studies, whiteness studies, or cultural studies, and their disdain for the volume is intense. Griffin is condemned as a white man entitling himself to speak for blacks while blacks are consigned to passive victimhood. As a cultural tourist glibly crossing racial boundaries, Griffin fed into preexisting clichés and fantasies of black life. As a Cold War liberal, Griffin presented the South as a site for otherness, one that can be transformed only by the ideals of American freedom and democracy. Griffin's book was published at the precise historical moment, in the summer of 1961, when heroic Freedom Riders were fanning out in the South to defy authorities and change the landscape of racial relations.[22] By contrast, Griffin was viewed as doing little more than voice empty universal sentiments about humanitarianism. Finally, Griffin's account was attacked as detracting from works by actual African American writers—ranging from Richard Wright to James Baldwin—who could deal more deeply and authentically with what it meant to be an African American in 1950s America.[23]

The vehemence of these condemnations arises from the racial politics of our time. They emphasize only the debits of empathetic understanding across racial lines, missing entirely how Griffin's act was marked by moral courage, conscience, and ingenuity. More important, it was undertaken with sufficient subtlety and implicit knowledge of the murkiness of moral stances. In the end, it did yeoman's work in educating white readers to feel the horror of racism and to recognize the false presumptions and entrenched ideals at its core.

Universalism

For Griffin to communicate empathy for African Americans, he first had to clear away illusions concerning the fixed nature of racial identity. He did so by employing a variant of what philosophers call "moral luck." Going as far back as Aristotle, and central to the recent work of philosophers Martha Nussbaum, Thomas Nagel, and Bernard Williams, the concept of moral luck has varied uses and implications. As Nussbaum indicates, character and virtue, so often considered fixed qualities, are sometimes fragile branches against the tragic winds of contingency. Nagel demonstrates how moral luck makes judgment problematic, since the same intentions and actions on the part of individuals may, through a chance happening, have quite different outcomes. Williams uses the notion of moral luck to batter down the fixed moral edifice constructed by the universalism of Kantian and utilitarian ethicists.[24]

Moral luck ideas bounce in different directions around Griffin's journey. One brilliant conceit behind his project was to demonstrate how a throw of the racial dice determined identity and the consequences of one's life. At the same time, moral luck can suggest that our identities are formed not only by circumstance but by other forces beyond our control, ranging from constitutive forces (temperament and capacity) to antecedent circumstances (what has happened to us before) to simple circumstance (being thrown into a situation). According to the theory of moral luck, the individual and his or her place in the world is both embedded and circumstantial. Griffin hammered these points home by example in *Black Like Me*. Moral luck, too, fit nicely with Griffin's universalist vision. After all, moral luck defines existence as much for whites as it does for blacks, without making racial identity an entity cast in concrete. Hence for Griffin identity was malleable and powerful at the same time, and all people were, at base, essentially the same, partaking of a shared humanity. By linking universalism and moral luck, and then by fostering empathy, Griffin intended to demolish justifications for racial prejudice and racial ideology. Here he was in sympathy with other white liberals of the period in maintaining that African Americans were no different from white people, except for degrees of skin coloration.

Historian Kenneth M. Stampp famously wrote in *The Peculiar Institu-*

tion (1956) that "slaves were merely ordinary human beings, that innately Negroes *are*, after all, only white men with black skins, nothing more, nothing less."[25] A similar view infused well-meaning studies that compared the effects of the concentration camp experience on Jews with the toll of slavery on African Americans. In *Slavery* (1959), Stanley M. Elkins, borrowing from psychologist Bruno Bettelheim's observations of Nazi concentration camp inmates, famously concluded that in a total institution (one that allows for no freedom, such as the concentration camp or slavery), the subject is reduced to a childlike existence. While Elkins and others spoke too little of mechanisms of struggle and collective agency on the part of Jews and blacks in horrendous situations, the upshot of the analyses was simple and hopeful: When an individual of any race, ethnicity, or religion is placed in a total institution of degradation, the results will be the same. We are, then, brothers under the skin in our suffering. Building on the culture and personality school of thought, Elkins maintained that culture was malleable; that since racial characteristics were neither innate nor necessary, then change could occur. Griffin, too, wanted to move cultural understanding in a new direction by blasting away at the stereotypes and clichés that inhibited cultural identification with others.[26]

While Griffin was preparing to embark on his tour of the South as a black man, Harvard philosopher John Rawls began building piece by piece the edifice of his great book, *A Theory of Justice* (1971). Rawls argued that problems in justice can be understood best when everyone is theoretically stripped of their identities, when everyone wears a "veil of ignorance" that prevents them from perceiving what is in their own best interests as a particular individual in favor of what would be in their best interests as a general individual. Everyone is placed in what Rawls called "the original position." Rawls's mode of analysis helped to illuminate many of the quandaries of injustice.[27] But it remained abstract.

In contrast, Griffin lifted the "veil of ignorance" through his temporary embrace of a black identity, an act that is particular rather than abstract in practice. Griffin wanted, through his experiences, to establish universal ideals of sameness and of rights. He sought to bear witness to the suffering of blacks.[28]

However, Griffin's temporary investment in blackness complicates matters. Rather than engaging in a simple quest for an empathetic understanding with African Americans, he is doing something both more daring and unsettling. He is transforming himself into an object for our empathy, an object removed from the normal depths of black experience. Perhaps the best formulation for his act is as follows: White readers identify with a white man who appears to others to be a black man. In the process, they come to appreciate the unfairness of how blacks suffer.

Empathy Gone Awry

Of course, Griffin's racial masquerade occurred in the context of a long, often torturous, history of white identification with blacks and other "outsiders" in America. As Eric Lott has demonstrated, white fascination with blacks, as in minstrelsy, has been ripe with desire and hatred.[29] In the late nineteenth and early twentieth centuries, middle- and upper-class whites harbored fantasies about the working and immigrant classes. Viewing themselves as afflicted with ennui, a sense of "weightlessness" in their increasingly mundane existences, these elites imagined that the immigrant and working classes possessed a natural and edifying vitality and primitivism. Their understanding of the other was motivated more by their own needs and desires than by any serious appreciation of the working class. However limited such excursions into the world of the working class might have been, on occasion they helped to break down barriers and fuel progressive reform and inter-class solidarity.[30]

Two years before Griffin's project, in a shocking essay titled "The White Negro" (1957), Norman Mailer presumed to have engaged the black psyche, and there he imagined his own spiritual and sexual liberation. Ignoring all aspects of African American life having to do with religion and community, work and probity, and the struggle for equality and dignity, Mailer presented blacks as quintessential hipsters. For Mailer, historical circumstances had consigned blacks in America to live under a sign of death, in an existential present. Mailer's fantasy granted African Americans a strange type of freedom that he equated with the figures of the hipster, drug dealer, pimp, and murderer. Identifying with these underworld figures, Mailer imagined the delight of radical transgression, going so far as to fantasize about the adrenalin rush experienced by a black teenage robber as he thrusts a killing knife into the body of a Jewish store-owner. Mailer's empathy with a vengeance was a primitivism gone wild that obscured black reality while illuminating the neurotic world inhabited by Mailer himself.[31]

A decade later, William Styron composed his Pulitzer Prize–winning novel, *The Confessions of Nat Turner* (1967). Whether novelists turn to historical characters for their material or invent characters from the broadcloth of their own imaginations, they create a reality. On entering into the world of imaginative empathy for a character, readers come to feel the pain—as well as the joy—of the characters depicted. This is central to the experience of reading and to feeling empathy. Normally, this is hardly controversial. But Styron, a white liberal, chose not only to write about a black historical figure but to frame his account in controversial ways. He readily admitted to taking "the utmost freedom of imagination" in his depiction of Nat Turner's life.[32] He presented Turner as a self-loathing neurotic, given to sexual fantasies about a young white woman. Styron's Turner was a complex man, but hardly a heroic one. Coming into print at the precise moment when the African American liberation movement was demanding its own heroes and the right to produce its histories, Styron's account ignited a bonfire of controversy.[33]

For some readers, Styron had in effect executed Turner a second time by projecting his own neuroses and creative needs onto the dead man. Ten black writers, in a volume summing up the criticisms of Styron's novel, challenged Styron's depiction. They characterized his act of empathy as another case of a white man appropriating the life of a black man for his own purposes. It was, in the view of black psychiatrist Alvin Poussaint, "slander" against Turner and generations of black Americans.[34] The great Southern writer William Faulkner, albeit in a different context, admitted that it was extremely difficult for a white man to enter into the reality of a black man. As Faulkner put it, "It is easy enough . . . to say glibly, 'If I were a Negro, I would do this or that.' But a white man can only imagine himself for the moment a Negro; he cannot become that man of another race and griefs and problems."[35]

Other works in this period and earlier had sought to present the complexity and reality of American racism and its psychological effects. Swedish sociologist Gunnar Myrdal's massive work, *An American Dilemma: The Negro Problem and Modern Democracy* (1944), studied how stereotypes and clichés about race-supported institutions—political, economic, and social—consigned African Americans in the South to second-class citizenship. His conclusions anticipated much in Griffin's own work: that Negroes are, in essence, "inherently not much different from other people," and that while whites and blacks lived in close proximity with one another in the South, whites had little understanding of the realities of black life. Racism, Myrdal concluded, was "a problem in the heart of America" and it needed to be resolved.[36]

White readers of Griffin's time could also enter into the world of African

American life in the works of Richard Wright. In Wright's autobiographical account of his early years, *Black Boy* (1945), they could learn how he suffered from the illness of his mother, forced and constant changes of homes, and disabling poverty. He wrote: "I had never in my life been abused by whites, but I had already . . . been the victim of a thousand lynchings."[37] His popular and powerful novel *Native Son* (1940) depicted the difficult circumstances of an African American living in the Chicago ghetto. Out of such engagement, white readers could come to understand why a young man like Bigger Thomas would hate whites, feel excluded from possibilities, and be able to kill. The novel's depiction of ghetto life is marked by images of the rat-infested tenement where the Thomas family tries to survive.[38] Philosopher Martha Nussbaum rightly notes: "We cannot follow the novel without trying to see the world through Bigger's eyes. As we do so, we take on, at least to some extent, his emotions and rage."[39] Yet we remain "spectators," distanced from his reality, limited in our identification.

The Challenge and Necessity of Empathy

Empathy is invaluable but difficult to achieve at a meaningful level. Depictions of suffering can take on an aesthetic beauty that limits our ability to identify with the pain of others. Too many images of suffering may actually numb us to that pain.[40] And empathy itself can be skewed: Empathy for an "unborn infant" as a human being may move someone to ignore the quandary of its teenage mother, or vice versa.[41] Moreover, a sadist can feel the pain and suffering of an innocent—an act of empathy—while at the same time taking pleasure in those feelings.[42]

Expressions of empathy even when achieved are often limited. Consider the story of the Russian countess who, on a freezing night in Moscow, attends a play. The drama is about the suffering of peasants, and it brings her to tears as she imagines the pain of another. It proves to be a strangely satisfying and painful experience for her. She has, at that moment, transcended her own privileged existence. While she weeps for the suffering of these fake peasants, she is unconcerned about her carriage driver, who freezes outside, tending to her horses after being ordered to await her exit from the theater. Empathy, therefore, can be limited in its scope, a form of self-indulgence without any commerce with the near-to-hand suffering of her own servant.[43]

Empathy is further challenged by our common inability to feel the pain of others or to identify with suffering, especially when it is undergone by people different from us—a point well appreciated by Griffin. Aristotle recognized that pity is greatest when we confront suffering in others who are like us "in age, character, disposition, social standing, or birth." This is so, according to Aristotle, because "generally, we feel pity whenever we are in the condition of remembering that similar misfortunes have happened to us or ours, or expecting them to happen in the future."[44] Rousseau asked in *Emile*, "Why are kings without pity for their subjects?" or "Why are the rich so harsh to the poor?" The answer is simple: Neither the king nor the wealthy man can imagine himself in the position of the other.[45]

Contemporary philosophers and social theorists agree that we draw the lines around our empathy in congruence with the perceived closeness to us of the objects of our compassion. Avishai Margalit and Richard Rorty have noted that the circle of empathy begins with family, then reaches out to ethnic and religious connections, sometimes encompassing national identifications. We are, in large part, what our cultures tell us we are. Culture thus enables us to understand the world, but it also limits appreciation for different cultural takes on the world. Hence to speak of empathy for humanity at large is empty and diffuse. The trick is to begin to widen the circle so it can be more inclusive of those who do not fit in neatly with our normal identifications. In Rorty's view, such a widening recognizes that our cultural understanding is contingent rather than foundational, simply one way among many of making sense of the world. And one aspect of such insight, in Rorty's liberal worldview, is to reject cruelty and to empathize with the suffering of others. This is why the concept of moral luck is connected with empathetic understanding.[46]

Even if empathy is too often limited in its scope, it remains a virtue of great value when accompanied by compassion. Adam Smith viewed compassion and pity as the central "social passions" that allow us to become closer to others.[47] Rousseau ranked pity or compassion as the chief virtue.[48] Through our ability to feel or appreciate the suffering and pain of others, we may moderate our own actions so as to cause less suffering to others. Out of natural feelings of pity and compassion for others, Rousseau continued, arise virtues of humanity and generosity. While political theorist Hannah Arendt disdained pity, she celebrated compassion as a more concrete feeling for a particular rather than general concern. In discussing the French Revolution, Arendt noticed how pity easily turned to cruelty.[49] "Pity, taken as the spring of virtue," Arendt wrote, "has proved to possess a greater capacity for cruelty than cruelty itself." But as philosopher André Comte-Sponville remarks, "Pity is neither a guarantee nor a panacea," but it can help us to appreciate and work to lessen the suffering of others.[50]

Today, we are comfortable with the term *empathy*, associating it with sympathy and compassion. Empathy represents a moral feeling or virtue, an attempt to identify with and to understand the suffering of others. As the scholar Robert L. Katz puts it, "When we empathize in everyday experiences, we enjoy a sense of membership [with others that] reduces social distance."[51] In a world of narrow interests and stunted virtues, this is no small matter.

Historians have demonstrated that the concept of empathy and compassion for others emerged as a motif, with the introduction of the novel in the eighteenth century. Through the experience of reading, a moral sensibility was stoked; readers came to understand how the suffering of fictional characters had analogues in the real world. Increased feelings of empathy also came from sources beyond the novel. In an age when physical suffering had lessened, thanks to advances in science and hygiene, empathy for the pain of others grew apace. Antislavery advocates used various means of depiction—from illustrations showing welts from whippings on the backs of slaves to stories of the separation of slave children from their parents—to show how slavery was a corrupting institution, inflicting unnecessary and unfair pain on innocent individuals. While most readers of these texts might fail to imagine themselves as slaves, they could recognize at least its inhumanity and, in some cases, dedicate themselves to its abolition or eventual demise. Without much hyperbole one could claim that empathy is a central virtue without which human solidarity and reform would be well-nigh impossible.[52]

"What Is It Like to Be a Bat?"

John Howard Griffin's challenge was to widen the circle of empathy, to make white Americans morally concerned with African Americans. He began with the common presumption that blacks and whites lived in separate worlds and that they "in reality know nothing about one another."[53] His racial masquerade was designed to widen this identification by contending that skin coloration in the Jim Crow South was in fact nothing more than a matter of luck. Thus even a white person suddenly possessed of black skin was subject to inhumanity in a purely contingent situation. Empathy for the plight of African Americans came less from understanding their daily lives as such than from identification with how those lives and realities resulted from nothing more than a flip of the racial coin.

The limits of our ability to identify with another were well illustrated by philosopher Thomas Nagel in his classic essay, "What Is It Like to Be a Bat?" (1974). Nagel confronts his readers with an old and central philosophical and moral problem: Can we understand a consciousness that is alien from our own? Bats, Nagel assumes, certainly have experiences, but we can never feel them *as a* bat does. What can we know? In Nagel's thought experiment, we can imagine ourselves as something like a bat.[54] We can embark on a masquerade of sorts by thinking of ourselves with webbed arms, some sort of sonar radar, and poor vision, and even to the extent of pondering what it would be like to hang upside down much of the day. But this "tells me only what it would be like for *me* to behave as a bat behaves." I remain me, but fail to comprehend the key question: "what is it like for a *bat* to be a bat"? And this we can never achieve, in part, because we cannot be anything more than human beings pondering what it would be like to be something other than what we are. We cannot experience "batness."

Griffin tangled in *Black Like Me* with a variant of Nagel's puzzle. While obviously blacks and whites were members of the same species, given the power of racism, blacks were often presumed to be radically different. Griffin in his encounters with white Southerners comes to this conclusion, or he comes, more properly, to believe that white Southerners perceive blacks as totally other—in effect, as an alien species like a bat. In his most telling formulation, Griffin states that, for whites, blacks are "a different species," more animal than human. This view of blacks, of course, coexisted with the recognition that African Americans had souls and could achieve much. But, as Myrdal also found, Southern whites often perceived African Americans as "a lower biological species," different in critical ways from themselves.[55]

One point, then, of Griffin's racial masquerade was to demonstrate the limits of this perception by becoming a black person. Through the simple act of dyeing his skin, Griffin comes to be viewed as a black person from the hateful perspective of Southerners. In that sense, he had bridged a divide, one certainly not as deep phenomenologically as that between a bat and a human, but within the parlance of racial identity in the South in 1960, a vast one nevertheless.

Readers of *Black Like Me* felt a connection with a pseudo-black man because Griffin's portrait is multilayered and strikes at the heart of identity and difference. When Griffin first espies himself in the mirror, in the late hours of his first night as a black man, he is revolted by the image that confronts him. "The transformation was total and shocking." Prejudices and fears about race well up in him that he had assumed were long rejected. Yet Griffin remains cognizant that he is the same person he has always been, except that now his skin color is darker. This tension between competing identities in Griffin—"I became two men"—is helpful for white readers of his account. It is an "as if" situation, a variation of Kafka's *Metamorphosis*, perhaps, where a person is transformed in most aspects while remaining the same in others. The ruse helps readers to assume another identity, to imagine themselves as a black person. And the evocation of the squashing of Kafka's bug of difference in the story has chilling anticipations of Nazism.[56]

Moral empathy, as Griffin understood, is limited by social bonds and sympathies. Following scholars of culture, Griffin interpreted cultures as relative, marked by certain dominant myths and characteristics. These concepts shaped our worldviews, allowing us to function but at the same time limiting our ability to penetrate into the reality of those from different cultures. Growing up in Texas, Griffin learned to be prejudiced; "we saw [blacks] as 'other' and 'different' and 'not like us'—and always that implied that they were somehow inferior to us."[57] While African Americans were close-to-hand in the South, they were perceived by many whites as living a different reality, residing literally in another world. As already noted, Myrdal had remarked that whites were so encased in their own cultural stereotypes and sense of superiority that they sometimes viewed blacks as part of "a lower biological species."[58] Griffin recognized that whites too often dwelled in cultural illusion and in the "cliché of stereotype" in their dealings with black Americans.

In a revealing essay, "The Intrinsic Other" (1966), Griffin explained how he had first penetrated the mask of stereotypes in a manner that was at once touching and naïve. During World War II he was on combat duty in the South Pacific, living on an island and working with aboriginal people. From his ingrained cultural perspective, Griffin viewed himself as superior—educated in musicology, fluent in various languages, well-read. But, within the context of the island and the demands of its environment, he was a cultural imbecile who could not even navigate a trail. He came to realize that cultures are relative to their environments and that we are all too often blind to the cultural realities and values of others.[59]

The Same Man

The power of Griffin's *Black Like Me* resides in how it establishes empathy through the device of moral luck. Griffin is a virtuous man. The adversities he faces are unearned, contingent on nothing more than his temporary adoption of a different skin color. He makes it clear, and this is central, that he remains, in all other aspects, the same man, no less educated, no less moral, no less religious, and no less humane than he was previously. He dresses and speaks exactly as he had before. But the sum total of all his qualities dissipates immediately in the face of his adopted skin color. Griffin anticipates the postmodern view that racial identity is a construction rather than a biological given. As Griffin changes identity back and forth from black to white, there arises a schizophrenia about the contingent nature of racial relations. How can the same person ("In truth, if you look at it objectively, I will be the same person, only dipped in a vat and changed in appearance") one day be endowed with the attributes of a human being and the next day find himself reduced to the level of an animal?[60] It is all because, as Griffin comes to realize, "My skin was dark" (116). What makes this so absurd, then, is that racial identity, rather than being etched in stone, is simply "superficial" and contingent.

The contingency of morality and identity defines Griffin's understanding of human suffering. First, it shows how suffering arises from artificial hatreds and social arrangements beyond the control of any individual. As Griffin writes in the preface to *Black Like Me*, the details about black suffering in the South are less important than the reality that an innocent group is being persecuted. Thus he universalizes their plight and identifies himself with it while also identifying them with other groups that suffer, all because of a roll of the genetic or sociological dice: "I could have been a Jew in Germany, a Mexican in a number of states, or a member of any 'inferior' group. Only the details would have differed. The story would be the same" (xiii). Second, if such suffering is distributed by pure chance, and if it could afflict anyone given a shift in circumstances, each of us then has a responsibility to oppose such suffering.

As we saw earlier, Griffin encounters hatred in the South just because he appears to be a black man. He withers emotionally under the stares of white hatred, suffers from economic discrimination, and realizes that he exists now in the white world as the despised Other. White readers feel for Griffin as a black man because we know that he is a white man, too. And this form of empathy at least makes it possible to identify more with the black figures in the story who, on a daily basis and without recourse to changing their skin color, also suffer the outrageous blows of an entrenched racial hierarchy. Thus Griffin's "innocent suffering"—after all, he has done nothing wrong, has no cultural differences from whites, is an exemplary father and husband, and so forth—by inference confers innocence and victimhood onto blacks.

Sexuality and Family

When Griffin does have one-to-one more personal interactions with whites in the South, the subject invariably turns to black sexuality. Here Griffin is suddenly seen as a fount of knowledge, as whites seek to have their stereotypes of black sexual hunger or lack of sexual inhibitions proven true. They want Griffin to sanction their own stereotypes about authentic black sexuality. Griffin invariably disappoints, upholding his universalist belief that black people are no different from whites. Such perverse harping by white men about black sexuality strikes him as "ghoulish" (88). It serves as another sure sign of the gap in understanding that separates whites from the realities of black people living in their midst.

Griffin admits to his own concerns about how his racial masquerade will affect relations with his white wife. He decides that he will not see her until after his journey has been completed. He worries that she will not see him as the man she married but instead as "some bald-headed Negro" seeking to share their marriage bed. If she sees him as such, Griffin believes that will be a "death sentence to me." Will he, in the eyes of his wife, come to assume the identity of a black man or something else? "At base," Griffin worried in his journal, "she would always see herself lying not with a Negro, but with a part-nigger."[61] When he does finally reunite with his wife, he discovers that his fears were unfounded, more or less. "There were . . . no 'Southern-nigger-rape' recesses deep in her as there are with so many white women; or if there were, she had somehow got rid of them while I was gone." Yet, "Will I ever know? I doubt it."[62]

Although acutely aware of his own sexual concerns and confusions about black sexuality, he is stunned by the hypocrisy of whites about race and sexuality.[63] White males talk about what they presume to be the sexual perversions of blacks, but they fail to see how their own rapacious actions against black women reveal a pathology of monumental proportions. Griffin is picked up by a white man while hitchhiking from Mobile to Montgomery,

Alabama. The white driver is married, in his early fifties, with grown children and grandchildren. He seems at first to be "a decent white" (103). Like clockwork, however, the conversation quickly takes a "salacious" turn. The white man relates nonchalantly about how he often hires black women to clean his house or work for his business. "'And I guarantee you,'" he boasts, "'I've had it in every one of them before they even got on the payroll.'" Faced with Griffin's understated disdain, the white man explains that "'everybody does it. . . . We figure we're doing you people a favor to get some white blood in your kids'" (104). How, Griffin wonders, can whites rant about the "Negro's lack of sexual morality" and about "racial purity" while they are, without apparent sense of contradiction or guilt, engaging in the most wanton acts of rape and potential "mongrelization"? Here Griffin comes face to face with white pathology, with how a churchgoing individual, an "amiable, decent American," possessed a "dark tangent . . . the sickness, the coldness, the mercilessness, the lust to cause pain or fear through self-power" (105).

Griffin wrote at a time when many sociologists sought to explain how racism stripped blacks of their confidence, agency, and humanity. While these works were intended to argue against racial prejudice and its effects, they also resulted, as Ralph Ellison complained, in a rather one-sided view of African American life and institutions. Instead of understanding the mechanisms of African American culture that made for a rich community, even in the face of discrimination, they reduced black folks to mere stereotypes of pathology.[64] In Griffin's account, almost all of the blacks he encounters are hurt by racism. But they are also able to ward off some of its indignities by forming a community predicated on mutual respect and assistance. Griffin records the many kindnesses that blacks offer him as a stranger in their midst. "Among Negroes I was treated with the most incredible courtesies, even by strangers" (40, 63). His visit with a dirt-poor black family depicts the quiet wisdom and generosity of the parents and the joyfulness of the children. Here Griffin finds no pathology, only the strength of a family confronting undeserved injustice and discrimination. Despite the impoverishment of this family, Griffin is impressed with "the bravery of these people trying to bring up a family decently, their gratitude that none of their children were blind or maimed, their willingness to share their food and shelter with a stranger—the whole thing overwhelmed me" (114).

Griffin inverts the presumed order of things. Whites become the pathological group. They are prisoners of racism as much as are blacks in the South. Even when Southerners are inclined to disdain racism, the power of institutions and culture draws them into it, or else they become bystanders, tacitly accepting the harsh realities of race as defined by bigots. The pathology of white racism engulfs all Southerners in a "vortex of evil."[65] The culture of the South and its institutions and best legal minds created a self-perpetuating system of white privilege predicated on gross hypocrisies.[66] With some exceptions, the common Southerner, as Griffin learns from his own travels in a strange land, is an amalgam of hatred and incivility, of stereotypical and contradictory views. He comes to realize that whites do not see that "the Negro is the same human as the white man": rather the Negro is seen as "a different species . . . something akin to an animal" (91–92).

Although he digs shallowly into how whites are conditioned to this racial superiority and hatred, he records his reactions to it as a white man in black skin. He comes to feel, in his new racial identity, revulsion for his "own" kind. Griffin wilts under "the withering horror" of the hate stare (52). He also understands why African Americans, in the face of such hatred and contempt, contemplate suicide, seek to lose themselves in drink or dissipation, or cling ever more tightly to religious community. "I had begun this experiment in a spirit of scientific detachment," Griffin claims, "now it has become such a profound personal experience, it haunted even my dreams" (117).

Griffin's *Black Like Me* establishes the depths of white contempt for blacks and demonstrates how such hatred is an artificial construction. As he reminds us, his "real" identity is as a white man. He undergoes daily indignities only because he has changed the color of his skin. Everything else about him remains the same. Thus Griffin performed a fascinating moral and philosophical maneuver for his white readers. He made the case for the likeness of all human beings under the skin. By his racial masquerade, he attempted to enter into the reality of another, presumably alien, species (at least from the perspective of some white Southerners and perhaps some Northern whites) to show that we can understand another's reality *and* that empathy is more telling when it is linked to contingency. But for a slightly different skin color, presentation, and circumstances, any white, no matter how pure his or her heart, or how valuable his or her contribution to humanity, can be reduced to a racial stereotype.

Legacy

Griffin understood by the mid-1960s that the notion of a white man speaking for African Americans was dated and unacceptable. "By '67," Griffin wrote without any sense of dismay, "the day was long past when black people wanted any advice from a white man."[67] He also realized that the weight of white intransigence regarding civil rights demanded more radical actions than simply unmasking abuses. Indeed, half-jokingly, he dreamed of a righteous Northern invasion of the South as the only adequate means to bring an end to racist injustice.[68]

Griffin should be remembered for his attempt to establish empathy in *Black Like Me* rather than for his increasing sense of frustration with Southern racism during the 1960s. He was, along with Lillian Smith and other white Southerners, a voice for upholding ideals of color-blindness and universalism.[69] Such calls failed, of course, to resolve problems of racial injustice and discrimination; they paid insufficient attention to the economic and institutional privileges associated with white racism. They undervalued black cultural history and identity.[70] But the actions undertaken by Griffin in *Black Like Me* convincingly discounted one of the most lingering misperceptions underlying white privilege: that there are innate and significant differences between blacks and whites. Griffin also advances, through his emphasis on the contingent nature of racial difference, the view that moral understanding is rooted in an appreciation for the essential community of man.

While this is sometimes a rather abstract and sentimental notion, it was also, within the context of the early days of the civil rights movement, a perception that enabled Northern whites to bridge the gap between them and the other, to view the actions of Southerners (if not themselves) as a form of pathology. As one reader wrote to Griffin, "The last pages of your *Black Like Me* have just been read. Thank you for reminding me of my responsibilities. In my weakness I had forgotten. . . . Thank you for understanding."[71] An Israeli reader was caught up by the universalism apparent in *Black Like Me*. "May your articles and your book," she wrote, "help finally to bring about the abolition from the world of this wound—racial discrimination." She had been forced for years during the German occupation of France to wear a yellow star. "The letter froze me," wrote Griffin, reflecting on how common are the "humiliations and dangers" inflicted on others.[72]

Despite its problems, especially to our modern eyes, Griffin's "journey into fear" stands as an imaginative intervention in the moral realm, an attempt to widen the circle of "we" to encompass fellow whites and black Americans. Thus, he proclaimed in 1977 that "there is no 'other.' All men face the same fundamental human problems of loving, of suffering, of fulfilling human aspirations and of dying."[73]

In 2001 Jay Copp, writing in the *Christian Science Monitor*, found that the "staying power" of *Black Like Me* was remarkable and ever expanding. He reported that lately the book had found "respect among African-Americans." Perhaps Copp was on target when he suggested that a text like Griffin's might be a powerful tool to push a new generation of whites to identify more with, and to understand, the injustice of racism, even in the age of Barack Obama.[74]

In terms of the moral virtues, empathy ranks near the top. But as noted earlier, empathy with and for whom remains a question of no small moment. We will see more of this problem in empathetic understanding in the next chapter, where we examine capital punishment. Can one feel empathy for both a victim and a murderer?

Chapter Five

Just Rewards? Capital Punishment

"A Man Full of Murder"

Max Jensen's summer job in 1976 was as an attendant at a Sinclair gas station in Orem, Utah. It was unexciting work but necessary to pay the bills. He worked the 3 to 11 P.M. shift. Married for one year, with a three-month-old baby, Jensen was a law student at Brigham Young University. He and his family lived in a trailer. While money was tight, the future looked bountiful for this hard-working, devout Mormon. Until Gary Gilmore barged into his world.[1]

Thirty-six years old, Gilmore had spent eighteen of his last twenty-one years incarcerated. Bright and wily, violent and willful, Gilmore had been released only three months earlier from the federal penitentiary in Marion, Illinois. The odds of his hewing to the straight and narrow after a slew of arrests for robbery and assault were slim to nonexistent. A friend who had served some time with him in prison remarked that Gilmore "was full of hatred, and he knew no boundaries. . . . You could tell that he was now a man full of murder."[2] Robbery and murder were on his mind that July evening in Orem.

Jensen offered no resistance, only a willingness to do as he was told and a desire to live to see his wife and daughter again. Brandishing a .22-caliber Browning automatic pistol, Gilmore told Jensen to get down on the bathroom floor, a surface Jensen had cleaned earlier that day. Jensen was prone, his hands beneath his stomach; he was no threat to Gilmore. Although Gilmore often was in a liquor- and drug-induced haze, that evening he was sober. He thrust the pistol against Jensen's skull and said, "This is for me." The gunshot reverberated in the green-tiled bathroom. A moment later, still not satiated, Gilmore announced that the next bullet was for his girlfriend,

Nicole. He fired again, at point-blank range, into Jensen's skull. Gilmore then hurried from the gas station with cash from the register and change from Jensen's coin changer. He left behind an innocent man lying in a pool of blood.

The next evening Gilmore struck once more in similar fashion. His victim, Ben Bushnell, was married, with an infant and another on the way. Majoring in business administration at Brigham Young University, this gentle giant of a man had worked various jobs to support his family and pay for his schooling. When a position managing the City Center Motel in Provo opened up, it seemed an ideal opportunity because it included free housing. Things changed in the flash of a gunshot, as Gilmore stood over the prone Bushnell and shot him in the head. He left this victim writhing with pain, slowly descending into death.

Within hours of the second shooting, Gilmore was captured. He readily confessed to his crimes, even if he was unable to explain why he had chosen to snuff out the lives of both men. Perhaps he saw the terror and hope in their eyes: the terror that gave Gilmore a sense of demonic power, and the hope for family and a bright future Gilmore realized he would never attain.

Mikal Gilmore hardly knew his older brother. Gary had almost always been in prison during Mikal's youth. When Mikal received a phone call from his mother alerting him to the evil Gary had just committed, he was shaken. He recalled his girlfriend saying to him, "But you know they won't kill him. They never put people to death in America anymore." In response, Mikal said, "You don't understand. He's going to die. They're going to execute him. He was born for it."[3]

Mikal Gilmore—later a writer for *Rolling Stone* magazine—was right. Gary Gilmore had murdered at a major moral moment in the debate over and practice of capital punishment in America. From 1960 through 1964, an average of 36.2 individuals were executed each year in the United States; from 1966 to 1968, only 3 people were executed in the nation, and no one was executed again until 1977.[4] In 1972, capital punishment was, at least temporarily, halted by the Supreme Court ruling in *Furman v. Georgia*. The court decided there was so much "capriciousness" in the imposition of the death penalty—regarding who was charged with capital offenses and who was not—that the entire system reeked of unfairness, most notably in terms of racial discrimination.[5] The court's decision did not sit well with the public, especially as crime rates soared in the 1970s. State legislatures quickly sought to plug holes in their death penalty statutes to better meet the requirements laid out by the Supreme Court.

In the case of *Gregg v. Georgia* in 1976, the year of Gilmore's murders, a divided court upheld the death penalty as not violating the Eighth Amendment to the Constitution, which outlawed "cruel and unusual punishment." In this decision, several justices also acknowledged the value of the death penalty to punish and deter criminal acts.[6]

Gilmore would be the initial beneficiary of this legal turn. He did not seem to mind and professed his readiness to die. To some observers, he harbored a strong "death wish." Many times, before and after the crimes, he had flirted with suicide by slicing at his wrists. But the state demanded that he live in order to be properly executed, in this case by a firing squad. The decision to execute Gilmore was, in effect, a case of state-sanctioned suicide.[7] In an interview after he had won a challenge to allow his execution to go forward, Gilmore accepted full responsibility for what he had done and admitted that he deserved fully the verdict of death. As he phrased it, "I do see the logic of an eye for an eye. I think that's acceptable."[8] He then boasted, "Dying ain't no big deal."[9]

On the morning of 17 January 1977, at 8:07, Gilmore was strapped into a chair. His last words reportedly were "Let's do it." Against Gilmore's wishes, officials placed a hood over his head. A red marker was then placed over his heart. Gilmore died quickly as the bullets thumped into him. The first man in nearly a decade had been executed in the United States.[10]

While Gilmore's execution was met with protests by the American Civil Liberties Union and other civil rights organizations, it also elicited enormous support around the nation. In Salt Lake City following the execution, a state legislator in Utah pondered whether to introduce a bill to abolish capital punishment. But he knew its chances of passing were nil.[11] Many cheered Gilmore's execution. In Los Angeles, police officer Mark Fuhrman, later to become famous in the O. J. Simpson case, wrote in a letter to the editor of the *Los Angeles Times*: "As a policeman, I say, One small step for Gary Gilmore—one giant step for mankind."[12]

Around the nation and in Utah, the public had begun to line up behind the moral rightness and necessity of the death penalty years before the Gilmore case. By 1969, public support for executions, for the first time since 1936, had inched above a majority. By the mid-1970s, the favorable response to capital punishment hovered closer to 60 percent, although sometimes it flirted with a figure as high as 76 percent.[13]

A new age of capital punishment was slowly dawning. In Florida in 1979, John Spenkelink was convicted of killing and then beating his traveling companion. Unlike Gilmore, Spenkelink fought his sentence. After his appeals had been exhausted, he became the first man in many years to be executed involuntarily. By 1983, only six people had been executed.[14] However, over the next seven years, executions climbed to 134 in the United States.[15] Capital punishment once again became well entrenched in the moral and body politic of America. Former Supreme Court Justice Lewis F. Powell, Jr., remarked in 1989, "A large majority of our people consider that capital punishment is appropriate for certain crimes," no matter what people in other countries might think.[16] While all of Western Europe and much of the world have outlawed capital punishment, it remains in place in the United States, with more than one thousand individuals executed over the past quarter-century.[17]

Moral considerations in most religions, as well as in Kantian ethics, depend on absolutes, moral imperatives, and either/or formulations. Moral rules are presumed to be unaffected by circumstance and contingency. From the late 1960s through the 1970s, American moral presumptions regarding capital punishment shifted a great deal. Rarely distant from conflicts about the morality of capital punishment were questions of whether it deterred potential killers, what constituted fair retribution for crimes, and whether the ultimate punishment of death could ever be fairly applied and humanely enforced. The question, as Michel Foucault understood it, was: Why is a particular "means of punishing" morally and practically superior to another set of possibilities?[18] In part, this was connected to and fueled by what was happening in the 1970s—a massive surge in crime, an undermining of authority along with a desire for certitude, and major crises in the American psyche. However, even after the turmoil of the 1970s had abated, capital punishment remained entrenched among many Americans as a moral necessity, a valuable marker of justice.

The Maudlin Seventies

Americans in the 1970s staggered in the face of what has been described variously by historians as a "nervous breakdown," a "moral panic," a "decade of nightmares," or a period of conflagration, when the capacious structures of American civility and optimism burned to the ground.[19] At the highest levels of national government, corruption and deceit were exposed. Vice President Spiro T. Agnew—who had made his reputation in part by skewering his opponents for their moral and political lapses—resigned from office in disgrace after it was shown that he had taken kickbacks from contractors as Maryland governor and then as vice president.[20] The Watergate scandal unleashed a flood of damning evidence about how President Richard M. Nixon and his cronies had used the armature of government to harass political opponents and cover up such actions. In August 1974, Nixon resigned the presidency of the United States. His successor, Gerald R. Ford, after only a month in office, granted Nixon a full pardon for any crimes he might have committed. In the eyes of some this was a reasonable move designed to unite the nation and cap the rancor associated with Watergate. To others it smacked of political chicanery; some even suspected that a deal had been struck between Nixon and Ford to allow the latter to become president. Bob Dylan seemed to have anticipated the new reality for American political leadership back in 1965, when he intoned, "But even the President of the United States sometimes must have to stand naked," in a song titled "It's Alright, Ma (I'm Only Bleeding)."

Americans were bleeding in other ways throughout the 1970s. If Watergate had damaged the authority associated with the office of the presidency, then the Vietnam War had challenged American illusions on a host of additional fronts. The war in Vietnam came to a grinding halt in 1975. Americans watched on television as embassy personnel and some Vietnamese supporters scurried onto the last departing helicopters before the victorious North Vietnamese army and National Liberation Front forces teemed into Saigon. The war had dragged on for ten years, at a cost of more than fifty-eight thousand American lives and hundreds of thousands of Vietnamese casualties. Although Nixon had promised "peace with honor," the war seemed for many Americans to have been a folly, a national and humanitarian disgrace, as well as a waste of lives. American confidence in its mission of spreading democracy and emerging victorious from all its wars had been lost. Moral authority—real and imagined—staggered under the dual blows of Watergate and Vietnam.

The American economy also tumbled in these years. After World War II, America had experienced unprecedented economic growth, without apparent end. By the early 1970s, Americans confronted a new economic challenge: stagflation. Productivity declined, unemployment and inflation rose. The government puzzled aimlessly over how to deal with the economic downturn. Problems were greatly exacerbated by the oil embargo of 1973, and later the steep rise in oil prices, engineered by the Organization of Petroleum Exporting Countries (OPEC). High oil prices fueled inflation, dampened economic growth and shifted consumer buying away from Detroit's gas-guzzling cars to energy-efficient Japanese models. Gasoline shortages during the embargo led drivers to wait for hours to get to a gas pump. Tempers flared as drivers sputtered without gas to the station only to find the gas supply had already been sucked clean by others. To improve efficiency, the government mandated in 1974 that speed limits on highways be lowered to fifty-five miles per hour—a sure signal that the American embrace of speed and confidence had come to a screeching halt.

Of course not all was doom and gloom in this period. America celebrated its bicentennial with exuberance. Relations with the People's Republic of China opened up new diplomatic possibilities in the Cold War. A rights revolution at home inaugurated federal legislation to protect many African Americans, women, and handicapped people. Building on an ethos from the 1960s, the therapeutic revolution, despite the economic downturn, suggested that personal liberation and happiness should be sought through meditation, new forms of spiritualism, therapy, and hedonism. Music tastes shifted as well. Some Americans sought release from the political protest and inner angst of 1960s music. Disco appeared as palliative, with its pulsating rhythms, syncopated dance moves, and political irrelevance.

Reign of Crime

However bright the lights of disco, they could not banish the problem of crime in the late 1960s and 1970s. Millions of people in New York City on July 4, 1976, went to nearby waterways to gaze at the massive collection of tall ships sailing to honor the bicentennial. People stayed into the evening to thrill at the fireworks display. But these same New Yorkers and their guests returned to their homes and hotels wary that they might become victims of crime. Crime was linked to the economic distress of the city. New York City had barely averted bankruptcy, and it remained in economic distress: 340,000 jobs had vanished in the city between 1974 and 1977.[21] Decay was everywhere. In the Times Square area, a famous hub of the city, pornography and massage parlors predominated. Crime seeped through the city's pores. Although by 1976 the rise in the crime rate had leveled off, there were still 95,652 reported felonies committed in the city in a two-month period early in the year.[22]

The shadows of crime and violence darkened the streets, literally and figuratively, in the summer of 1977. A massive power failure, beginning on a sultry July night, plunged the city into darkness and inaugurated a day of urban rioting and crime. Undermanned police forces could barely contain the violence; stores were looted and buildings were set afire throughout the city. National television coverage showed images of marauding bands carrying television sets and any items they could find in retail stores. About four thousand rioters were charged with crimes; they represented at best only a small part of those engaged in misdeeds on that hot evening and the day that followed. An urban breakdown had occurred.[23]

As if New Yorkers did not have enough to worry about, they were also at this time beset by a serial killer. David Berkowitz, then known only as "the Son of Sam," held the city in terror from the summer of 1976 to the fall of 1977. He was suspected in the deaths of six people and wounding of seven others. His victims were typically young women with long hair. Sometimes at point-blank range he would murder a woman and the man who was with her. Warnings were issued for New Yorkers to be on the lookout for this killer and to avoid putting themselves in situations that might permit him to strike.[24] The bottom line was that New York City lived in fear of Son of Sam specifically and violent crime in general throughout the mid-1970s.

Popular culture fed on the anxiety over crime and urban breakdown. The mentally unhinged newsman Howard Beale, in the film *Network* (1976), after ranting about lost jobs, economic depression, and punks running amok in the streets, hits on the line that will ignite his viewers and become a mainstay of popular culture of the period. He urges viewers to get up from their seats, open their windows, and shout as loudly as they can: "I'm mad as hell, and I'm not going to take this anymore!"

Such outrage and the willingness to do something radical about it had already surfaced in popular culture in the film *Death Wish* (1974). Stolid actor Charles Bronson plays Paul Kersey, a successful, law-abiding businessman living in New York City. His world is shattered one night when a gang of punks rapes and kills his wife; they leave his daughter fatally traumatized. Kersey finds the criminal justice system dysfunctional, unable and unwilling to prosecute the villains. He decides to take matters into his own hands, becoming a self-appointed avenger. He wanders the littered streets and grim graffitied subways at night, at first looking to prevent crimes from happening but in time willingly placing himself in situations where criminals ply their trade. Much to the dismay of the criminals, and to the delight of audiences, Kersey is armed and prepared to retaliate. Horrible criminals are dispatched with regularity and stoicism as Kersey becomes a hero for many in the crime-ridden city and a symbol for the nation at large.

Attitudes of fear and anger captured national perceptions. Throughout the country, Americans were victims of violent crime. Between 1966 and 1971, "crimes per 100,000 persons" had risen by 74 percent, with robbery rates up 133 percent.[25] A 1975 article in *Time* magazine was headed, "Crime Boom," and it recited the grim statistics. In the space of a single year, crime in seven major categories had climbed 17 percent. If popular perceptions were that the crime wave was limited to urban areas, the new statistics proved otherwise. Suburban crime soared 20 percent in the space of one year. But the ultimate figures reflecting the jump in crime were no doubt even more harrowing. Statistics captured only the reported crimes; estimates were that "about one-third of all violent crimes go unreported."[26]

Beyond the horror of increased crime was the reality that fewer criminals were being caught, prosecuted, and imprisoned during these years. This became a rallying cry for politicians and others railing against liberal do-gooders who were painted as soft on crime. Increases in the size of police forces proved unable to keep pace with the explosion in crime, which was largely due to demographics, economic downturn, and heroin addiction. Some began to speak of the criminal justice system as bankrupt, nothing more than a "revolving door" that criminals enter and quickly exit without indictment or punishment. In a highly influential book, *Thinking About Crime* (1975), James Q. Wilson reported that during a three-year period in Manhattan in the 1960s, only 3 percent of those indicted were convicted after a trial. While 80 percent of them pled guilty, plea bargaining led to very minor penalties or probation: "slaps on the wrist" was the often-used term. Criminals were back on the streets almost in seamless fashion. According to Wilson, "In New York State the chances of the perpetrator of a given crime going to prison fell" in the 1960s "by a factor of six." Only 27 percent of convicted robbers with serious prior offenses in Los Angeles County were sent to prison.[27] No wonder Americans were joining in the chant, "I'm mad as hell . . . !"

Such violent and criminal shocks to the moral and political nervous system pushed many Americans to rally around their established or implicit moral beliefs. While the 1960s are sometimes viewed as a period of moral relativism and experimentation, the mode of discourse of the 1960s—on both the right and left—was dominated by absolutism and utopianism. The New Left condemned the existing liberal ideology as morally corrupt and politically impotent. Their view of the world, often marked by an Age of Aquarius ideal of freedom, cut a chasm between those blessed with enlightenment and those consigned to darkness. The popular phrase of the period, "Don't trust anyone over thirty," may have fit the demographics of the youth movement, but it revealed hubris of immense proportions. Among the right, and the emerging Christian fundamentalist movement, moral certitude ruled as well. One was either right or wrong, saved or damned. "America, love it or leave it," "America, right or wrong" captured their own sense of apocalypse and desire for clarity. This 1960s style of either/or thinking in moral and increasingly political terms set the stage for the hardening of positions on capital punishment in the 1970s.

Celebrating the Death Penalty

Citizens expect the criminal justice system to mete out proper retribution. This funnels the urge toward revenge into a socially controlled response. While justice need not always exact "an eye for an eye," the notion that certain types of murder demand the death penalty became a particularly lively moral and practical issue in the 1970s, in part because the Supreme Court had in 1976 reopened the legality of the death penalty and in part because of the crime wave and public fears over it. Capital punishment might be a form of state revenge or retribution in the name of justice; it might also be a way of preventing other murders from occurring. In the minds of proponents of capital punishment, this latter point was the clinching argument. In the view of opponents of capital punishment, since it failed to deter, it was unnecessary and excessive. Capital punishment became a moral and political litmus test.

Ernest van den Haag quickly emerged as the nation's leading advocate for the death penalty. He refused to yield to any study, no matter how sophisticated its regression and aggregate analysis, which claimed that capital punishment failed to deter murder. With his clipped European accent, stylish clothing, and a thin cigar held upward while he debated on television and radio, Van den Haag was an odd but powerful spokesman for capital punishment. He relished debate and possessed an eviscerating wit. Born in Holland, he came to the United States in 1940 to escape from fascism. Van den Haag attended the University of Iowa and received a Ph.D. in economics from New York University in 1952. An eclectic thinker, Van den Haag was also a psychoanalyst. He also taught law and criminology at various New York–area universities. His political bent sometimes came close to that of a crusty reactionary. He not only favored capital punishment but dismissed the groundbreaking *Brown v. Board of Education* decision of 1954 and child labor laws as undermining state prerogatives and as unnecessary intrusions.[28] From the late 1960s well into the 1980s, his focus was riveted on making a case for capital punishment.

It was a particularly opportune time to lobby for the death penalty. As Van den Haag well realized, the American population had lost faith in the power of the prison system to rehabilitate criminals. Our society, in Van den Haag's view, had in recent years tended to romanticize criminals or come to see them as victims of social forces against which they had no defenses. The utopianism of the therapeutic movement in psychology, and some strands of liberalism and radicalism from the 1960s, presumed that anyone, even hardened criminals, could be rehabilitated. If so, then the logic of the death penalty was weakened, since murderers might be redeemed rather than wasted by state-imposed death. A crisis of confidence in the nation undermined such presumptions. People had come to doubt that the death penalty was a deserving punishment for murder and were confused by statements that the death penalty did not deter potential murderers. Presidential candidates Richard Nixon and George C. Wallace wowed "silent majority" crowds in 1968 with their proclamations that criminals too often went unpunished, that crime was out of control, and that liberal nostrums were not working.[29] Van den Haag built on this base by emphasizing that capital punishment worked as a deterrent for criminals.

Van den Haag presented an essentially utilitarian logic in his defense of capital punishment. His writings before 1975 noted that although statistical studies did not prove the deterrent effect of capital punishment, they did not necessarily disprove it either. It stood to reason and "common sense," at least in Van den Haag's mind, that the greater the penalty, the more likely the deterrent effect of the penalty. Criminals' "fear of death" is stronger than their fear of life imprisonment; if not, then why would most of those on death rows across the nation be fighting against their sentences? Since "only death is irrevocable," it is more feared than life imprisonment and has a better chance of deterring a murderer.[30]

But the very notion of the "irrevocable" nature of the death sentence and the obvious fact that it was imposed in an erratic, often racist, and economically biased manner, deterred Van den Haag not a whit. In Van den Haag's view, all prosecutions for crimes at any level had biases built into the structure of accusation, defense, and conviction. Did that mean that we should jettison all punishment? Errors do occur, and innocents are executed. If a trial was unfair, and the distribution of the penalty skewed according to race and economic circumstances, wouldn't that cast problems on the imposition of the death penalty? No, thundered Van den Haag, because the presumed deterrence of the death penalty, whatever injustices might be found in the system, remained valuable for saving the lives of innocents.[31]

Proponents of the death penalty such as Van den Haag got a research boost in 1975. Economist Isaac Ehrlich published an extensive analysis claiming that capital punishment did indeed deter murder. A recent Ph.D. from Columbia University, Ehrlich announced that he was morally opposed to capital punishment. His model of analysis—a version of marketplace thinking—was highly technical, but it was essentially based on a simple assumption: murderers, even when in the throes of passion, remain rational creatures. The potential killer weighs the cost of the act against its presumed benefits. In most cases, the potential murderer recognizes the death penalty as sufficient incentive to halt the killing. Ehrlich came to the startling conclusion that "the tradeoff between the execution of an offender and the lives of potential victims it might have saved was of the order of magnitude of 1 for 8 for the period 1933–67 in the United States."[32]

Ehrlich's surprising conclusion was extremely controversial. In quick order, statistically sophisticated academics crawled over his data and conclusions like ants at a picnic. Hans Zeisel, emeritus professor of law and sociology at the University of Chicago, noted that Ehrlich's conclusions differed from almost all previous studies, which had argued either for a lack of deterrent effect for capital punishment or the impossibility of sufficient statistical data to draw any compelling conclusions. Zeisel cited one study, done in Canada and using Ehrlich's method; it found no clear evidence that capital punishment deterred murder. After citing a number of counterstudies, including submissions to a special issue of the *Yale Law Review* devoted to Ehrlich's hypothesis, Zeisel argued that the preponderance of evidence demonstrated that the death penalty was without deterrent effect on potential murderers. Of course, given the rather firm lines that had been drawn around the question of capital punishment in the 1970s, those in favor of the death penalty regularly trotted out Ehrlich's findings to support their stance, while opponents of capital punishment relied on their own studies negating its deterrent effects.[33]

Following publication of Ehrlich's research, Van den Haag proclaimed the logic of deterrence with even greater vehemence and frequency. In a *Los Angeles Times* editorial, Van den Haag was in an exultant mood. All arguments against the death penalty seemed to have been crushed, because Ehrlich had demonstrated "that for each non-execution of a convicted murderer we do in fact run the risk of between seven and eight murders by other murderers who could have been deterred by the execution." In simple utilitarian terms, then, "the loss of a convicted murderer's life weighs less heavily in the balance than the risk of losing seven or eight additional victims."[34]

In a flurry of books and articles, Van den Haag presumed the value of capital punishment for deterrence but also entertained other criticisms. He acknowledged that the criminal justice system sometimes made errors. Issues of fairness, however, should not have priority over retributive necessity. Misapplications of the death penalty failed to lessen the penalty for murder for those others deserving of it. Even if many murderers were undeterred—because they decided the cost-benefit analysis still leaned in their favor or because they were irrational—the existence of the death penalty, tied to the ingrained habit among most citizens to obey and fear the law, would have an overall deterrent effect. Deterrence would be even more effective if punishment for crimes was applied with greater frequency and alacrity.

Van den Haag pricked liberal assumptions about rehabilitation. He announced that it was a waste of time and funds to rehabilitate criminals. Indeed, it was "morally" distasteful: "I do not believe that having done something wrong entitles an adult to rehabilitation. It entitles him to punishment. Murder entitles him to execution." And on the issue of torturing the murderer, or dispatching him with a slow death, Van den Haag opined, "If I were convinced that innocent lives could be saved by torturing guilty men, I would favor torture." Van den Haag thus consistently stood behind the death penalty as deterrence rather than for reasons "as metaphysical as justice." He proudly announced, "I value the life of innocents more than the life of murderers."[35]

Execution as a Moral Imperative

If Van den Haag almost wantonly strayed from morals and metaphysics, political theorist Walter Berns championed capital punishment on those very grounds. He was uninspired by the deterrence argument central to Van den Haag's work. The issue of deterrence, for him, was unsettled by conflicting studies of its effects and irrelevant to the larger moral imperatives he wanted to investigate.[36] Berns sought to frame his support of the death penalty as a moral issue, based on the assumption that retribution, even when fueled by anger, was just and necessary for the preservation of a moral community.

Berns had been a student of the conservative theorist Leo Strauss at the University of Chicago. He inherited from Strauss an obligation to think in abstract terms about the nature of justice. But in his popular volume, *For*

Capital Punishment (1979), he melded abstraction with gruff obeisance to popular desires. As an immensely popular teacher of government at Cornell University, Berns had been shocked when African American students took over various campus buildings to pressure the administration to meet demands for, among other things, a separate Black Studies program. Berns's anger overflowed when the administration at Cornell negotiated with the students and refused to lodge any charges against them. Berns fled to the University of Toronto. From that vantage, he regarded American political life as being in a state of chaos, in large part because Americans had surrendered core values.[37]

With erudition and a hint of populism, Berns argued for the morality of the death penalty. He began by acknowledging anger and a desire for retribution as fair responses to criminal activities. Retribution was part of a system of justice: "Anger is the passion that recognizes and cares about justice" (152). Thus the community of law-abiding citizens, in the name of justice and morality, accepts the task of punishing those who transgress the laws. To do otherwise would be to mock the very laws on which the community had been established. Retribution, based on ancient doctrines of "just deserts" or "an eye for an eye," might not always be easily transferable to the modern community, but they retained logic and vigor (144). In making a case for retribution, Berns followed in Kant's footsteps. Kant, as Herbert Fingarette correctly notes, "was a 'fierce' retributionist if ever there was one." Respect for the law as an abstract good required that penalties be imposed in the name of justice and right.[38]

The death penalty struck Berns, much as it did Kant, as a dignified and necessary response to the worst transgression, the murder of another human being, as an assault on justice. Capital punishment, he proclaimed, "serves to remind us of the majesty of the moral order that is embodied in our law and of the terrible consequences of its breach" (172–173). While capital punishment was an abstract good, it paid dividends for the maintenance of the moral order. Within the context of 1970s America, this was no small matter.

For all the "majesty" of Berns's case for the justice inherent in capital punishment, his work was anchored in the anti-elitism, crisis of authority, and crime wave of the 1970s. The crime spike in this period threatened the American moral community. Berns announced that almost all criminals avoided conviction for their crimes: "96.5% of the crimes committed go unpunished" (108). He excoriated psychologists and death penalty abolitionists who proclaimed that justice was served when criminals, even murderers, were objects for rehabilitation, pity, or celebration as rebels. The "intellectual community" in America was a force for moral disintegration because it failed to support the "ordinary American" who feels "morally indignant at the sight of crime and criminals." Unfortunately, liberal intellectuals, as Berns understood them, preferred to lecture that the public should feel it is "shameful" to experience anger and desire just deserts (149). But the public had spoken. In the wake of the Supreme Court ruling of 1972, which found state capital punishment statutes lacking, thirty-five state legislatures had passed new rules for capital punishment. Berns made it clear that he sided with the people against elites and intellectuals.

Yet Berns's enthusiasm for capital punishment strangely lacked anger and depth. He believed that executions should not be antiseptic, viewed only by a handful of prison officials and the families of the victim and the murderer. But he was against televising the executions, believing that such a presentation would be "vulgar" (187). How then to "impress upon the population the awesomeness of the moral order and the awful consequences of its breach"? Let selected representatives of the public witness the executions. To maintain "decorum," Berns suggested that members of the legislature be present at these executions rather than the angered public at large. After praising state legislatures for reasserting the death penalty, he argued that it should be employed against only "extraordinarily heinous crimes." What constituted crimes of such magnitude?

Here Berns was a bit vague. He could imagine a case of rape where capital punishment was worthy. However, by and large, he seemed to find that criminals who struck out against figures in public life were most deserving of the death penalty. Thus the murderers of President John F. Kennedy and Martin Luther King, Jr., had earned the death penalty. Jack Ruby, who had gunned down Kennedy's assassin, Lee Harvey Oswald, in a Dallas police station, was viewed as less culpable and less deserving of the death penalty, perhaps because he had acted out of anger. But how to distinguish between the anger of Ruby and the racist anger exhibited by King's killer, James Earl Ray? On this score, Berns was silent. Nor did he explain how the wisdom of the state legislators, in their rush to pass legislation mandating capital punishment, would be reasonable about limiting its applications (179, 182–183).

Of course, even liberal commentators agreed with Berns that crimes deserved to be punished.[39] The question remained open as to what constituted proper punishment. As criminologist Norval Morris wrote in 1974, "To say that a punishment is deserved . . . is not to say that it ought to be imposed."[40] In 1983, in *Wild Justice*, a wide-ranging analysis of revenge and retribution,

Susan Jacoby deeply appreciated the power of "just deserts" without coming to the conclusion that justice was served only by reinstitution of the death penalty. No less than Berns, Jacoby realized that justice and revenge were intertwined. Why shouldn't a Holocaust survivor demand that justice be done for outrages committed, even when the criminal had aged and become distanced from such crimes? Her answer was that revenge was a natural feeling and, more important, that justice should be served, no matter how tardy in coming. The law served to mediate the anger and desire for revenge on the part of the individual. Otherwise, we would return to long, drawn-out blood feuds and affairs of honor. In contrast to Berns, Jacoby supported what she called "measured retribution." It was impractical to demand the old measure of the *lex talionis*, "an eye for an eye." Debates about capital punishment diminished the reality, in Jacoby's view, that life imprisonment was a severe punishment, even for murders.[41] The chance elements of murder conviction, the racial and class elements in prosecution and conviction, along with a host of other factors, made capital punishment justice a drawn-out and flawed process. Better to have speedy convictions with murderers forced to spend their natural lives in maximum-security prisons. This would channel the desire for revenge without compromising a sense of justice, at least in Jacoby's view.

The problem of unfairness in the death penalty was vexing. Of course, unfairness is part of the criminal justice system in general, as Van den Haag often asserted. But the irrevocability of the death penalty, once enacted, made it a particularly pressing concern.[42] Statistics overwhelmingly demonstrated that an African American accused of killing a white person was almost assured of the death penalty. In contrast, black on black murder or the murder by a white person of a black person was less likely to elicit the death penalty.

Van den Haag acknowledged this. He hoped for greater fairness in distribution but remained adamant that justice was served even when innocents were punished. For Van den Haag, acknowledging discrimination and chance as factors in conviction and sentencing did not contradict the ideal of justice, nor undermine the power of capital punishment for deterrence.[43] Van den Haag recognized this, too. While some might see execution as a fitting and just punishment for a murderer, it undermined the righteousness of revenge. What was the moral claim involved in life imprisonment when the murderer, now fifty years of age, had become in effect a person quite different from the man who had murdered at age twenty-one? If the individual showed contrition and was reformed, what purpose was served, even in the name of justice, by imprisoning someone who was no longer a murderer, in the sense of his current personal identity? Van den Haag's solution, rather coldblooded if logical, was to impose the death penalty quickly on the accused so that he would not have time to stymie the logic of executing a categorically more "deserving" person.[44]

Politics of Death

In the view of most anti–death penalty activists, no person was deserving of death, especially at the hands of the state. To enact the death penalty was to relinquish hope for redemption and rehabilitation. Such views may be naïve, but they are logically connected. In contrast, advocates for the death penalty seemed unconcerned with how missteps and moral evasions during the war in Vietnam and during Watergate might have tarnished the reliability of the justice system in meting out the death penalty. Perhaps they had nowhere else to turn other than to cheer the on-screen vigilante exploits of Charles Bronson. A foolish consistency, as Emerson long ago pointed out, may be the "hobgoblin of little minds," but it also needs to be explained in terms of the reality death penalty abolitionists faced.

Skepticism about government grew throughout the 1970s, culminating in the anti-government rhetoric and politics that elected Ronald Reagan to the presidency in 1980. Talk of getting the government out of people's lives became the *soupe du jour* on the menu of conservative politicians. But then the numbers of citizens supporting the death penalty rose steeply, from just below 60 percent in 1977 to an incredible high of 80 percent in 1994.[45] This was proof positive for many that the government remained the proper instrument for exacting justice. Abolitionists claimed the issue was more ambiguous. They argued that statistics failed to tell the entire story: How many in favor of the death penalty in the abstract would personally be willing to condemn someone to death? It remains to be explained how these numbers continued to rise so steeply. After all, crime rates had already topped out, and by the 1990s, the economy was booming.

America in the late 1970s and 1980s was stirred by cultural wars fought over college curricula, religion in the schools, abortion, gay rights, and many other issues.[46] While little attention has been paid to the death penalty in terms of its place within this cultural war, the impetus behind the conflicts and the rise of fundamentalist religion are central to understanding why public support continued to grow for capital punishment. First, as Berns recognized, there was a divide between the views of the intellectual elite and the working-class white population on punishment and the death penalty. Support for the death penalty blended with populist calls for taking back rights from and exerting stronger controls on those perceived as dismissive of traditional values. Juries and prosecutors, in this view, needed the power to exact retribution for the crime of murder. Second, politicians often confronted an electorate that expected them to approve the death penalty. In the 1960s and 1970s, opposition to the death penalty often came from governors who found it both morally troubling and unfair. By the 1980s, however, few of those politicians were willing to confront the issue or to oppose the popular will. State officials excused their passivity by saying they were simply following the law and desires of the voters. Many others, as we shall see in the case of George W. Bush in Texas, invoked the death penalty as a political and moral yardstick to measure their strength of character and stance against crime. The need to be strong on the death penalty colored the actions of politicians from both parties. The most famous example of this was when Governor Bill Clinton, running as a Democrat for the presidency in 1992, rushed back to Arkansas to approve the death penalty for Ricky Ray Rector. Although Clinton personally supported the death penalty, this was hardly a prime case for its imposition. Rector was mentally retarded. Clinton was acting politically, not morally, seeking to convince the public of his toughness on crime. The specifics of the case and the justness of the verdict seemed of no consequence to him in his rush to the White House.

Religion and Death

The strongest and most contradictory force that kept the fires burning in favor of capital punishment may well have been the upsurge in fundamentalist religion in the United States. The fundamentalist movement gained national attention in 1976 with the election of one of their own, Jimmy Carter, as president. At that moment, fifty million Americans, or 34 percent of the population, referred to themselves as born-again.[47] *Newsweek* magazine ran a story declaring 1976 to be the year of the fundamentalists. While fundamentalists did not emphasize support for the death penalty as one of their crucial issues—in contrast to their fevered opposition to abortion, drugs, and homosexuality, and enthusiastic support for morality, family, Israel, and religion in schools—they did help to set the tone for the discourse surrounding it. Moreover, fundamentalism was centered in those regions of the South and Southwest where support for capital punishment was most resolute.[48]

The politics of most of the fundamentalist leaders were, to put it mildly, conservative. They were waging a war of apocalyptic proportions against Satan and his minions, often referred to as "secular humanists." According to a publication from the Family Foundation, secular humanists held "that there are no absolutes, no right, no wrong—that moral values are self-determined and situational."[49] In contrast, the fundamentalists presented a world that was absolutist, anchored in the inerrancy of the Bible. This meant that issues were either right or wrong, moral or immoral. After the ravages of Watergate and Vietnam, and in response to the moral changes ushered in by the 1960s counterculture and its penetration into consumer and mainstream culture, many longed for a sense of certitude. As Earl Shorris argues, fundamentalists found in religion a palliative for their fear, a way of discerning the movement of history, the placement of their lives within a larger context of certitude, and with the promise of salvation, a way of enduring in the world. Minister Jerry Falwell, a leader in building the movement, proclaimed that he wanted to bring "America back to God, back to the Bible, and back to moral sanity."[50] While fundamentalists did help to put moral values on the political agenda, as Robert Wuthnow has observed, they did so in a manner that studiously avoided moral complexity.[51] Black and white, rarely gray, were the colors on their moral palette.

Despite the movement's stated adherence to biblical truths, there is no clear position on capital punishment in the Bible. On the one hand, Catholics and other Christians found in the Bible, especially in the message of Jesus, an emphasis on mercy, forgiveness, and redemption, along with respect for the sanctity of life. On the other hand, a religious perspective drenched in the rhetoric and reality of the Old Testament could translate into a chorus in favor of retribution, "an eye for an eye" policy. Thus, the fundamentalist Lutheran minister Michael Bray—who had spent time in jail for destroying seven abortion clinics in Washington, D.C.—happily embraced capital punishment and the role of the state in enacting it, claiming for it divine sanction in the Bible. Yet he also believed it was proper to kill abortion doctors because the state had refused to prevent the "murder" of "innocent" fetuses. For Bray, the killing of an abortion doctor "is directed toward the evil" and saves the lives of others—a rather simple utilitarian viewpoint, whatever his moral bearings.[52]

For many Catholics and some Protestants, however, there was tension between a position in favor of capital punishment and opposition to abortion. After the Supreme Court decision *Roe v. Wade* (1973), which made abortion legal under certain circumstances, Catholic and fundamentalist opposition to abortion skyrocketed, predicated on the simple argument that the unborn fetus was human and that to destroy it was to exterminate human life. Of course, this seemed to contradict the support many abortion opponents had for capital punishment or for an expansive war machine, as Randall Balmer has pointed out.[53] But contradictions are as much a property of the right wing as of the left. After all, those on the left who opposed capital punishment often favored abortion. Van den Haag considered abortion a personal matter, but never wavered in his support of capital punishment, indicative of a more libertarian position—although libertarians might naturally have hesitated to give government the power over life and death.[54] And one could argue on behalf of conservatives that the unborn fetus was innocent, while the murderer had responsibility for his or her crime and therefore had earned the ultimate punishment. To not punish, in the fundamentalist view, would have been to allow sin to flourish and to set a weak example for others.

The Varieties of Opposition

Against the fundamentalist tide swam dedicated opponents of capital punishment. Some of them refused to wade in the muddy waters of morality as much as their pro-death penalty counterparts. Karl Menninger, a well-known psychiatrist without much background in criminology or social psychology, attacked the very notion of punishment in a well-known book, *The Crime of Punishment* (1968).[55] He was certainly on target with some observations: Current modes of punishment had failed to rehabilitate criminals, and crime was not diminishing, despite ever-expanding funding for anti-crime measures. The criminal justice system was a disgrace. From a suspected criminal's point of arrest to the years of imprisonment to the moment of release, abominations of injustice prevailed. Not only was the system corrupt in practice, it was immoral in intentions, concerned only with "sadistic" punishment (25–58, 205).

Menninger turned the tables on public perceptions, announcing that we are all criminals. How is the individual who steals towels from a hotel, or cheats a bit on taxes, or misrepresents facts on an insurance claim uninvolved in criminal activity? Instead, we focus our ire on those who are poor, ignorant, and riddled with problems, who steal to survive, who kill out of misplaced anger, or who are simply unlucky enough to fall headlong into the arbitrary system of criminal justice in the United States. Menninger evinced little sympathy for the victims of crime, claiming that "sometimes the victim himself is partly responsible for the crime that is committed against him" (181).

Criminals were not responsible for their acts in most cases, according to Menninger. Hence imprisoning them added to the potential for future wrongdoing. Capital punishment was a simplistic solution, one based on outmoded notions of retribution. And it was only the most obvious symptom of a system and approach that was bankrupt. Imposing the death penalty was, in effect, doing to the criminal what he or she had done to the victim, except this time the motivation was cloaked in the name of justice (190–191).

Menninger's solution was therapeutic and educational. Through "education, medication, counseling, training," the lives of criminals could be transformed. Instead of spending massive amounts of money on prisons and crime prevention, funds should be diverted into a therapeutic paradise.[56] The focus should be on treating the problems of poverty, dysfunctional families, and a violent culture. Menninger always believed that proper psychological therapy could, with few exceptions, rehabilitate and redirect criminals. Often, killers strike at symbols rather than specific individuals, as they are impotent to deal with the hurts perpetrated on them in their youth. Childhood needs and fantasies, in Menninger's clinical opinion, gain fleeting satisfaction in robbery; rape is a matter of inadequate men attempting to exert sexual power over women (181–184).

Not all death penalty opponents agreed with Menninger's utopian position. Hugo Adam Bedau accepted the reasonableness of an "appeal to a general principle of desert," and he acknowledged unfairness throughout the criminal justice system. But there were more pressing questions. Were other options available that could be considered as retribution and "just deserts," that were less final than the death penalty? Even more important, could one make a case that the death penalty violated the Eighth Amendment to the Constitution outlawing "cruel and unusual punishment"?[57] Bedau worked tirelessly throughout his academic career at Tufts University to engage with the death penalty. He published volumes containing different points of view, and he wrote in many venues, both popular and academic. Bedau always tried to be respectful of the moral muddiness involved with the death penalty. Menninger's simplicities did not cut it for him. He refused to stomach arguments for capital punishment that—in addition to recognizing the weakness of the argument for deterrence—overlooked other possibilities. Nor did he ever stray from a horror of executions themselves.

If there was no alternative form of retribution other than execution, then one could make an argument for the justness of that act. But this ignored the potential efficacy of life imprisonment. By the 1980s, almost the entire Western world had, in keeping with international human rights declarations, outlawed the death penalty. Such movements, however, had little resonance in the defiantly exceptionalist United States. Nevertheless, Bedau tried to convince anyone who would listen that the death penalty was unnecessary. Studies indicated that it failed to deter criminals, so the utilitarian argument must fall by the wayside. He summarized: "Neither utilitarian nor retributive considerations require us to use the death penalty, and so no rational purpose of punishment in a just society is more effectively served by the death penalty than by the less severe punishment of long-term imprisonment. . . . To continue to use the death penalty is to persevere in using an excessively severe punishment."[58]

The crux of Bedau's case, then, was to argue the unconstitutionality of the death penalty because it was "cruel and unusual punishment." He was not the first to argue this. The Supreme Court had in previous rulings on the death penalty admitted that what might have been deemed a proper form of punishment in the eighteenth century might now be deemed cruel. But the Supreme Court negated the notion that the death penalty per se was either cruel or unusual punishment (917).

After reading Philip Hallie's powerful work, *Cruelty* (1969), Bedau came to view capital punishment as cruel because it occurred within an essentially unequal power relationship (918). Hallie had argued that sadism inhered in the power exercised over the life of another. Such unequal distribution of power personified cruelty.[59] More important, even the most vicious killers should not be required to forfeit their humanity. The state and its citizens cannot, as the death penalty did, work for the "total obliteration" of any human being; by so doing, the state "offends our moral imagination" (919). Bedau engaged the issue most originally on moral grounds, asserting that three arguments suggested to him that the death penalty was cruel and inhumane, and hence unconstitutional: First, no one can "do anything that utterly nullifies his or her 'moral worth' and standing as a person" (920). Second, however morally deficient the murderer might appear to be, "these capacities do not overwhelm all capacity for moral agency—for responsible action, thought, and judgment, in solitude and in relationship with other persons" (921). Third, human beings are more than biological entities; they are "moral beings," thus "even the worst and most dangerous murderer is not a fit subject for annihilation" (923). To obliterate or annihilate a moral being, argues Bedau, in close alignment with Hannah Arendt, was to partake of an evil action (922).

Turning the Tide

However compelling Bedau's arguments, they were incapable of quelling the desire for retribution on the part of many Americans. Far more successful were the actions of Sister Helen Prejean, a nun in the order of the Sisters of St. Joseph of Medaille. While Sister Prejean has never wavered in her absolute rejection of the death penalty, she came to appreciate the moral complexity of the issue, especially for relatives of crime victims. She had been working with poor African Americans in New Orleans when she was suddenly thrust into direct contact with capital punishment by way of a death row inmate awaiting execution. In January 1982, she was asked if she would care to be a pen pal for Patrick Sonnier, a young man on death row. He and his younger brother, Eddie, were convicted of a particularly brutal crime in 1978. David LeBlanc (seventeen years old) and Loretta Bourque (eighteen years old) had been in a car at the local lovers' lane. Posing as security officers, the Sonnier brothers forced the couple from their car and handcuffed them. Loretta was subsequently raped, then she and David were shot to death. Although it would remain unclear which of the brothers actually pulled the trigger, both were involved in the crime's vicious chain of events. Patrick claimed that he did not rape Loretta Bourque. At one point, however, Patrick confessed to the murders, as part of a rather bizarre deal he claimed to have worked out with his brother. But Eddie apparently failed to comprehend the specifics of the pact, and Patrick took the rap. In any case, Eddie ultimately received a life sentence while Patrick was condemned to die in the electric chair.

The Catholic nun and the Cajun killer began to correspond, and soon their relationship blossomed into friendship. In Sister Prejean's account, she becomes his spiritual adviser, talking with him about the Bible, redemption, and responsibility. She emerges as an intensely energized activist trying to overturn Patrick Sonnier's murder conviction and that of others in subsequent years. Prejean believed that no one deserves to be executed by the state, no matter how horrible their crime. In her view, it diminishes the sanctity of human life, fails as a deterrent, brutalizes the culture, and gives up on the potential for good within everyone.

What makes her narrative of Patrick Sonnier's life on death row and his eventual execution so compelling is that she paints him as neither saint nor victim, but as a human being in all of his complexity. He is mean spirited at times, but also capable of compassion for the families of the murder victims. He comes to embrace with especial interest a psalm that reads: "I am contemptible, loathsome to my neighbors . . . as they combine against me, plotting to take my life. But I put my trust in you, Yahweh."[60]

Since he claimed neither to have pulled the trigger nor to have raped Loretta, Sonnier is unrepentant. He regrets what happened, but he can acknowledge only his moral weakness in deciding to join his brother with the intent of robbing the young couple. He remains, to the end, unwilling to recognize that even in the best scenario, his initial act is inextricably linked with the unnecessary deaths of the young couple and the horror visited on their families. He may not have pulled the trigger but, at the very least, he supplied the gun and created the situation. Nonetheless, Sister Prejean works tirelessly on his behalf; but her efforts and those of his legal defense team ultimately fail. They had hoped the Catholic governor of Louisiana, Edwin Edwards, would commute the death sentence. But commutation proved to be too politically controversial in the pro–death penalty atmosphere of the 1980s.

Finally, all appeals are exhausted, and Patrick Sonnier's day of reckoning arrives. Hour by hour, Sister Prejean takes us through his last day. She will be with him in his cell and one of those cleared to witness his execution. His final words to the families of the victims express regret over what happened, but without acknowledgment of his guilt for the crime. Sister Prejean carefully describes how Patrick is strapped into the chair, a "metal cap is placed on his head and an electrode is screwed in at the top." Another electrode is attached to his leg. A strap on "his chin holds his head tightly. . . . He cannot speak anymore. A grayish green cloth is placed over his face." The executioner pulls the required levers. The electricity makes "the fingers [of Sonnier's right hand] curl up." He is pronounced dead (94).

Prejean's book is a powerful morality tale about the injustice of capital punishment. She not only considers Sonnier innocent of the crime, but also believes it is wrong to take his or anyone else's life. The execution is cruel and unusual punishment, a form of torture that denies individuals their human rights. As her narrative proceeds, however, Prejean comes to realize that she had erred badly by failing to reach out to the families of the victims. She had considered doing so when she first got deeply involved with Sonnier's case. But she perhaps rationalized away the issue because it had been five years since the Bourque and LeBlanc families had lost their loved ones. She soon learns this was both a tactical and a moral mistake.

Murder usually involves more than two people. Families of the victim often cling to their need for and presumed right to vengeance, closure, and justice. However ambiguous or difficult these concepts may seem, in theory and practice they are valid and compelling. Loretta Bourque's stepfather is driven by outrage and desire for revenge. Why, he demands, has this nun interjected herself in the case without even contacting the still-grieving families? While Prejean seems to feel at times that the Bourque family is avoiding dealing with the reality of their daughter's murder by focusing so hard on vengeance, she also comes to appreciate the depth of their grief. "The victims are dead and the killer is alive," she notes, "and I am befriending the killer. Have I betrayed his victims?" She denies this. Instead, she feels she is following Christ in rejecting hatred and revenge, and offering love and sustenance to the killer (21). Still, "their hurt and anger sting," she admits (65).

The hurt of the families highlights questions that continue to stir the death penalty debate. Does the death penalty help the families of murder victims to achieve closure? And is it proper and relevant to have testimony from victims' families during the sentencing stage of a murder trial? These are tough, unanswerable questions, although psychologist Robert Jay Lifton, who has done extensive research into survivors of the atomic bombs in Japan, states that "closure is an illusion."[61] Wendy Kaminer claims that our therapeutic culture has given too wide a berth for the families of the murdered to play out their victimhood. Such pure emoting and parading of pain, she thinks, skews the potential for justice. The serendipity already inherent in the justice of the death penalty only increases: Is it a greater crime to have killed a beloved mother than to have killed a lonely woman?[62]

These are complex legal and moral problems. Since the victims' families are, through no choice of their own, implicated in the courtroom drama, how are their needs to be honored? There is, whether one likes it or not, a long tradition—perhaps even evolution-based—of revenge and retribution. Moreover, as some writers contend, one of the weaknesses of the justice system is that it eschews narratives and emotions in favor of simple procedures and presumptions of what constitutes relevant facts. If so, then where does one draw the lines between what is appropriate and what is inappropriate for enunciation during a trial?[63]

The parents of Loretta Bourque were convinced that they deserved a voice. They spoke out strongly against Patrick Sonnier and claimed retribution as their right. Indeed, philosopher Jeffrie G. Murphy brilliantly points out that resentment and a desire for revenge are natural in human beings, part of a sense of the self. Without them, we would lack autonomy. One can argue, Murphy recognizes, that "retributive hatred" can be satisfied not only by the death penalty, but his point is valid. Families of victims should feel resentment and even hatred for the person(s) responsible for the crimes. Whether in the long run these feelings for revenge are as palliative as forgiveness is another question (and beyond the scope of my inquiry here).[64]

Bourque's parents feel vindicated or compensated in some fashion by Patrick Sonnier's death. They soon become death penalty advocates, present outside prison gates for other executions.[65] For them, the equation is simple. If someone takes a life, then his or her life should be taken in turn. It is a simple logic and, in its own way, compelling. Against this view, often eyeing the Bourques from a picket line protesting the death penalty, is Sister Prejean. For her, the sanctity of human life, even the life of the killer, should never be compromised. Retribution can be exacted, but not at the cost of another death. The moral divide between them remains unresolved.

Prejean's book, *Dead Man Walking,* became a bestseller and a popular text in schools, especially after it was turned into a powerful film. Activist and actor Susan Sarandon had read the book. While she was in New Orleans shooting another film, Sarandon arranged to chat with Sister Prejean about producing the film version. *Dead Man Walking* premiered in 1995, starring Sean Penn as Michael Poncelet (an amalgam character based largely on Patrick Sonnier as well as another death-row inmate, Robert Lee Willie, who was also ministered to by Prejean) and Sarandon as Sister Prejean.[66] While the film focused only on the details from the Sonnier case (in the book, Prejean relates Willie's as well), it effectively charted the inmate's growing sensitivity and potential for redemption. The film did not slight the pain of the victims' families, but it argued that capital punishment was an abomination against humanity and the value of life. The scenes where Poncelet is prepared for his death and the execution were powerful blows against capital punishment. But did the book and film deepen the debate or change minds about the death penalty?

As Sister Prejean noted in her follow-up book, *The Death of Innocence* (2005), there were positive signs that the death penalty was losing ground in the United States. In 1999, there were 98 executions, compared to 66 in 2001, 71 in 2002, and 65 in 2003. The total number of death sentences had declined, from 320 in 1996 to 231 in 2000, to 143 in 2003. Most executions in the United States were taking place in the South and Southwest, especially in Florida and Texas. It appeared, in Prejean's analysis, that thirty-eight out of the fifty states were "letting the death penalty slip into disuse."[67] Other analysts of the death penalty were equally confident that the curtain had fallen. Writing in 1986, Franklin E. Zimring and Gordon Hawkins predicted that capital punishment would be gone by 2001. In 2003, Zimring, in a new book, still thought it would vanish in the not-too-distant future.[68]

Thus the film rode on a wave of popular concern with capital punishment and during a period when the crime wave that had bedeviled Americans in the 1970s appeared to be on the wane. The film, in any case, set up something of an all-too-easy scenario to allow viewers to come away horrified by the death penalty. In presenting Poncelet as misguided but essentially human—someone with feelings, with the potential for rehabilitation and even grace—the deck was stacked. Few could avoid identifying with his humanity and resist the logic of condemning his execution. But what if the film had focused on a less captivating individual, someone without any apparent hint of innocence or concern for redemption? What if the murderer was simply brutish, thuggish, and mean spirited? Given such a murderer, would the public favor a reprieve?

New Doubts

Thanks in recent years to the increased scientific accuracy of DNA testing in death penalty cases, it has been demonstrated that many inmates on death row had been wrongly convicted. While in the 1970s the imposition of the death penalty attempted to establish a sense of certitude and closure, now the opening up of cases revealed a system that was erratic and mistaken. Certainly, as Van den Haag always admitted, some innocents would be executed, but the perception had always held this would be a mere handful of cases. And if one accepted the view that such deaths allowed for deterrence and justice to endure, then they were unfortunate but permissible. Beginning in the 1990s, however, more cases came to public notice that indicated that miscarriages of justice, irrevocable in the case of the death penalty, were more common than previously imagined. In a *New York Times* op-ed piece, sociologist Richard Moran argued that more than simply unfortunate "errors" being the cause of wrongful convictions and executions, there was also the problem of "malice" on the part of prosecutors. Moran concluded that between the 1973 and 2007, 80 of the 124 exonerations of death row prisoners "resulted not from good-faith mistakes or errors, but from intentional, willful, malicious prosecutions by criminal justice personnel."[69] How many innocents, then, should be killed before doubts can be raised about the logic of the death penalty?

Consider the case of Joseph M. Giarratano. A former police officer and drug abuser, Giarratano had been convicted of murdering his girlfriend. He could not recall the crime, and he pled innocent. He was convicted and sentenced to death. Six years later, he became convinced that evidence at the crime scene proved he had not committed the murder. Giarratano, now a highly skilled jailhouse lawyer, began working on his own behalf, finally filing a writ of habeas corpus. Twelve years after his 1979 conviction for murder, Giarratano's death sentence was commuted to life imprisonment. In Giarratano's opinion, "The inescapable risk of executing even one innocent individual should be enough to abolish capital punishment."[70]

A flurry of cases has surfaced demonstrating that death penalty convictions were obtained unlawfully or that investigations were flawed. In two bestselling books, John C. Tucker's *May God Have Mercy* (1997) and John Grisham's *The Innocent Man* (2006), we are brought close to how justice is poorly served. In both cases, inadequate police work, prosecutorial zeal to achieve a conviction without sufficient evidence, and the willingness of juries and judges to accept contrary evidence led to the convictions of two men for crimes they did not commit. One of them was executed, the other spent years on death row before being exonerated. In the latter case, the innocent man finally won his release, but died not too long afterward, broken by the dysfunctional wheel of justice.[71]

Growing doubts about the fairness of the death penalty sometimes led to action from unexpected quarters. Conservative Illinois Republican Governor George Ryan, occasionally referred to as "Governor Grumpy," issued a moratorium on the death penalty in his state in early 2000. He had voted for the death penalty as a legislator in 1977, in the wake of the Supreme Court decision telling states to rewrite their death penalty statutes. Ryan was an increasingly unpopular governor, tainted by charges—later upheld—that as Illinois secretary of state his office had been issuing commercial driver's licenses for the right price. Only a bit past halfway in his term as governor, he announced that he would not seek reelection. Two days before he vacated the governor's office, Ryan commuted all Illinois death sentences. The numbers were staggering: "163 men and 4 women who have served a collective 2,000 years for the murders of more than 250 people." In addition, he granted a full pardon to four men and reduced the sentences of three others convicted of murder to the same lower penalty that had been meted out to their accomplices. As Ryan put it, "Our capital system is haunted by the demon of error: error in determining guilt and error in determining who among the guilty deserves to die."[72]

What had happened? In 2000, Ryan, once a small-town pharmacist, had been shocked by findings that some men on the brink of being executed (in one case, within forty-eight hours of meeting his death) had been innocent. In addition to issuing his moratorium, he appointed a high-level panel to look into the entire system of capital punishment in the state. The panel was composed of former United States Senator Paul Simon, former CIA and FBI director William H. Webster, and bestselling crime author and lawyer Scott Turow. Their report was a sustained indictment of the presumably improved Illinois system of justice. They suggested that perhaps 160 people on death row should receive clemency. And they also noted that in the previous decade thirteen death row inmates had been exonerated for crimes for which they were scheduled to be executed. The report indicated that standards for seeking the death penalty and imposing it were erratic, and that African Americans were most likely to receive the death sentence when their victims were white. The system, in essence, stunk.[73]

Building on this report and perhaps seeking to ensure a legacy as a humanitarian and gutsy politician, Ryan commuted all of the state's death sentences. In a powerful speech at Northwestern University—where law and journalism classes had investigated death penalty cases and found many flaws in the system—Ryan thoughtfully ran through his arguments for why the death penalty, however justified it might be in the abstract, was a failure in practice. He put the brunt of the burden on the high number of errors in the system, finding that, had he not pardoned the four condemned men he believed to be innocent, a total of seventeen people over a decade would have been wrongly executed. So many executions in a fairly liberal state not known for its calls for vengeance were unconscionable to Ryan. Nearly half of "300 capital cases in Illinois had been reversed for a new trial or resentencing." Of those on death row, close to two-thirds were African Americans. Further, Ryan found that forty-six men on death row had been convicted based on testimony given by jailhouse informants. The entire system, he concluded, "is an absolute embarrassment."[74]

Yet other governors, legislators, and citizens did not and still do not find the death penalty to be an embarrassment. Many prosecutors in Illinois were "outraged" by Ryan's commutation of the death sentences.[75] In the liberal state of Massachusetts, Republican Governor Mitt Romney pushed for a bill to institute capital punishment. He argued that it was possible in death penalty cases to attain "a standard of certainty."[76] In 2004, efforts were made in New York State to reinstate the death penalty. Governor George W. Pataki had a decade earlier defeated incumbent governor Mario Cuomo in part on the basis of Cuomo's opposition to the death penalty. While the bill was stalled, it had the support not only of Pataki, but of Eliot L. Spitzer, then state attorney general and later to serve briefly as governor.[77] Of the candidates running in early September 2007 for the Republican and Democratic nominations for president, most were in favor of the death penalty. Among the eight in contention for the Democratic nomination, four supported the death penalty, even while reserving it for "heinous" crimes. The four candidates in favor—Hillary Clinton, Barack Obama, John Edwards, and Bill Richardson—were generally acknowledged to be the leading candidates. In the ranks of the Republicans, only one out of eight candidates was opposed to the death penalty. In the presidential election of 2008, the death penalty was a nonissue between John McCain and Barack Obama. Supreme Court rulings have consistently refused to reopen death penalty cases, tossing them back to the state courts even when major evidentiary materials have been introduced. The death penalty lives on in twenty-first-century America. The greatest force at present working against the death penalty might be its high administrative costs in a time of economic recession.

Bush and Death in Texas

The chief executive of the state of Texas, George W. Bush, appeared deaf to the chorus of moral and practical complaints about the death penalty. Rather than accepting the moral responsibility to examine death penalty cases carefully for problems that might warrant either mercy or reconsideration, Bush and his counsel, Alberto Gonzales, studiously avoided such complexities. During Bush's term as governor, 152 people were executed. Records indicate that Bush granted clemency in one case, and in only one other case does it appear he spent more than thirty minutes contemplating what to do.[78] Nonetheless, Bush stated that "for every death penalty case," he was fully briefed and relevant questions were raised.[79]

As brilliantly reported by Alan Berlow in an article in the *Atlantic Monthly*, Alberto Gonzales (later to serve and ultimately resign as Bush's U.S. attorney general) prepared summaries of each capital punishment case for Governor Bush.[80] Then, usually on the day of the scheduled execution, Gonzales would meet with Bush to discuss the memorandum. These memoranda were generally brief; much of the content repeated, often in grisly detail, the facts of the crime. Berlow reports that even in cases where there was an egregious problem—the condemned person might be mentally retarded or have suffered from a horrendous upbringing; evidence had not been introduced; counsel had been incompetent—this material was omitted from or downplayed by the reports. On only a handful of occasions did Bush even glance at the text of a petition for clemency. The meetings avoided in-depth consideration of cases because only one half-hour of the governor's time was allocated for these life-and-death decisions.[81]

As it appears, half an hour was more than enough time for a decision, given that Bush and Gonzales had already rejected the principle of intervention. As Bush phrased it in his autobiography, he had no desire to "second-guess" the jury or to interfere with the court's decisions. Hence Bush viewed himself as nothing more than a rubber stamp. Unlike the governor of Illinois, who could commute death sentences, the governor of Texas can issue a reprieve only for a three-month period. But that does not mean the governor's power is limited. Such a reprieve would send the case back to the Board of Pardons and Paroles, a body made up of political appointees; at one point, each board member had been appointed by Bush. If he had chosen to return cases to them, they would have been politically motivated to reconsider. But for Bush there was no need since, by definition, the courts had adjudicated; nothing was left to consider.

Bush began with the strong conviction that the death penalty is justified morally, drawing on his reading of the Bible, his gut instinct about morality, and his taking of the political pulse of Americans. As governor he worked assiduously to speed along the death penalty, without much concern for the seriousness of the mandate. He approved a measure that streamlined the appeals process so that the condemned would be executed more quickly, with fewer permissible appeals. And he announced that capital punishment served as a deterrent for potential murderers. "I support the death penalty because I believe, if administered swiftly and justly, capital punishment is a deterrent against future violence and will save innocent lives."[82] When challenged on the facts behind this premise, Bush replied: "I can't prove it. But neither can the other side prove it's not."[83] Despite many cases nationally where it had been shown that justice had gone astray, where men and women on death row had been exonerated, Bush refused to take seriously his ultimate moral responsibility to consider that the system might be corrupted, especially for those men and women who had been selectively targeted, poorly represented by counsel, and doomed by lives of deprivation and debasement.

Since the return of capital punishment in 1976, seven death row prisoners were found to have been mistakenly condemned to death in Texas. A story in the *Dallas Morning News* reported that incompetent attorneys had represented one-quarter of those convicted and on death row in Texas. Yet Bush never wavered: "All that I can tell you is that for the four years I've been governor, I am confident we have not executed an innocent person, and I'm confident that the system has worked to make sure there is full access to the courts."[84]

In only one case did Bush fret about the death penalty. This happened in the well-publicized case of Karla Faye Tucker, who had killed two people with a pickaxe in 1983. When her time for execution came in 1998, Bush considered the case carefully. This was in large part because she had become a born-again Christian while in prison and had deep remorse about her act. She also had among her supporters for clemency such powerful figures in the Christian right as Pat Robertson and Jerry Falwell. However much Bush stewed over this case, he allowed it to move forward because, he argued again, commutation lay in the hands of the Board of Pardons and Paroles and the court system. He refused to take any responsibility for delaying the execution.[85]

The point of moral action is less to act with decisiveness, especially when the issues are contested and complex, than with careful consideration. People of conscience can disagree about the morality of the death penalty. A strong moral case can be made for retribution; vengeance may well flow in our veins. A strong case, as well, can be made that it is wrong to take a human life, even an evil one, especially since life imprisonment is a severe punishment. As to the practical effects of capital punishment, that debate will continue ad nauseam, I suspect. But there should be consensus about the responsibility of George W. Bush, and all Americans, to think seriously about the death penalty. In practice, as governor of Texas, Bush failed miserably. The way he and Gonzales worked out the logic and set up the system in Texas allowed them to cede authority and eschew complexity. Mitigating circumstances were ignored; flaws in the system of justice were shunted aside. Morality as avoidance and absolute overrode any pretense to morality as process and responsibility.

To be a "decider," as Bush referred to himself during his presidency, requires that one be open to different points of view, that one considers fully the moral and legal complexity of cases. Bush announced that this was his procedure: "I am a decisive person. I get the facts, weigh them thoughtfully and carefully, and decide," acknowledging his "awesome responsibility."[86]

Within these parameters, Bush could have acted morally while approving the death penalty. But all the evidence indicates that his attention span and concern about death penalty cases were minimal. Poor data and immature consideration lead to faulty decision-making. The same mode of approaching the situation in Iraq would have far-reaching consequences.

PART III

Present Problems

Chapter Six
Muddiness and Moral Clarity: The Iraqi Situation

Two Meetings with President Bush

On being ushered into the White House Oval Office on 10 January 2003, Kanan Makiya must have experienced tremendous awe and satisfaction. Standing under the nearly nineteen-foot ceiling, Makiya, trained as an architect, no doubt understood how such an imposing space added to the power and prestige of the president. George W. Bush was ensconced behind the *Resolute* desk, made from timbers of a British ship given to the United States in 1880. Bush greeted Makiya warmly. With Bush were Vice President Dick Cheney, National Security Adviser Condoleezza Rice (soon to be secretary of state), and Zalmay Khalilzad, from the National Security Council.[1]

Makiya was a man with a mission. His meeting with President Bush might be viewed as the culmination of a long campaign to bring the attention of the world to the crimes against humanity committed by Saddam Hussein, the dictator of Iraq. Much to his elation, he would find Bush an eager, receptive listener.

The son of an important Iraqi architect and a British mother, Makiya had spent most of his fifty-four years living in Britain and the United States, eventually settling in as a professor of Islamic and Middle Eastern studies at Brandeis University. After years as a political radical, he had evolved into a proud humanist, convinced by political theorists Hannah Arendt and Judith Shklar that cruelty was the centerpiece of totalitarianism. Experience, too, had educated him in this position. Under the pen name Samir al-Khalil, Makiya had detailed how Saddam and the ruling Baath party had created a totalitarian state in Iraq and should be held responsible for the deaths of millions of Iraqis.[2] He also used his fine-tuned aesthetic sense to describe how monuments to Saddam expressed the vulgarity of Saddam's self-created cult of leadership.[3] Faced with such crimes, Makiya, who had revealed his identity as a leader of the opposition to Saddam only a few years earlier, was clear about his objectives: removal, by any means, of Saddam and the Baath party from power and the establishment of a democracy in Iraq. Call him a romantic or utopian, but clearly his dreams and the policy of the United States government seemed to have merged in the early months of 2003.

Any nervousness Makiya, along with two other Iraqi exiles, may have experienced in the Oval Office that day was dispelled by the president's enthusiasm for his views.[4] Three months prior to the American invasion of Iraq, the president opened the meeting by stating that Saddam's heart "of stone" made war inevitable. Bush was convinced Iraq's dictator was in possession of weapons of mass destruction, and that he was aiding and supporting Al Qaeda terrorists in violation of United Nations sanctions and undermining the development of democracy in the Middle East. Given such "realities," the president bolstered Makiya's confidence by welcoming the end of Saddam Hussein and the Baath party. Bush did not hold the floor for the entire meeting; he solicited information about the life experiences of each of the Iraqis present. Makiya and his fellow exiles gave the president a quick lesson in the differences between Sunni and Shia Arabs. As to how American troops would be received in Iraq, Makiya confidently prophesied that they would be greeted with "sweets and flowers."[5] The Iraqi exiles, quite as much as President Bush, left the meeting pleased with the prospect that soon Saddam Hussein would be removed from power and Iraq propelled on the road to democracy. Makiya later related that, looking Bush in the eyes, he saw that when the president spoke about democracy he "genuinely meant this . . . on a personal level, on a one to one level."[6]

All present in the Oval Office that day had achieved what they believed was moral clarity, something especially treasured by President Bush.[7] For Makiya, without doubt, it was "a morally just war."[8] Saddam was a force for evil in the world, the Iraqi people wanted democracy, and the United States should employ its military power—even if it had to act alone—to transform Iraq. The details of how this would occur, alas, appeared to be less than clear. At one point, Bush turned to National Security Adviser Rice and asked her if American preparations for the rebuilding of Iraq after the invasion were "well advanced." According to Makiya, "Rice looked down. She could not look him in the eye. And she said, Yes, Mr. President. She looked at the floor."[9]

Spreading democracy became something of a mantra for Bush and other members of his administration in the days leading up to and after the invasion of Iraq in 2003. This dedication to the dream of democracy—connected with a policy, at least in Iraq, of humanitarian intervention—was bolstered by another meeting that occurred in the Oval Office more than a year later. On 11 November 2004, Natan Sharansky, a famous former Soviet dissident, was ushered into the White House. Sharansky had become in the 1970s a human rights activist, a refusenik demonstrating for the right of Soviet Jews to immigrate to Israel. He'd helped physicist Andrei Sakharov, a winner of the Nobel Peace Prize, with translations of his writings into English. Such activities led to Sharansky's arrest in 1977 for "treason." After a mock trial, he was sentenced to spend thirteen years in Soviet prisons and labor camps. Yet Sharansky continued to challenge Soviet authority in prison. He went on hunger strikes, one of which lasted more than one hundred days; he spent more than a year in freezing and forbidding punishment cells.[10]

Worldwide attention and agitation on the part of Sharansky's wife and others, including President Ronald Reagan, won him his freedom after nine years. Following his release, Sharansky became a well-known human rights activist and staunch supporter of his new Israeli homeland. He was also well connected to the White House. He knew Elliott Abrams, a key figure in the National Security Council, and other neoconservatives both within and outside the Bush administration.[11] Abrams helped to open the door for Sharansky to various members of the Bush administration.

President Bush, fresh from defeating Senator John Kerry in the national election of 2004, had been relaxing at Camp David. He had with him an advance copy of Sharansky's new book, *The Case for Democracy: The Power of Freedom to Overcome Tyranny and Terror*, and by the time he met with Sharansky, Bush had read most of it with enthusiasm. Condoleezza Rice, whose expertise was in Russian studies, was also reading the book because, she told Sharansky, "It's my job to know what the president is thinking."[12]

In clear, crisp prose, Sharansky and his co-author, Ron Dermer—an American from Miami Beach who had become an Israeli journalist and later Israel's minister of economic affairs in the United States—made a case for the significance of moral clarity in foreign policy. This contrasted strongly with the realist tradition of foreign policy practiced by former Secretary of State Henry A. Kissinger and others. Realists generally contended that governments act on vital interests. Interests are powered by strategic, economic, and political needs. Stability is treasured more than uncertainty. Thus for the realist, the Soviet Union and Communist China are acknowledged as antagonistic to American interests, but ground is found for mutual cooperation and competition. The key for the realist is, in a sense, to do business with the enemy or to deal with the enemy in a manner that allows business to be conducted. Peripheral issues, such as human rights, are less central, especially when a nation that is denying them to its people might function as a useful ally in global rivalries (69–72).

Moral clarity replaced realism, in Sharansky's account, without undermining vital interests. Moral clarity meant a willingness to confront and condemn totalitarian governments and practices anywhere in the world. While Sharansky acknowledged that democratic governments did, on occasion, commit inhumane acts, the America ideal was to support freedom for oppressed people. In contrast, totalitarian and thug regimes relied on cruelty and oppression, war and censorship, to survive. These appeared, as Arendt had suggested, as the hidden rationale for the state's existence. Moral clarity meant one recognized the distinction between governments based on freedom and regimes based on fear (243). Human rights became a cause for political action. But Sharansky and Dermer warned against naïveté. Even dictators sometimes preach human rights or celebrate the proletariat while they murder millions (xxxiii). The realistic humanitarian, armed with moral clarity, fights for democracy around the world. In Sharansky's view, "*All* peoples desire to be free. I am convinced that freedom *anywhere* will make the world safer *everywhere*" (17). Each victory for democracy, in turn, becomes a stepping stone for the growth of democracies and greater freedom around the globe. In the process, the United States—as a democratic and freedom-loving nation—benefits greatly by having allies dedicated to such values. Human rights become realism by morphing into strategic advantages.

In their Oval Office meeting, Sharansky regaled Bush with stories about how Soviet dissidents, armed with moral clarity, managed to persevere in a totalitarian atmosphere. Their desire for freedom kept them going despite horrible punishments. People everywhere, he told Bush, want freedom, even in the Middle East. At one point Sharansky told Bush, "You are a real dissident." Bush seemed uncertain what Sharansky meant by this, but the forthcoming explanation must have stroked his ego. "You see, unlike most democratic leaders in the world, you really believe in the power of democracy. . . . Dissidents are usually alone in their struggle." But history is on the side of those with moral clarity, courage to forge ahead with their convictions, and belief in democracy (xiii). Although the meeting with Sharansky was scheduled for forty minutes, it went on for more than an hour and a quarter. Bush refused to let the session end, holding off four interruptions, until he had been fully energized by Sharansky's human rights vision and the dream of his own role in making the world anew (xiii).

Bush exulted in finding his own gut morality expressed by Sharansky, a man whose experiences in Soviet gulags had taught him the value of democratic freedoms. As Bush later stated, "I felt like his book just confirmed what I believe."[13] Each man, in his own manner, was convinced he had achieved moral clarity. For Bush, such clarity—as we saw in his death penalty decisions as governor of Texas—cut through false or unnecessary complexity and confusion. Things were often clear, black and white, good and evil. Bush had famously stated that he believed not only in his God but also in his own intuitions. Thus, in an initial meeting with Russian president Vladimir Putin, Bush sized the man up and was immediately convinced he could be trusted. Bush's gut feelings were an instantaneous form of moral clarity—at least to him.

Some moral commentators go so far as to suggest that following one's moral instincts, or gut feelings, may work better than exerting too much energy in ratiocination. Journalist Malcolm Gladwell in *Blink* (2005) celebrates "the power of thinking without thinking." He illustrates this with various examples of how psychologists have found that proper decisions come most often from the gut and intuition. We feel what is right.[14] In like manner, only with more scientific data, Gerd Gigerenzer suggests how evolutionary development has armed humans with an intuition for moral behavior. Gut feelings and unconscious motivations, rather than endless packets of information to mull over, translate into better decisions.[15] The famously nonintellectual president found in Sharansky's moral clarity regarding democratic freedom the foundations for his own, previously unconscious faith in his moral clarity and righteousness.

Bush's new perception of himself as a moral crusader, acting from his gut and heart, did not stay behind the closed doors of the Oval Office for long. The themes were transferred almost verbatim into his second inaugural address and into what then became known as "the Bush Doctrine."

"The moral choice," Bush stated in his address, is "between oppression, which is always wrong, and freedom, which is eternally right." Human rights and world peace are dependent on freedom: "The best hope for peace in our world is the expansion of freedom in all the world." Bush volunteered America to help in that drive; with courage and conviction in its ideals, America would also help itself. Bush acknowledged that Sharansky's views coincided with what he'd felt in his gut; now they had become official policy, expressed in his Doctrine of Freedom—part of his "presidential DNA" and personal "philosophy."[16]

That philosophy had already begun, and would continue, to stake out its raison d'être by engaging in a fight against evil.[17] Bush had famously declared certain states—Iraq, North Korea, and Iran—as constituting an "axis of evil." Such morally tinged language was a perfect vehicle for Bush's either/or view of the world. To a degree, Sharansky agreed. Along with Bush, he contended that the most significant step an individual could take was in "finding the moral clarity to see evil."[18] To see evil afoot in the world and to leave it to its own purposes was to traffic in sin. Bush, Sharansky, Makiya, and others came to feel they had found such moral clarity—and it necessitated the invasion of Iraq, the disposal of Saddam Hussein, and the establishment of an Iraqi democracy.

Making Evil Known

Makiya was resolute in acting on his moral clarity. With equal amounts courage and conviction, he made it his responsibility to rivet the attention of the world on the crimes of Saddam Hussein. For him, there was nothing muddy about the immorality of Saddam's sending hundreds of thousands of soldiers to die in a senseless and unjust war with Iran from 1980 until 1988. Nor was there anything muddy about how Saddam had used chemical attacks and other means to eliminate many thousands of Iraqi Kurds and Shiite Arabs in the southern marshland region.[19] Nor was there anything muddy about the torture Saddam had unleashed against many Iraqis. And Makiya was right.

Saddam Hussein's reign in Iraq from 1977 to 2003 was evil, in both senses of Arendt's term. Iraq in these years was a textbook case of the radical evil of a totalitarian state with a hunger for horror. According to the organization Human Rights Watch, Saddam and his Baath party had erected a network of terror that infiltrated every part of Iraqi society. In addition to a huge standing army, the Baath party had its own military wing, the People's Militia, which numbered 750,000 members at its highpoint.[20] The Mukhabarat, the Iraqi state intelligence agency, in 1978 employed more than 150,000 people, with another 57,000 connected to another internal spying agency (18). In totalitarian Iraq, citizens informed on their friends and colleagues, even on their family members, either because of coercion or desire for gain. No one felt safe; no one was safe. This pervasive bureaucratic state fit well into Arendt's model of evil as banality.

The numbers of dead and maimed at the hands of Saddam Hussein and his state terror apparatus are staggering. An estimated 200,000 died from torture and execution in Iraq over his near thirty years of rule. The death penalty applied to twenty-four offenses ranging from acts deemed prejudicial to the internal or external security of the state to general categories of "offenses constituting a danger to the public" (27). Constraints on the power of the state—such as an independent judiciary or uncensored press—were nonexistent.

During his years as president and head of the military, Saddam Hussein launched two wars: first his eight-year war against Iran and then his short-lived takeover of Kuwait in 1990. Estimates of Iraqi dead in these conflicts vary widely, but a figure of 750,000 would not be far off the mark.[21] Following the Gulf War in 1991, which drove him out of Kuwait but left him in power, Saddam unleashed attacks against his internal opposition. In the northeastern part of the country, the government forces used chemical and conventional weapons against Kurdish cities and villages. Thousands of innocents died in these attacks. Saddam also ordered Kurdish villages razed and their inhabitants relocated. At least one-half million Kurds were uprooted from their ancestral lands. Saddam also orchestrated an assault against Shiites in the marshland area of Iraq. This area, the presumed home of the Garden of Eden, near the Tigris and Euphrates rivers, was damned up at various points, drying up the marshland and forcing the inhabitants to starve or relocate to areas where they could be better watched and controlled by Saddam's bureaucracy of terror.[22]

The Soviet dictator Joseph Stalin once joked coldly that when we hear about a million people dying it is a statistic, but when we learn that one person has perished it is a tragedy. Perhaps the figures in the preceding account fall short of personalizing the horror of Iraq over a quarter-century, so let's follow Makiya's example by filling in the details.

In 1988 various cities and villages in the northwestern part of Iraq known as Kurdistan were subjected to poison gas attacks. Those killed by poison gas were mostly women, children, and the elderly. Odd-colored clouds followed in the wake of Iraqi warplanes flying over towns such as Guptapa. A teacher of chemistry survived the gassing, but he found most of his extended family dead. Many of them had been choked to death by the chemicals or had drowned when they fainted in the river nearby. The chemist discovered the dead bodies of twenty-five members of his family strewn in the vicinity of his home, "blood and vomit running from their noses and mouths."[23] Poison gas was also dropped on the city of Halabja. A "yellow-white cloud" from the chemicals engulfed parts of the city, according to one report. A photograph in the *New York Times* shows a baby, mouth agape, dead from the gas. An adult, also dead, cradles the child. Tallies of the numbers of people who died in the attack vary widely, from 100 to 5,000.[24]

Sometimes the methods used to eliminate Kurds were strikingly reminiscent of those German Sonderkommando units employed to kill Jews during World War II. Taimour, a young Kurd, was seized from his village with his family—father, mother, and three sisters, as well as various relatives. His father was quickly separated from them by authorities, his murder all but assured. The rest of the family was placed in trucks to be escorted elsewhere; the heat was stifling, and at least three children died en route in the vehicle, which was packed with at least one hundred people. When the doors of the truck finally opened, Taimour had his worst fears confirmed: close by were six to seven open pits—ready for their bodies. Taimour and the others were ordered to enter the pits. The troops began shooting them. Taimour was first hit in his left shoulder, with a flesh wound. As people wailed and died all around him, he managed to scramble out of the pit, only to be pushed back in and hit again with another flesh wound, this time in his back. Eventually, the shooting ceased. His immediate and extended family all lay dead in the bloody pit. Miraculously, Taimour climbed out and made for a sheltered area. After seeking aid from local residents, he was cared for by a Bedouin family. He slowly recovered from his physical scars, although his mental wounds will never heal.[25]

When not resorting to outright genocide, Saddam's regime employed torture. Authorities tortured many for crimes imagined by a state bent on oppression. Consider the case of the poet Nabil Jamil al-Janabi. His crime: reading one of his poems to a Kurdish audience in Sinjar. There are no indications the poem was in any manner incendiary in content. It was Jamil's bad luck to have been caught in the spider's web of the Iraqi terror machine. He was thrown into "a single, cold, dark cell with no bedding," and soon taken out, blindfolded. Then, the torture began: Electrical wires were attached to his body, one to a toe, the other to his penis. After an hour of electrical shocks, Jamil passed out. Barely awake, he found himself being tortured with cigarettes stubbed against his flesh. More indignities were heaped on the naked, shivering Jamil, as he passed in and out of consciousness. His ordeal continued as two men beat his testicles with electric rods.

By this point, Jamil was broken; he was willing to do anything to stop the pain. He signed a piece of paper thrust before him and received a jail term of five years for a poem that, he "admits in his statement," was "calculated to incite people to act against the government" (44).

Jamil was hardly alone in the injustice of his suffering. In a wrenching documentary account, another young man survived torture only to be plunged into a catatonic, paralyzed state. With his tongue cut out, he spends his time staring into the distance, perhaps looking for his lost self.[26] Stories such as these are the cruel, barely concealed face of Saddam's totalitarian state. And they only begin to scratch the surface of the pain Saddam imposed on the minds and bodies of Iraqis throughout the 1980s and 1990s.

Era of Humanitarian Intervention

The decade of the 1990s witnessed the end of the Cold War. The breaking down of old, relatively stationary power blocs, however, helped to unleash ethnic conflicts that often bordered on the genocidal. In the face of such horrors, humanitarian intervention came to the fore, both in principle and, at times, in reality. Foreign policy expert Richard Falk remarked: "The 1990s were undoubtedly the golden age of humanitarian diplomacy."[27] Many activists proposed that human rights be enforced by the United Nations, the North American Treaty Organization, or other regional security groups. Human rights were seen as having their roots in the United States in the Atlantic Charter of 1941. Thus, to call for humanitarian rights to be preserved and protected, even with American force of arms, was fulfillment of a policy rather than a quixotic intervention in the world. Indeed, as some argued, humanitarian ideals had a long history in the United States, stretching back to the Declaration of Independence and Woodrow Wilson's Fourteen Points in the aftermath of World War I.[28]

Throughout the 1990s nongovernmental agencies (NGOs) sprouted up, vying with one another for funds and riveting the world's attention on hotspots of inhumanity. Organizations as varied as Doctors Without Borders, Amnesty International, the International Rescue Committee, Oxfam, and many others leaped into the bloody territories where human rights were being violated. With the help of CNN coverage, attention was focused on the suffering, and humanitarian agencies were able to build large networks of support and funding for their work. Even when these NGOs failed to stem the tide of violence, they at least were not passive against its cruel face. They had, as they emphasized, acted to make the world a better, more humane place.[29] Passivity did not appear a valid option.

No one was more directed in promoting humanitarianism and celebrating interventions for human rights than Michael Ignatieff. In countless books and articles, Ignatieff (trained as a historian and serving in the 1990s as a director of the Carr Center for Human Rights at Harvard University) detailed the importance of human rights for the dignity of people around the globe. Alas, in too many places—Rwanda, the Congo, the former Yugoslavia—the most basic of human rights were in grave jeopardy. Genocide and cruelty against innocents must be stopped—even if it meant trampling national sovereignty. Human rights were "universal" and sacrosanct, according to Ignatieff. Societies must embrace pluralism and tolerance. When these fine ideals were violated, then it behooved other democracies to intervene. In Ignatieff's vision, America and other democracies would become the core of a "new kind of empire," one dedicated to human rights.[30] Ignatieff was not a naïf, despite this somewhat utopian dream. He knew that history often played tricks with the best of intentions. Tragedy was part of the burden of the human condition. But he upheld the moral imperative for powerful democracies to act against genocide and oppression. Since intervention would often be rejected by some of these democracies for various reasons—political wariness, dislike for violating the sovereignty of other nations, or failure of will—such interventions would be rare and often not legitimated by the United Nations. Nonetheless, when human suffering was abundantly on display, as in Rwanda, intervention remained a moral imperative.[31]

This perspective was bolstered with stinging moral clarity in Samantha Power's Pulitzer Prize–winning book, *"A Problem from Hell": America and the Age of Genocide* (2002). Born in Ireland and raised in the United States, Power (a colleague of Ignatieff's at Harvard's Carr Center) was passionate and erudite, turning heads and hearts toward her position. She chronicled America's unwillingness throughout the twentieth century to face evil with moral energy. All too often, the United States had dismissed—as in the case of the ethnic killing in the states that had composed Yugoslavia—violence as either endemic to the region or as being practiced with equal rigor by both sides. In such situations, government officials suggested, there was nothing that could be done by the United States. At other times, government officials evaded labeling atrocities as genocide, fumbling around with bureaucratic language that obfuscated reality. Power also dissected claims that no vital interests of the United States were at stake in such faraway places as Rwanda, where close to a million people were killed. Such moral parsing and deception halted American interventions. In contrast, her post–Cold War vision of American power was as a force for justice, morality, and liberation in the world. This would be achieved if only the American people and its leaders were willing to face the task. Power was hopeful that the United States, in the wake of the 9/11 attacks, would become an activist force against genocide, using its moral, diplomatic, and military capital. "The attack might enhance the empathy of Americans inside and outside government toward peoples victimized by genocide."[32] Empathy was at the core of humanitarianism and foreign policy.

Such blanket endorsements of humanitarian intervention seemed a bit naïve and dangerously romantic in the minds of some leftist thinkers. David Rieff, the son of intellectuals Susan Sontag and Philip Rieff, had initially been fascinated throughout the 1980s by how immigration was transforming the world. Soon he was traveling to war-torn Bosnia, settling into Sarajevo and other hot spots to examine the weakness of the United Nations' response to pure genocide. By the early 1990s, Rieff was vociferous in his calls for a vigorous United States and United Nations intervention to stop Serbian atrocities in Bosnia. He knew of the suffering in Sarajevo because he had experienced it. He warranted intervention in the case of Bosnia because it had been an exemplary pluralistic society that demanded protection. But with each passing year and the failure of humanitarian interventions, Rieff became more cynical and pessimistic about the potential for such engagements around the globe.

He arrived at the presumably hardheaded and hardhearted position that, since the United States itself was an imperial power, its interests in the world were largely confined to actions that supported that power. Unless compelling within the logic of strategic interests, United States intervention in hot spots of cruelty was unlikely. Or if it did occur, it would result in a different form of hegemony being exercised over the population. Indeed, by the time of the September 11 attacks, Rieff's appreciation for human suffering around the globe was equaled by his skepticism about the potential for American and humanitarian relief organizations to do much to combat it. By 2005 Rieff's perspective emphasized the dangers of good intentions in a complex world, suggesting that the success of humanitarian interventions—especially "at the point of a gun"—were a form of utopian dreaming.[33]

Humanitarian interventions (sometimes referred to as "military humanism") in the 1990s had usually, as Rieff noted, been unsuccessful.[34] United Nations forces, with explicit orders not to intervene with military force, stood by helplessly while Hutus slaughtered Tutsis in Rwanda, and as

Serbians killed thousands of Bosnian Muslims in Srebrenica. United States intervention in Somalia ended ignominiously when Somali rebels attacked special unit military forces, killing and dragging some of their victims through the streets; UN forces sustained serious losses as well, leading the United Nations to withdraw in 1995, leaving Somalia in a state of chaos. All too often, humanitarian assistance diverted attention from the root problems or, in some cases, unintentionally buoyed the forces of oppression. As Rieff put it in 2006, "Crusades have a way of backfiring and—however good the intentions of those who call for them—causing harm in places where it is least expected."[35]

However, humanitarian interventions did bring relief in some cases. After many miscues in the former Yugoslavia, NATO and the United Nations in 1999 finally intervened to stop ethnic cleansing in that region. NATO bombing against Yugoslavian and Serbian forces and military installations halted Slobodan Milosevic from realizing his dream of a "Greater Serbia." Unfortunately, the intervention occurred late in the game, after many thousands had perished and hundreds of thousands of Kosovars had fled to Albania. Nonetheless, intervention did bring surcease to 1.9 million people who had been living under threat of Serbian violence.[36]

Empathy and Action: Liberal War Hawks Against Saddam

Many intellectuals on the left asked how America could stand by and allow a dictator like Saddam Hussein to remain in power. These intellectuals were not naïfs or romantics; they knew that, for example, the United States had supported Saddam and Iraq in his war against Iran. Realpolitik and fears of a dominant Iran in the region had led earlier administrations to soft-pedal Saddam's tyranny. But after 9/11, the Bush administration had come to the conclusion—albeit initially with little support—that Saddam's regime of evil was dangerous to the peace and security of the United States. In time, thanks to the efforts of Sharansky and Makiya, Bush would build on the perspective of his deputy secretary of defense, Paul Wolfowitz, regarding intervention and the imposition of democracy as moral imperatives.[37] Before this happened, liberal intellectuals pondered long and hard whether it would be proper to align themselves with a conservative Republican administration they generally abhorred. And, they wondered, would the loss of lives in a military endeavor to oust Saddam and establish a structure for democracy in Iraq be justified? Indeed, they also worried about whether it would work.

The position of liberal war hawks on the logic and necessity of going to war with Iraq is at once appealing and disconcerting. It is also understandable only within the context of the challenge of 9/11 and the spirit of humanitarianism that informed the 1990s. In contrast to Makiya, liberal war hawks had no ties to Iraq. In contrast to Sharansky, they had not suffered totalitarian torture. In contrast with Bush, they usually lacked the moral clarity that comes from believing God is on your side. In thinking about those marching to oppose a war in Iraq—something he had done many times against previous wars—Paul Berman mused, "It's something of a scandal in my eyes that hundreds of thousands of people are not marching in support of the oppressed Iraqis."[38]

From his apartment building in Brooklyn, Paul Berman grimly watched the World Trade Center buildings burn and collapse on September 11, 2001. Later that somber day, winds carried into his neighborhood shards of existence—scraps of charred documents, pieces of cloth—from the victims of the terrorist attack. That day redirected Berman's life. With passion and conviction, he determined to meet head-on the challenge of what he saw as an attack on democracy by a totalitarian movement fired by dreams of a "war of Armageddon."[39] His favored weapons in this new battle against terror and totalitarianism would be ideas. We must "persuade tens of millions of people around the world to give up their paranoid and apocalyptic doctrines about American conspiracies and crimes, to give up those ideas in favor of a lucid and tolerant willingness to accept the modern world with its complexities and advantages."[40] With a brittle combination of moral outrage and moral clarity, Berman went to war.

Berman was well prepared for battle. Born in 1949, he had long been a participant and critic of radical politics in the United States, Europe, and Latin America. He grew up in a leftist Jewish family, feeling an especial affinity for the Jewish anarchist movement. His early exposure to this brand of radicalism, he later claimed, gave him the "habit of an independence of mind." He had been a student of the radical Palestinian exile and literary critic Edward Said at Columbia University in the late 1960s. After spending time in rural areas of Nicaragua in the 1980s, he stunned *Mother Jones* editor Michael Moore and other leftists by detailing how the Sandinistas, rather than being a radical's wet dream, were in fact in the process of imposing their own brand of authoritarianism. Berman continued in the 1990s as an independent social democrat, with bylines in many leading journals of political opinion. His attention up to this point had been focused on the radicalism of the 1960s.[41]

Berman appreciated how some in the generation of 1968, as he often called it, had matured. He disdained, however, those factions of the generation who had lost themselves in revolutionary enthusiasm and violence. Cadres of Weathermen and Progressive Labor Party radicals had failed to appreciate the necessity of democratic socialism. They had misread the historical moment in their revolutionary zeal by entering into a romantic world of fantasy, summoning up demons of a capitalist Leviathan and dreams of a Leninist revolution from above.

Not all had been lost, however. Out of this failed moment, some of the leaders of the generation of 1968 came to maturity, accepting their responsibility to push for reform and humanitarian enterprises. Some of them had even, in Germany and France in particular, entered into the halls of governmental power. They had also come to realize, as the anarchist-inclined Berman had, that totalitarianism—in the Soviet Union, China, or elsewhere—had no human face; it was a system of horror. And it must be opposed.[42]

The generation of 1968—exemplified by leaders such as Adam Michnik in Poland, Vaclav Havel in Czechoslovakia, Bernard Kouchner in France, and Joschka Fischer and Daniel Cohn-Bendit in Germany—became powers in the new Europe that emerged in 1989. One-time street-fighters in the 1960s, these men by the 1990s were leading a new revolution. After the fall of the Soviet Union, some like Michnik and Havel labored to build independent nations predicated on democratic principles. Cohn-Bendit helped to form the European Union and the Green party in Germany, while Fischer rose to be German foreign minister. Kouchner, after obtaining a medical degree and hanging out with Fidel Castro, formed the organization Doctors Without Borders and eventually settled into a position in the French government. All of these former radicals had taken up the bright banner of liberal society, in Berman's perspective, praising its openness and condemnation of totalitarian dreams of utopia. They had, in effect, become moral exemplars of human rights in spirit, thought, and action.[43]

Maturity and understanding about politics and totalitarianism had come to Berman out of his experiences with the left. He also found it exemplified in certain key texts by Hannah Arendt and Albert Camus. From Arendt, Berman came to appreciate how she unflinchingly bundled fascism and communism together as modes of totalitarianism. She also understood how the logic of these systems was anchored in a mad form of self-fulfilling, romantic destruction. Their ideological foundations explained away apparent contradictions with mesmerizing force. Their cult of leadership responded to the spiritual malaise of many. Those perceived as bumps in the road to utopia—such as Jews or dissidents—the totalitarian state sought to consign to "holes of oblivion," to literally write them off the pages of history and to execute them with fiery righteousness. From Camus, Berman, like other 1960s radicals including Tom Hayden, came to appreciate the necessity of revolt while realizing that moderation was always required. It was easy to become an executioner in the name of justice. One was to be engaged with the problems of the world; Camus' politics were without resignation. But they were peppered with a strong sense of tragedy and limit, with respect for debate. These positions guided Berman on his journey into the world of modern terror that came into being on 9/11 in New York City.[44]

To understand what he was up against, Berman threw himself into the study of the ideological foundations of his enemy. Although without any background in the history of Islam, Berman consumed a steady diet of works on radical Islam. He read in translation various volumes by the Egyptian scholar Sayyid Qutb, a founder of the Muslim brotherhood. Qutb had been a thorn in the side of Nasser and his vision of a modern, secular Egypt in the 1950s. Qutb spent many years in prison before being hanged in 1966 (63). In the 1950s Qutb had been a graduate student at the University of Northern Colorado, and he translated his experiences there into a general critique of Western civilization. Qutb's younger brother Muhammad, also a scholar of note, was one of Osama Bin Laden's teachers in Saudi Arabia (63).

In Berman's analysis, the elder Qutb emerges as someone with deep religious conviction and an abhorrence of Western civilization's lax morality. He fears that Islam is being weakened by the spread of this debased Western culture. The only solution, from his perspective, is to reinvigorate Islamic society, to cast off democratic pretensions in favor of Islamic tradition and order. Western civilization's appreciation for plurality and the division between church and state was rejected by Qutb. He maintains that Islam demands that religion define all aspects of existence; anything less than this is blasphemy. The secular must be folded into the totality of the sacred; otherwise both will suffer. Society must be ruled by a strict moral code, that of Sharia, which is fully religious in its essentials (95). Moreover, Qutb—along with other radical Muslims such as Tariq Ramadan—stress obedience to authority in contrast with the heady freedom (and license) that is part of Western society. These are not matters simply of style in Qutb and his followers; rather they are essential to the survival of Islamic culture and society. While acknowledging that notions of a clash of civilizations, made popular by American political scientist Samuel Huntington, are too pat, Berman does argue that Qutb's worldview is strikingly bifurcated in upholding the confrontation between Islam and Western modernity. In Qutb's view, and especially in the minds of his followers dedicated to a cult of suicide and destruction to achieve purity, the stakes are immense. While admitting that Qutb's vision has aspects that are "rich, nuanced, deep, soulful, and heartfelt," Berman finds it burdened by urges that are narrow, demonic, and dangerous (77).

Qutb and his followers were but one side of the coin of Islamist fascism, in Berman's view. Equally dangerous and allied with them was the fascism of the Baath movement in Iraq. Berman tried to demonstrate how Iraqi Baathism shared qualities of practice and streams of thought with European totalitarianism. He even attempted to sketch a direct lineage between Baathism and Nazism, in theory and practice. His overall analysis of Iraqi totalitarianism was beholden to the generalizations Arendt had drawn between Nazi Germany and the communist Soviet Union. Totalitarian states, whatever their surface dissimilarities and geographic distance from one another, were joined by a logic of destruction and ideological fervor.

Berman did not contend, as did President Bush and others in his administration, that Saddam and his ruling party had been involved in the 9/11 attacks. But he was clearly arguing that the worldviews of Qutb and those of his spiritual followers who had joined Al Qaeda and Saddam were similar; they were, in effect, totalitarian fellow travelers in violence and hatred. This seems jarring at first, given Saddam's generally secular outlook. But Berman tried to demonstrate how Saddam shared an essential vision of the world with Qutb, a sort of romantic longing for an earlier ideal of an Islamist empire, one purified from outside Western interests. Saddam's embrace of a cult of leadership, his emphasis on obedience, and his utopian fantasies steeped in bloodshed and violence all fit well into a general outline of a rising Islamic fascism. Berman believed that in drawing these parallels with broad strokes, he was alerting his readers in the West to the nature of its enemy. The question remained: What was to be done about it?

In general, Berman believed that the United States and its allies needed to win the hearts and minds of the Arab world in this fateful "clash of ideologies" (183). He noted how, after the defeat of Germany and Japan in World War II, the United States had engaged in strenuous efforts to educate and lead the defeated nations away from authoritarianism and into democracy. They had succeeded in nation building. The revolution of 1989, as evidenced in Poland and elsewhere in Europe, indicated that years of totalitarian rule could be shed; with leaders such as Michnik, Lech Walesa, and Havel, new, pluralistic, and democratic societies, beholden to human rights, could be erected. Berman, armed with moral clarity and enthusiasm, called for "the Terror War" to be waged "on the plane of theories, arguments, books, magazines, conferences, and lectures." The ideals of 1989 needed to take root in Islamic nations and cultures, and Berman proposed that he and other liberal intellectuals become their Johnny Appleseeds (185).

Berman knew this would be a difficult undertaking. He recognized that many Islamic nations were authoritarian; the circulation of ideas was limited by censorship. And he was well aware, as a leftist, that the reception of the United States in the region as anything but a staunch ally of Israel made progress uncertain. But, drawing on the experiences of dissidents in the former Soviet Union and other totalitarian societies, he also knew that subversive ideas could filter in. Underground networks of closeted Arab democrats should be encouraged. The role of Berman and other intellectuals was—in a form of paternalism—to take on the enemy of Islamic fundamentalism and to promote a vision of democracy among Arab intellectuals, as if those intellectuals were somehow ignorant of them. The United States government, too, falling under the sway of such visions, would employ its diplomatic and economic power to support dissidents abroad and to reform authoritarian governments. Berman hoped that, over time, democratic ideals would spread across the Islamic world, as initially Arab intellectuals and then the masses would opt for freedom and human rights, which he perceived as universal desires. The West needed "a politics to out-compete the Islamists and Baathi . . . a politics to fight against poverty and oppression; a politics of authentic solidarity for the Muslim world, instead of the demagogy of cosmic hatred." In sum, Berman's utopia of the twenty-first century, which he imagined beginning with the liberation of Kabul in the war against Afghanistan fascism, would spread throughout the Arab world, and, in time, bring forth the flowers of reason, freedom, and liberal ideals (189–191). But by 2003, the notion of ideas battling in the Middle East had been drowned out by the drumbeat for a new war, undertaken by the United States to remove Saddam Hussein from power and to insert in his stead a new democratic Iraq.

War with Iraq

Ideas in this case traveled along the wings of a warplane. Berman was intrigued with humanitarian interventionism; it had been the proper response to the situation in Kosovo. He considered the intervention of Western forces in Afghanistan to have been a success as well. The reactionary fascist regime of the Taliban was overthrown; women and others were enjoying rights previously unimaginable in that nation. Of course, such accomplishments were limited largely to the capital city of Kabul. But the ideals of humanitarianism upheld by Berman and others had gained a foothold. The ensuing years, in his view, would be a test to see how well the initial gains of freedom might stretch into the countryside. The verdict of history in Afghanistan had yet to be fully rendered, but the initial results seemed to him to be positive, if incomplete (175f). Military intervention, rather than simply being a sign of the defeat of humanitarian ideals, now appeared the way to freedom in nations that were under the totalitarian thumb.

Nowhere did this seem more true than in Iraq. Berman agreed fully with Kanan Makiya's evaluation of the totalitarian nature of Saddam and his Baath regime. He was sadly cognizant of how Saddam had eliminated many thousands of political opponents over the nearly thirty years of his dictatorship, how he had squandered lives in an absurd war with Iran, and how he had crushed the uprisings of the Kurds and of the marsh Arabs in the south in the days after the 1990 Gulf War. Indeed, he once spoke of Saddam as being "like Hitler and Stalin rolled into one."[45] As talk swirled around Washington and the United Nations in 2002 and 2003 about Saddam's possession of weapons of mass destruction, of his refusal to allow United Nations inspectors full access to his secrets, and about how his hijacking of food aid during the blockade was contributing to the starvation of his population, Berman listened intently. He concluded that removal of Saddam from power was required. It boded well for the human rights of the Iraqi population and for its potential to install a democratic pluralism in the nation, which Berman and other liberal war hawks hoped would become a beacon for rebels against other authoritarian regimes in the area.[46]

Some war hawks, such as Christopher Hitchens, viewed it as a responsibility of those on the left to seek solidarity with the suffering Iraqi masses. He expressed empathy for the horrors they continued to endure. Hitchens had for many years been the equivalent of an intellectual street-fighter for the left in both England and the United States. A literary critic of great range, Hitchens was also a fierce polemicist and debater with an ability to head straight for the jugular of his opponents. In books and articles, he had eviscerated Mother Teresa, Henry Kissinger, and many others. But as he increasingly supported military intervention against Iraq, he and his leftist allies moved toward divorce. Finally, in October 2002, Hitchens parted company from the left journal of opinion, the *Nation*, because it had become a mere "echo chamber," in his view, for avoiding the threat of Saddam. As a leading voice of antiwar sentiments against intervention in Afghanistan and now in Iraq, the *Nation* had, for Hitchens, failed as a voice of engaged and enlightened anti-fascism.[47]

Hitchens bought fully into the Bush administration conceit that Saddam was an immediate threat to the region and to the world because he was hoarding chemical and other weapons of mass destruction, and because he was actively building, or at least contemplating erecting, a program to develop nuclear weapons. In addition, for Hitchens, claims about the connections between Iraq and Al Qaeda terrorists were both true and certain to grow worse with time. The removal of Saddam, Hitchens argued, along with America's taking responsibility to build a new Iraq, became the marks of moral thinking and responsibility.

Saddam Hussein's megalomaniacal vision of his totalitarian government's gaining such weapons—especially in the years after 9/11—sent a collective shudder down the backs of the Bush administration and many liberals as well. Berman worried about the potential danger Saddam represented. Saddam was first and foremost a war criminal, a totalitarian, and a force for Islamic fascism in the world. Berman argued further that, after 9/11, there was an additional "good reason" to go after Saddam: Saddam was part and parcel of a new form of Islamic totalitarianism. As such, he represented "an extreme danger" to democracy and peace in the region.[48]

Yet Berman also granted himself an escape clause. While he was enthusiastic about overthrowing Saddam by military means, he never actually supported outright the Bush administration as the force to achieve this. This view represented something of a tightrope act for Berman, and it is unclear how intellectually compelling it is. In effect, Berman believed that the Bush administration would fail at the ultimate mission of bringing order and democracy to Iraq. The Bush administration, up to the time of the invasion, had shown little understanding of the realities involved in military engagement, especially in the Middle East. Moreover, the administration, with its cowboy mentality of going it alone, undermined the potential for success by failing to create a coalition in favor of democratic and humanitarian war. Finally, at least in hindsight, the Bush administration, while correctly predicting that Saddam would fall from power quickly in the face of a swift military offensive, terribly underestimated the complexities, costs, and complications involved with the occupation of Iraq.

Thus Berman wrote about how badly "the Bush administration had bungled the promoting of democracy" in Iraq, leading to nothing less than a "disaster."[49] He even sometimes appeared to crow about his prescience:. "I approved on principle the overthrow of Saddam," he wrote, but "I never did approve of Bush's way of going about it. . . . Bush was leading us over a cliff" without "moral leadership."[50] Certainly, these criticisms of the Bush administration were valid, but Berman nonetheless must have realized that the Bush administration was the only entity ready and willing to do the bidding of the war hawks. How could one dissociate toppling Saddam from the Bush administration as the vehicle for accomplishing it?

We know what happened from various accounts of the Iraqi war. The plan to remove Saddam Hussein from power went rather well. Bombing on a large and often precise scale—with more than a touch of "shock and awe"—weakened the superstructure of Iraqi resistance. A scaled-down, highly mobile American military force—with British help and scattered military support from other nations—sprinted toward Baghdad. At least initially, they met with relatively little opposition. The Iraqi government was soon toppled; Saddam and his ruling thugs fled, hiding underground or recouping to fight a guerrilla war against the occupational forces. America suddenly found itself in charge of a nation, one that was sagging in its infrastructure, dispirited, and less than enthusiastic about a long American occupation. Makiya's vision of the American forces being greeted with "sweets and flowers" proved, at best, transient.

The very structure of the American invasion and occupation, predicated on a minimal commitment of forces, meant that those forces were stretched thin. In the absolutely critical early days of the invasion, these forces proved unable to impose order. Widespread looting of national treasures and important infrastructures occurred. An administration blinded by hubris and ignorance appointed L. Paul Bremer, a man without experience in the Middle East, as the nation's ruler. Complicating his mission was the reality that he was surrounded by others equally ignorant of the region and often powered only by an ideology of free-market capitalism. One of Bremer's most significant initial acts was to decapitate the armed forces in Iraq. This made for many angry and suddenly impoverished former soldiers, as well for the loss of the very forces capable of bringing about order. At the same time, Bremer banished individuals with Baath party credentials from governmental agencies. While there was a political logic to this, many of those dismissed were Baath party members only because it had been a prerequisite for employment. And with these experts in various governmental functions gone, the nation quickly tumbled into chaos. Iraqis who had cheered Americans initially found their enthusiasm for the intervention diminished as long-simmering ethnic and religious tensions erupted into the streets. Liberation had, in these dark days, brought little freedom and much bloodshed. The president of the United States may have later deceived himself when he helped to land a plane on an American aircraft carrier and then told those assembled on deck that the conflict, or at least serious fighting, in Iraq was over. This statement, and its lack of understanding of the conditions in the nation and the problems inherent in nation-building, hardly surprised Berman.[51] But at least Saddam Hussein was gone from power, later to be tried on Iraqi soil in a court of law and hanged for crimes against his own people.

It is easy to argue that the American intervention in Iraq in 2003 was a monumental mistake, rife with tactical and political errors. The relative stability of Saddam's regime was, for at least five painful years, replaced by chaos. The nation tottered on the edge of civil war among different religious and ethnic groups. The presence of Al Qaeda terrorists, nonexistent in Iraq before the conflict, grew as a direct result of the conflict. Often it seemed the only buildings and services erected by the massive United States funds flooding into Iraq were edifices of corruption and waste. Private security firms mushroomed in Iraq, acting often in an imperial and uncontrolled manner. Fighting in the nation was redolent with blood. In May 2008, the number of Iraqis who perished in the "humanitarian intervention" was estimated at 83,000 to 90,000 people.[52]

The troop surge of 2007, with its infusion of 20,000 soldiers into Iraq, coupled with a wilier strategy for dealing with the various powerbrokers in the nation, has brought, as of early 2009, some degree of stability to the nation. American troops are scheduled to be reduced; elections have been and will be held. Violence has dipped. The future of Iraq, however, remains uncertain.

Was the invasion of Iraq to remove Saddam Hussein and the Baath party from power, then, an enormous miscalculation on the part of liberal hawks? Are they guilty of capitulating to utopian dreams and romantic fantasies rather than taking an ironic or nuanced view of the realities of foreign intervention, no matter how justified by empathy for Iraqi suffering?

Berman demanded that America travel the moral high road. No less than Makiya and Sharansky, he worshipped at the shrine of humanistic interventionism. He empathized with the suffering of the Iraqis under Saddam. Berman liked to remark about how easily Adam Michnik, the Polish reformer and social democrat, could decide about where he stood concerning the invasion of Iraq. According to Michnik, it was simply a matter of "being on the side of those who are being whipped."[53] And, in further agreement with Michnik and others, Berman believed that "this is a war for democracy, not for oil. An anti-fascist war." It was, in effect, equivalent to the civil war in Spain nearly seventy years earlier, the initial battle between the forces of Nazi evil and democratic good. In its newest form, the battle against Islamic totalitarianism had to be engaged. Berman, as a humanitarian interventionist, maintained that "severe oppression justified intervention, no matter what other explanations Bush may have offered." Thus Berman considered the protests against the war in Iraq, undertaken by many of his former comrades on the left, to be "a moral scandal," a collective failure on their part to understand the value in removing from power a regime that had orchestrated horrors on a monumental scale.[54] Even without any weapons of mass destruction found, even without any hint of a serious nuclear program, and even without an iota of connection between Saddam and Al Qaeda, the war was justifiable. So Berman argued.

Mea Culpa?

Liberal war hawks like Berman and Makiya blew it. At the most obvious level, Makiya's belief that American forces in Iraq would be showered with "flowers and sweets" did not happen, or not often and long enough to pay dividends. The removal of Saddam Hussein and the Baath party from power did not segue smoothly and quickly into a peaceful and democratic Iraqi nation. Iraq had become for five years a big muddy of problems. The blame showered on the liberal war hawks appears to have been well earned.[55] Indeed, the war hawks have been more than willing to blame themselves for prewar naïveté, romanticism, and foolishness.

Blame, as some philosophers contend, is absolutely necessary for moral philosophy, no less than for political judgments. Without it, we would be unable to evaluate actions—those of ourselves and others. Without blame, accordingly, or some form of rigorous criticism, how could we presumably learn from our mistakes? While blame may, as sociologist Charles Tilly argued, make for a "them versus us" situation more than does the assessment of credit, it remains a normal and necessary human activity.[56] But the assessment of blame is complex. Does it lie in a consideration of intentions, of the gap between those intentions and the "reality" of a particular situation, or in the results that transpire because of actions one helps, in some manner, to initiate?

"I was wrong on the facts" and "on the theory" to support the Iraq war effort, announced Peter Beinart, one-time editor of the *New Republic*.[57] Beinart admitted that he had been duped by the idea that Iraq was building a nuclear weapons program and that it was a threat to the United States and Israel. And he recalled that he should have realized the United States lacked the moral credibility and political sophistication to engage in regime-changing in Iraq. As with Berman, he acknowledged how absurd it had been to support a narrowly partisan administration in a war that required nation-building abroad and uniting the people at home.[58] Makiya, who more than anyone else pushed for American intervention, admitted that he had "made many mistakes of evaluation and judgment" about the totalitarian toll that had been exacted on the Iraqi people under Saddam. Saddam's brainwashing made it difficult for Iraqis to embrace pluralism and American leadership. He further charged the Bush administration with having made "every mistake you can imagine." This did not mean, however, that Makiya regretted Saddam's removal; simply that it had ushered in a period of danger and chaos rather than of celebration and happiness into his nation.[59] George Packer, who always referred to himself as a reluctant war hawk, acknowledged that he was guilty of buying into rosy pictures of easy American success, such as those painted by his friend Makiya. But he was enticed mostly by the abstract idea of bringing freedom to the Iraqis. The horrors that followed the invasion, however, had proven that the occupation had, at the very least been bungled.[60]

Michael Ignatieff, to a degree, seconded Packer, admitting that his desire to unseat a totalitarian thug in the name of humanistic intervention had clouded his vision of complex realities. He seems to argue that he allowed his empathy for Iraqi suffering and passion for a future democratic Iraq to taint his reasoned analysis of the difficulties involved in such an undertaking. This presumes a strict division between powers of reason and emotion. Psychologists in recent years have demonstrated that such Cartesian separations are figments of the imagination, without basis in science. Thus, Ignatieff's reasons and emotions were mutually supportive, pushing him toward intervention. It was not a case, as he would have it, of his emotion overpowering his reason.[61] "So supporting the war," Ignatieff admitted, "meant supporting an administration whose motives I did not fully trust for the sake of consequences that I believed in."[62]

An issue of the *New Republic* was devoted to admitting that its editorial policy and much of its writing had been wrong to cheerlead for the war in Iraq. The editors had been duped about weapons of mass destruction as a starting point in their litany of errors. They had fallen in line with an administration ill-equipped for the subtleties of diplomacy and reconstruction in Iraq. Although Saddam's regime was "a moral cancer" in the Middle East, it was not, at the time of the invasion, life threatening. A botched American invasion had proved to be counter-productive, a tragedy because the United States had "undermined and delegitimized" itself. The journal's editors sighed, "It will take years for America to regain the moral credibility it needs to effectively champion human rights."[63]

Yet the more one reads apologies by liberal war hawks for their mistakes, the more it appears an open question about how much blame they should place on their shoulders. On a moral level, their intentions in favor of bringing peace and democracy to Iraq were admirable. Their essential points that Saddam was a totalitarian dictator—"a megalomaniacal fascist," according to Thomas L. Friedman—and it is a good thing he is gone, are banal and beyond dispute.[64] Moreover, the invasion, "in some meaningful sense" had brought freedom to the Iraqi people, a smattering of elections, the rise of political parties, and freedom of the press. In the words of Leon Wieseltier, "I can imagine no grander historical experiment than the effort to bring a liberal order to an Arab society." Even in embracing error, then, the war hawks remained convinced of the nobility of their efforts and the righteousness of their cause.[65]

The self-criticism of the war hawks was focused mainly on how they had erred in supporting the Bush administration and accepting its main rationale for the war—that weapons of mass destruction made Iraq into an immediate threat. But then things get confusing. Berman, Makiya, and Ignatieff leave themselves in the rather odd position of being correct in wanting to depose Saddam but mistaken in thinking the Bush administration was the proper vehicle to achieve this end. This does not, however, mitigate any of their responsibility for cheering America's entry into this moral morass. After all, Berman recognized that the Bush administration was going to be the mechanism to liberate Iraq. How could the means that this administration was willing to employ be separated from the ends that it promoted, even if one of them, at least in a minor key, was democracy for the Iraqis? Berman applauded when Bush, after his meetings with Sharansky and Makiya, emphasized that the war in Iraq was about democracy, both in that country and in the region. Here was an exemplification of Berman's goals. The fact that those goals were being driven into a morass of a five-year bloody failure, alienating many in the Arab world and therefore undermining hopes of reform, seemed to have been figured into the initial calculus of this war effort. If so, then what did it mean for Berman to withhold his support for the Bush-led invasion of Iraq? Not much, it appears.

Berman and his war hawk allies did not violate the Kantian moral warning about how impure means pollute pure ends. The problem with Iraq was not in the justness of the war nor was it in the violent means employed to achieve victory. Even if another administration had engaged in the war, they would have used violent means in pursuit of the justified end of eliminating Saddam. Of course, it would have been better had the invasion come with the support of the United Nations and Arab neighbors of Iraq. Somewhat ironically, the means of war to the just end of freedom were underutilized, as the surge later suggested. And for the war hawks here is where the ultimate blame is to be leveled. The Bush administration, following the swift army vision of Defense Secretary Donald Rumsfeld and Vice President Richard Cheney, employed insufficient troops to secure victory and till the ground to allow democracy to grow. Had they been more astute and less ideologically blind, the war might have been brought to a successful conclusion in a reasonable time frame. Since Berman is not responsible for the failures of the Bush administration, then he has slim reason for assessing blame for himself. Whatever blame he should properly embrace seems to be centered on his willingness to reject war at the time, since it was going to be embarked on, in his view, by this inept administration. But to have rejected this chance, as Makiya and others would argue, was to allow the Iraqis to continue under a corrupt and vicious dictatorship for a longer time. And that, too, was unacceptable to Berman. Hence, as with most moral issues, the muddiness of the alternatives forced a choice. Berman made it; and things turned out horribly, he would admit.

In terms of the issue of intent, the motives of the liberal war hawks were relatively spotless.[66] With the exception of Makiya, none of them had much of a personal interest in Iraq. Makiya's devotion to a democratic Iraq hardly seems blameworthy or marred by self-interest. The liberal war hawks correctly condemned the repressive totalitarianism of Saddam; they justifiably felt empathy for those whose human rights were daily being violated. They had no interest in securing oil reserves or in turning a war profit. They had no racist animus against Arabs, other than in upholding a universalist pretension that those in the Middle East had as much of a right to freedom and democracy as anyone residing elsewhere in the world. To be sure, they harbored a strong desire to employ American military power to transform Iraq and the region, but this hardly seems a deep moral flaw. It may show hubris, naïveté, or romanticism, but hardly anything bordering on imperialism or malefaction.

No, the moral intent of the war hawks was pure. One might even argue that it was more empathetic and morally engaged than that of their severest critics. For the war hawks raised the essential moral question, as had John Howard Griffin with regard to civil rights in the 1960s: How wide the circle of we? What is to be done when sympathy with the suffering of others has been established? Is it moral, when such suffering is undeserved and sustained, to stand aside and allow it to happen? Does passivity in the face of such suffering condemn the outsider? These are difficult questions, and the liberal war hawks clearly felt that they, and the United States, would be morally lax not to topple Saddam. They knew there were dangers involved; there always are with resort to arms. But if there was a reasonable chance of success, with proportionate casualties, then would this not attain some aspects of being a justifiable war? When Makiya thought back on this issue, despite the sobering effects of what had happened after the invasion, whether the invasion would be worthwhile even if it stood only a "5 percent chance" of success. Admittedly, this was succumbing to a politics and morals of "hope over experience." But such hope, he averred, is the point of politics: to make moral things happen.[67] And, with casualties in Iraq reduced and American troops planning to exit, might Makiya's hopes have fitted well with his experience, to some degree?

The imperative for the American war hawks to act might even have been more compelling because blame for Saddam could, to a degree, be placed on the United States. The United States had readily supplied him with chemical and other weaponry when Iraq was at war with Iran in the 1980s. This was a textbook case in the amorality of Realpolitik. Although the liberal war hawks had not themselves played off one side against the other, as Americans they believed that the nation's cynical politics undermined democracy, both at home and abroad. Even if the United States had not been part of the problem in the 1980s, the nation in the post–Cold War world had the military power to act. And there was, in the minds of the hawks, sufficient reason for action. Tying humanitarism and military might together was ideal. The liberal principles and programs that he favored at home should also be shared with the world.

But as the liberal war hawks have admitted, and as their critics have pointed out, good intentions are insufficient warrant, especially in a complex world. A fair argument can be made that American intervention—especially after the tortures American soldiers committed against Iraqi civilians at Abu Ghraib became known—has done little to further the moral authority of America in the region. Despite its current relative calm, Iraq remains on the brink of ethnic and religious explosions, perhaps due in part to the American intervention. As "chastened" one-time liberal interventionist David Rieff puts it, the path to humanitarian intervention is littered with broken dreams and dead bodies.[68]

Counterfactual Thinking

Nothing is more central to moral thinking, and to the practice of moral history, than engaging with a counterfactual situation. Although many in the historical profession condemn "as-if" scenarios as the stuff of popular history, best consigned to the History Channel or works of fiction, there are historians who find counterfactuals embedded in the practice of history, and as such, valuable.[69] After all, in wondering about the variety of potential causes for the American Civil War, for example, the historian is implicitly suggesting that one cause was more critical than others in a complex chain of events. Implicit in such reasoning is the presumption that what did happen might still or might not have occurred if that one factor had not been present. This does not require a great leap of historical practice into the realm of fantasy. Nor is it merely idle speculation without practical value. By thinking about alternative courses of action, we better understand what did transpire and better understand how and why other roads were not taken. The reality of history often pivots on a rather thin surface of possibilities.

What if, then, Saddam had been deposed with the same alacrity as did happen, *but* American and British forces, numbering more than 400,000, had quickly sealed the borders and protected museums and ministries? Might have the chaotic five-year occupation been kept at bay? Might have another administrator, perhaps General Ira Garner, decided to follow more closely the model of denazification by keeping the army relatively intact and refusing to banish all those with Baath party credentials from administration positions? If these relatively minor but monumental changes had been made—even acknowledging that old wounds between Shiite, Sunni, and Kurd remained raw and at the surface—would the invasion have been a success? Certainly, in terms of the liberal war hawks and the ideals of democracy held by Sharansky and Makiya, it would have been a moral victory of the highest order. Liberal interventionism, but for a few minor changes—would have altered the political landscape of Iraq, as if in the blinking of an eye, without the large numbers of postwar casualties. Opinion polls taken of Iraqis in the immediate aftermath of the invasion indicate that they would have had "flowers and sweets" aplenty for the invading forces had order been imposed and, as a result, the forces had left quickly.

A reasonable counter argument comes quickly to hand, even if, on a simple utilitarian moral calculus, it could be shown that casualties from the overthrow of Saddam were minimal. Even without being a pacifist, or at least an aficionado of Just War theory, one could protest that the war was wrong for a host of other reasons. Was its ostensible goal—to prevent Saddam from building up his stockpile of chemical and nuclear weapons—something that could have been achieved through greater emphasis on allowing United Nations inspectors to do their jobs? Even if there was a United Nations resolution condemning Saddam's refusal to cooperate with arms inspections (in part, the United States claimed sanction for its actions because of this "precedent"), it is clear that the United Nations had not sanctioned the invasion. The coalition forces amassed by President Bush may have included many nations, but they were certainly unjustified—except in the oddest interpretation—to act on the behalf of the United Nations. Moreover, the sovereignty of other nations is a critical principle in international law. And at least in the light of retrospection, the presumed threat of Saddam's possession of weapons was not only horribly incorrect but also insufficient in and of itself to sanction the invasion.

Morality and Timing

No scholar has pondered some of these moral questions, especially in the light of Just War theory, more fully than Michael Walzer. Recall how, in Chapter 2, Walzer's notion of "supreme emergency" tied ethics and the timing of certain wartime actions together. To reiterate his argument in the context of the early days of World War II: Nazi Germany presented a threat of immense proportions to the survival of civilization. In the first year or so of the war, the only way for Great Britain to pursue the war was through saturation or area bombing of German cities. While Walzer acknowledged that such bombing of civilians violated the principles of Just Warfare, it was, at that particular moment in history, justified by circumstances. Two horrible choices presented themselves: Bomb innocent civilians or face the victory of Nazi totalitarianism on the European continent. Moreover, even though the choice to bomb civilians in Germany was justified, it was tragic, something not to be celebrated; it was and it remains a moral wrong. Hence it should have been undertaken with a deep sense of the sin and violation of what is right and proper in the practice of warfare it represented. The bombing of German civilians was, in the early years of the conflict, wrong and evil; the officials who sanctioned it did so with "dirty hands," with the necessary stain of moral declension. Such sin, while necessary, cannot be washed away by the ends that it achieved.

Circumstances, therefore, color moral perception and action. At the most mundane level, moral psychologists have demonstrated that someone is more likely to give spare change to a beggar if they have just passed by a bakery, having their sense of smell aroused pleasurably by the aroma of fresh-baked bread. The moral imperative to help the destitute is present at all times. It is, however, more or less likely to happen under particular circumstances.[70]

Armed with moral and political hindsight, the liberal hawks have offered their mea culpas. But they have ignored central ethical issues: timing and circumstance. Even if their intentions were pure, the timing of the invasion was off, and in a fashion that goes beyond, but includes, allowing more time to build a coalition and gain U.N. support for regime change. No amount of time would have changed the basic forces willing to go to war with Saddam. In addition, the argument that the United States was picking and choosing which evil dictator to remove forcibly from office is true but not quite compelling. One does not have to be consistent in choosing to remove all dictators in order to be correct in removing one. Just because some speeders do not get a ticket does not mean that others guilty of speeding are undeserving of their punishment. It is a good thing to rid the world of bloodthirsty tyrants like Saddam, even when there are costs to be paid.

But the timing of this invasion was out of synch with the immediate threat of Saddam Hussein, not simply in terms of his presumed holdings of weapons of mass destruction, but with regard to the evil he was presently engaged in. Moral choices are often situational, more pressing at a particular moment. Thus, to return to Walzer's analysis of the notion of "supreme emergency" in terms of the violation of human rights, the argument was less than compelling in 2003. As Walzer explained at the time, "The Baghdad regime is brutally repressive and morally repugnant, certainly, but it is not engaged in mass murder or ethnic cleansing." Had there been convincing rumors of continued human rights or genocidal abuse, then invasion in 2003 would have been, at least abstractly, morally warranted. But, in point of fact, the invasion of 2003 was mistaken in terms of the power of humanitarian intervention, because repression in Iraq at that moment was relatively quiescent. While the sovereignty of Iraq, or any other nation, is not sacrosanct, it deserves to be respected in all but the most outrageous and immediate of circumstances. The time for intervention in Iraq, then, had passed a decade earlier. It might have arisen anew, given Saddam's track record of abuses, but that was a matter of speculation rather than reality in 2003, when the invasion did occur.[71]

According to such a moral calculus, humanitarian intervention would have been on a higher moral ground in 1991. Yes, in retrospect, it might have been better had President George H. W. Bush ordered American troops to proceed to Baghdad to remove Saddam from power. Saddam had, after all, already been responsible for political murders and tortures beyond the imagination. But the politics of such a change of regime, in terms of our stated intentions and the desires of other Middle Eastern nations, mitigated that possibility.

In contrast, in the early 1990s, when Saddam Hussein was practicing what amounted to genocide against the Kurds in the north and the marsh Arabs in the south, the United States could have made a strong case for being morally bound to intervene—even without United Nations sanction. As Samantha Power has pointed out, when significant military pressure and attention are directed against those engaged in such activities, they tend to stop, and lives that were in imminent danger are saved. This meets a crucial demand for valid humanitarian intervention: immediacy of the danger and reasonable chance for the success of the intervention (which would apply to any military undertaking). The moral imperative behind intervention was furthered by the fact that the senior president Bush had, in some of his comments immediately following the end of conflict in the first Gulf War, encouraged the Kurds to take up arms in a futile struggle for their freedom only adds to the moral burden for the United States. Hence, the strongest case—both moral in terms of humanitarian intervention and obligatory in terms of responsibility—occurred in the early 1990s rather than in the early years of this century. Had Saddam begun a new campaign of repression against innocents, on a sufficient scale of horror, then the moral imperatives of the war hawks might have been more valid *and* pressing. Such was not the case.

The moral high ground, to a significant extent, then, was held by the war hawks. Their moral instincts were good; their moral clarity about the horrors of Saddam and his totalitarian state were on target. Their empathy was valid. The rather scattershot case made by the Bush administration, and their humanitarian credentials, rightfully should have given greater pause to enthusiasm for military engagement. But even under such circumstances, and with Kantian imperatives near to hand (that others are "*not merely* . . . *means* to be used by this or that will at its discretion"), the moral logic of the war hawks for using the Bush administration to achieve humanitarian ends appears reasonable.[72] Reasonable, in part, because but for a few circumstantial changes of policy, the action might have succeeded. In this case, there was moral clarity aplenty on the part of the war hawks—and even among some in the administration—about the righteousness of a war to liberate Iraq. Unfortunately, moral clarity and reality clashed at this juncture. More moral cloudiness about the ability of the Bush administration's military and postwar plans would have been valuable to the war hawks. A greater sense of wanting to remove a vicious dictator like Saddam on the part of many antiwar protesters might have usefully muddied their own positions. Perhaps out of that, if nothing else, a more full debate—on the interlocking levels of morality and policy—would have ensued.

Moral clarity of problems and of purpose, of the sort embraced by the war hawks and certainly by President Bush, might not have been achieved. But a little moral muddiness, under the circumstances, might have proven invaluable.

Conclusion
Torture and the Tortured

I am often at a loss for words when, early into a class that I teach titled "Morality and History," an enthusiastic student asks if history has anything to say about a particular moral problem, for instance, about our responsibility to others, or whether it is correct to employ violent means to achieve august ends. Any historian worth his or her salt will tell you, nothing quite so specific. But that answer does not exhaust the topic. Historical analysis, if nothing else, suggests that things have been—and no doubt will continue to be—complex and often muddy. This is a lesson one may take from area bombing during World War II as much as from debates about the morality of capital punishment. It is easy to think and speak in moral absolutes; indeed, we cannot live easily without them. In the case of bombing during World War II, such absolutes were quickly buried beneath the rubble.

Given that reality, what is one to do when faced with competing moral goods or evils? Even when we realize the value of empathy, as in the case of John Howard Griffin, we shiver at its hold over the war hawks. There is much to be said in favor of intervention in various spots around the world, and there always will be. But at what point must we, as a matter of survival, sanity, and self-interest, pull back? Or is such thinking little more than a sign of surrender to the forces of power and custom that consign our fellow human beings to suffer needlessly?

Sometimes not knowing what to do may be best; at the very least it implies an attitude of openness to complexity, a degree of flexibility in terms of means, and a willingness to compromise, if necessary, over ends. As Michael Walzer has remarked wisely, "I am inclined to think that the moral world is much less tidy than most moral philosophers are prepared to admit." Ditto for most politicians, pundits, and often, ourselves.[1]

One might dismiss this imperative by noting that we can sink into the big muddy of moral complexity, so deeply in fact that we are unable to extricate ourselves. While we thrash about wildly to balance competing moral claims and paths, the world chugs along. Passivity in the face of moral challenges does nothing. Fretting endlessly about moral niceties while people are slaughtered is an immoral stance of defeat.

Act we must. But as this book has demonstrated, such action should be based on empathetic understanding, careful consideration, and humility above all. Rather than rendering us into quivering pieces of indecisive flesh, recognition of the muddiness inherent in many solutions to problems helps us to avoid inevitable bumps and potholes along our chosen path of action.

In the past few years, there has been a resurgence of interest in theologian Reinhold Niebuhr. Accepting irony and sin, Niebuhr recognized the dangers of hubris. No one should act as if he or she were exempt from historical and human constraints. Niebuhr found it invaluable to begin by acknowledging these facts, for they might help us to arrive at better answers to pressing problems. It is a hopeful sign that Barack Obama is a professed fan of Niebuhr. As he puts it on the back cover of a new edition of Niebuhr's classic, *The Irony of American History* (1952), "I take away [from his works] the compelling idea that there's serious evil in the world, and hardship and pain. And we should be humble and modest in our belief we can eliminate those things. But we shouldn't use that as an excuse for cynicism and inaction." These are inspired and appealing words, coming hard on the heels of George W. Bush's politics of gut-level certitude. However many tricks the cunning of history may play on President Obama, at least they will be engaged within a useful context of moral acuity.[2]

Students in my classes, as might readers of this volume, often ask about moral absolutes. Can we exist without holding them close to our hearts? Students with religious convictions occasionally beseech me to recognize the sufficiency and inerrancy of the Ten Commandments to the moral life, while secular students uphold the strictures of the Geneva Convention or Just War theorists. All are valuable. It is wrong, immoral if you prefer, to bomb civilians intentionally. I accept that in the last two years of World War II, when the bombing of civilian centers in Germany and Japan was most devastating, it was disproportionate to the advantages to be gained. That is clear enough. Such actions are immoral.

But, the *big but*, is that such bombing had already emerged as a common custom of war, starting in the 1930s, with the Japanese bombing of Chinese cities or the Nazi destruction of Guernica. It had emerged as a given practice of warfare in this period and following: Nations bombed and attacked enemy cities if it could be done with minimal loss to their own forces and without necessarily bringing forth similar destruction on their own cities. This is unfortunate, to be sure; it is a horrible part of modern warfare. Perhaps it has always been the case for war.[3] The killing is ordered and accomplished by men and women who pledge allegiance to absolute values, given to them by God or ideology or their own gut feelings about what is necessary and just. As the means of destruction have grown apace, the arguments made in 1945 by some of those involved in the use of the atomic bomb have become more prescient: We must prevent wars before they begin or spiral out of control.

Torture

This brings us to the evil of torture. Since the photographs of the abuse of prisoners at the Abu Ghraib facility became public in the spring of 2004, many analysts have defended or denied the efficacy of torture. Perhaps even more than the destruction of cities in wartime, torture is an evil that appears to be without mitigating circumstances. As the infliction of pain on a person who cannot defend him- or herself, it is an absolute evil because its main purpose is to hurt and humiliate a human being. Some contend, however, that it is at times a necessary evil, just as in the case of area bombing of civilians.

The argument in favor of torture is invariably posed as a counterfactual: What if torture, of the most severe nature, were the only means of extracting information from a hardened terrorist that could prevent the loss of thousands of lives? Would it then be justified? According to Harvard law professor Alan M. Dershowitz, it would be. But only when it was undertaken with the sanction of a "torture warrant," issued by a judge affirming the use of torture. Dershowitz rightly recognizes torture as a momentous choice; hence it should be allowed not under the cloak of secrecy, but within the structure of the judiciary. Permitting torture, in such a legal framework, would grant its exceptional use a certain amount of "accountability" heretofore lacking. Although Dershowitz does not tie the use of torture to a simple utilitarian calculus, it is implicit in most analyses of the question. Is it morally acceptable to inflict immense pain on one person to deter potential pain inflicted on thousands or millions?

The problems with this approach are manifold. First, most studies of torture indicate that it is singularly unsuccessful in eliciting valuable intelligence information; under torture individuals will say whatever they can to appease their interrogators. In so doing, they may actually, by throwing out false leads, deter or diminish a timely response. Second, torture is a terrible public relations strategy. Once it becomes known that a nation claiming to be fighting a war based on humanitarian foundations uses torture, the moral high ground of its cause begins to erode. Third, the argument leads to new calculations of the value of torture and hence a very slippery slope indeed. So long as one maintains that torture is a valid technique, then what number of potential lives saved is required for torture to become justified? Are five too few, are ten enough?[4]

The belief in the absolute evil of torture is strong and compelling. There is no confusion about torture as a degrading form of cruelty. But is it barred morally, as a practice, as a means to attain a moral end? How is it different, in the end, from other immoral actions, such as using an atomic bomb on helpless and innocent civilians, especially when one believes that such an act will hasten the end of a war and, in the long term, save lives? We are no closer to satisfaction. Actions may be immoral in the abstract, but in certain situations and customs, they are readily employed by individuals who do not feel their moral reputations at stake or who do not think they are acting in a morally problematic manner. Moral arguments against them have power, and they must be aired, but do not expect them to score a knockout blow, no matter how much we think they should.[5]

Solutions often fail to meet precise criteria for moral or immoral action. Yet we must learn to recognize that when we embrace a moral evil, we do so knowingly and take moral responsibility for doing it. Thus, if government officials are convinced that the security of the nation, that the saving of a city from destruction, can be avoided by the vicious torturing of someone, they should sanction it. But they must do so, as Walzer avers for the early days of World War II, with the recognition that they are sanctioning a sin of the highest register. Whether torture proves invaluable or fails to secure life-saving information, the individuals who have sanctioned it are morally compromised. They have, in existential terms, created themselves, and they now have dirty hands. This means they must accept responsibility for their actions as well as the consequences that come from them. For the good of the society they govern, they must recognize that they have done wrong, although they may, in some cases, cloak themselves in the rationale of having done what was necessary.

What should follow from such a recognition, either by the individual agent or by the judging populace after the action? This is a difficult question.

Moral absolutists point out that if someone in power orders torture, then that person has committed a crime. They should be tried and punished, just as were leading figures in the Nazi and Japanese hierarchy following World War II. But such punishments were imposed from without, by a victor on a vanquished nation. Is it realistic—is there much historical precedent—for a nation to punish its own leaders for actions that were, in all probability, undertaken without evil intent or that seemed quasi-valid means to deter even more terrible ends? Might such punishment lead to intemperate rents in the social fabric? Clearly, the American public at the time of the Vietnam War had decided it was time to move on, no matter how much destruction had been wrought in the often empty name of freedom. Was this willed national avoidance correct, or at least reasonable?

My reflections on the muddiness of morality in history bring me to a different avenue of resolution, one that harkens back to notions of virtue. Individuals and leaders alike need to hone the virtues (moderation, justice, generosity, mercy, prudence). This does not mean we fool ourselves into believing that in certain horrific situations they may prove flimsy, mere shards of empty vessels. But what of after the fact, when the winds of war have moderated, when the terrorist plot has been deterred or found nonexistent? What then? Perhaps it is a naïve hope, or a utopian one, that when leaders and individuals make their choices, they constitute themselves as virtuous by acknowledging that they have acted with "dirty hands." Such a self-perception, it seems to me, accepts the necessity of acting in the complicated realm of politics while recognizing that there are evils that cannot be washed away. President Harry S. Truman famously said of presidential responsibility, "The buck stops here." While the buck of dropping atomic bombs may have rhetorically stopped at his desk, it never really entered into the chamber of his mind, either before or after the event. As historians we must come to understand how and why this was so. This does not absolve him, or us, from responsibility for the choice made. When we, and our leaders, make such morally "tainted" choices, a cost should be paid, an accounting must be undertaken. Otherwise, we stand guilty of dirtying the waters of our own virtue.[6]

We are responsible for our acts. This is a tremendous burden, but one that cannot be avoided. This is why existentialists talk so readily of the dreadful nature of freedom. By studying historical events, armed with moral concepts and concerns, narratives emerge that help us to see how actors in the past have chosen or avoided moral issues, how they have taken the path of evil or refused it. It is naïve to think that history is a corrective for us in the present, but it is often a palimpsest for our own problems, both moral and practical. By engaging with our past, we may, at the very least, embrace more wisely our choices and responsibilities in the present. Perhaps we can arrive at something suggestive of moral modesty? Maybe, in time, we will better learn to steer morality's boat through muddy waters.

Notes

Introduction

1. While much of the work in this area panders to our conceits, there are serious books that attempt to engage the issue. Among them are A. C. Grayling, *What Is Good? The Search for the Best Way to Live Life* (London: Weidenfeld and Nicolson, 2003); Arthur Kleinman, *What Really Matters: Living a Moral Life Amidst Uncertainty and Danger* (New York: Oxford University Press, 2006); Jacob Needleman, *Why Can't We Be Good?* (New York: Jeremy P. Tarcher/Penguin, 2007). Perhaps the best way to achieve moral action is through a form of misdirection. See Richard H. Thaler and Cass R. Sunstein, *Nudge: Improving Decisions About Health, Wealth, and Happiness* (New Haven: Yale University Press, 2008).

2. Some take a different approach, positing morality as present thanks to evolution, grounding it in biology and psychology, and testing presumptions about hypotheses through experimentation. That is, obviously, not the approach adopted in this historically grounded volume. For some of the best in this literature, see James Q. Wilson, *The Moral Sense* (New York: Free Press, 1993); Robert Wright, *The Moral Animal: Why We Are the Way We Are: The New Science of Evolutionary Psychology* (New York: Pantheon Books, 1994); Marc D. Hauser, *Moral Minds: How Nature Designed Our Universal Sense of Right and Wrong* (New York: HarperCollins, 2006). Suggestive in many useful ways is Jonathan Haidt, *The Happiness Hypothesis: Finding Modern Truth in Ancient Wisdom* (New York: Basic Books, 2006).

3. See the popular exposition of the claim that instant reactions may be most useful in Malcolm Gladwell, *Blink: The Power of Thinking Without Thinking* (New York: Little, Brown, 2005).

4. Trilling, "Preface," *The Liberal Imagination* (New York: Viking Press, 1950), xii.

5. Nussbaum, *Poetic Justice: The Literary Imagination and Public Life* (Boston: Beacon Press, 1995), 5. Very much in keeping with the general arguments of my book is Susan Neiman, *Moral Clarity: A Guide for Grown-Up Idealists* (Orlando, Fla.: Harcourt, 2008). Neiman has more faith in certain ideals to keep us on a steady course, but she does understand that too much moral clarity, too easily arrived at, is a dangerous thing.

6. Harvey Cox, *When Jesus Came to Harvard: Making Moral Choices Today* (Boston: Houghton Mifflin, 2004), 25, 37–38. In a similar vein, see Kleinman, *What Really Matters.*

7. There are, of course, many examples of historians with a moral imperative, and often their work is exemplary and open to complexity. Particularly impressive in this regard is the work of David Brion Davis. For his reflections on his work as a moral historian, see Davis, "Intellectual Trajectories: Why People Study What They Do," *Reviews in American History* 37 (2009), 148–159. Also, William Cronon, "A Place

for Stories: History, Nature, and Narrative," *Journal of American History* 78 (March 1992), 1347–1376. For a discussion of the moral turn, see George Cotkin, "History's Moral Turn," *Journal of the History of Ideas* 69 (April 2008), 293–315, with responses from Neil Jumonville, Michael O'Brien, James Livingston, and Lewis Perry, in the same issue, pp. 316–337. For my reply to the criticisms, see Cotkin, "A Conversation About Morals and History," *Journal of the History of Ideas* 69 (June 2008), 493–497.

8. Exemplary of this new philosophy is Jonathan Lear, *Radical Hope: Ethics in the Face of Cultural Devastation* (Cambridge, Mass.: Harvard University Press, 2006). Also, A. C. Grayling, *Among the Dead Cities: The History and Moral Legacy of the WWII Bombing of Civilians in Germany and Japan* (New York: Walker, 2006); Jonathan Glover, *Humanity: A Moral History of the Twentieth Century* (New Haven: Yale University Press, 1999). A classic in the genre is Michael Walzer, *Just and Unjust Wars: A Moral Argument with Historical Illustrations* (1977; 2nd ed., New York: Basic Books, 1992).

9. See the excellent work by Harry S. Stout, *Upon the Altar of the Nation: A Moral History of the Civil War* (New York: Viking, 2005); Michael Bess, *Choices Under Fire: Moral Dimensions of World War II* (New York: Alfred A. Knopf, 2006); Drew Gilpin Faust, *This Republic of Suffering: Death and the American Civil War* (New York: Alfred A. Knopf, 2008). Also, *The Problem of Evil: Slavery, Freedom, and the Ambiguities of American Reform,* ed. Steven Mintz and John Stauffer (Amherst: University of Massachusetts Press, 2007). An example of politically admirable and morally tinged history done poorly is Nicholson Baker, *Human Smoke: The Beginnings of World War II, the End of Civilization* (New York: Simon and Schuster, 2008). For more indications of this new emphasis on moral history, see the symposia: "Moral Judgment and the Practice of History," *Historically Speaking: The Bulletin of the Historical Society* 8 (Nov.–Dec. 2006), 29–33 and "Moral Progress in History: A Forum," *Historically Speaking: The Bulletin of the Historical Society* 9 (Sept.–Oct. 2007), 11–19.

10. Ruth Barcan Marcus, "Moral Dilemmas and Consistency," *Journal of Philosophy* 77, no. 3 (March 1980), 127.

11. This existentialist recognition informed my previous book. See Cotkin, *Existential America* (Baltimore: Johns Hopkins University Press, 2003).

Chapter 1. The Problems of Evil

1. "Wedding Rings of Buchenwald Victims," *New York Times,* 11 May 1945, 6. On the liberation of the camps and American reaction, see Robert H. Abzug, *Inside the Vicious Heart: Americans and the Liberation of the Nazi Concentration Camps* (New York: Oxford University Press, 1985); *The Liberation of the Nazi Concentration Camps 1945,* ed. Brewster Chamberlain and Marcia Feldman, intro. Robert H. Abzug (Washington, D.C.: United States Holocaust Memorial Council, 1987).

2. On the narrative of evil, see Maria Pia Lara, *Narrating Evil: A Postmetaphysical Theory of Reflective Judgment* (New York: Columbia University Press, 2007). Also, Lance Morrow, *Evil: An Investigation* (New York: Basic Books, 2003), 94, 234–235.

3. Thomas Harris, *Silence of the Lambs* (1988; New York: St. Martin's Press, 1998), 19.

4. Arendt, "What Remains? The Language Remains: A Conversation with Gunter Gaus," in Arendt, *Essays in Understanding, 1930–1954,* ed. Jerome Kohn (New York: Harcourt Brace, 1994), 5–6; Elisabeth Young-Bruehl, *Hannah Arendt: For Love of the World* (New Haven: Yale University Press, 1982), 102–106. Arendt was lucky. Her interrogation occurred before the police had come thoroughly under the control of the Nazi party. Indeed, her interrogator had been a criminal investigator, only recently moved to the "political division." He had no idea what he was supposed to be doing.

5. Levin, *In Search: An Autobiography* (Paris: Author's Press, 1950), 276.

6. Levin, *Compulsion* (New York: Carroll and Graf, 1996). A popular film version of this novel appeared in 1958. On Levin, especially his maniacal relation to *The Diary of Anne Frank*, see Lawrence Graver, *An Obsession with Anne Frank: Meyer Levin and the Diary* (Berkeley: University of California Press, 1995). On the trial and psychology of child rearing, see Paula S. Fass, "Making and Remaking an Event: The Leopold and Loeb Case in American Culture," *Journal of American History* 80, no. 3 (Dec. 1993), 919–953.

7. On existentialism in this period and on Wright's novel, see George Cotkin, *Existential America* (Baltimore: Johns Hopkins University Press, 2002), 169–172.

8. William March, *The Bad Seed* (Hopewell, N.J.: Ecco Press, 1997).

9. H. Trevor-Roper, *The Last Days of Hitler* (New York: Macmillan, 1947).

10. Niebuhr, *Christian Realism and Political Problems* (New York: Charles Scribner's Sons, 1953), 62–63.

11. Niebuhr, *Beyond Tragedy: Essays on the Christian Interpretation of History* (New York: Charles Scribner's Sons, 1937), x–xi.

12. Macdonald, "The Responsibility of Peoples," *politics* 2 (March 1945), 83, 84.

13. Macdonald, "The Bomb," *politics* 2 (Sept. 1945), 257–260.

14. Mumford, *The Conduct of Life* (New York: Harcourt, Brace, 1951), 18.

15. Mumford, *Condition of Man*, (New York: Harcourt, Brace, 1944), 3, 4, 111, 156–160; *In the Name of Sanity* (New York: Harcourt, Brace, 1954), 2–8, 68, 127, 131, 148, 199–200; *The Transformation of Man* (1956, Gloucester, Mass.: Peter Smith, 1978), 12, 21, 47, 119.

16. Cousins, *Modern Man Is Obsolete* (New York: Viking Press, 1945), 7, 12, 44–47. The piece originally appeared in the *Saturday Review of Literature*, 18 Aug. 1945. In a similar vein, see Dorothy Thompson, *The Development of Our Times* (DeLand, Fla.: John B. Stetson University, 1948).

17. Liebman, *Peace of Mind* (New York: Simon and Schuster, 1948), xi.

18. Elisabeth Young-Bruehl, *Why Arendt Matters* (New Haven: Yale University Press, 2006), 36–38.

19. Ribuffo, "Moral Judgments and the Cold War: Reflections on Reinhold Niebuhr, William Appleman Williams, and John Lewis Gaddis," in *Cold War Triumphalism: The Misuse of History After the Fall of Communism,* ed. Ellen Schrecker (New York: New Press, 2004), 27.

20. Gleason, *Totalitarianism: The Inner History of the Cold War* (New York:

Oxford University Press, 1995), 109. On the discourse of totalitarianism, see Benjamin L. Alpers, *Dictators, Democracy and American Public Culture: Envisioning the Totalitarian Enemy, 1920s–1950s* (Chapel Hill: University of North Carolina Press, 2003), 293–302; Ira Katznelson, *Desolation and Enlightenment: Political Knowledge After Total War: Totalitarianism and the Holocaust* (New York: Columbia University Press, 2003).

21. Excellent on Arendt is Gleason, *Totalitarianism*, 108–113.

22. Arendt, *The Origins of Totalitarianism,* new ed. (New York: World Publishing, 1966), 74. Unless otherwise noted, all citations in the text will be to this revised edition.

23. Mark Edmundson, *The Death of Sigmund Freud: The Legacy of His Last Days* (New York: Bloomsbury, 2007).

24. Lederer, *State of the Masses: The Threat of the Classless Society* (New York: W. W. Norton, 1940), 18. On Lederer and Arendt's analysis, see Wilfred M. McClay, *The Masterless: Self and Society in Modern America* (Chapel Hill: University of North Carolina Press, 1994), 215, 218.

25. Fromm, *Escape from Freedom* (New York: Rinehart, 1941). On Fromm, see Cotkin, *Existential America*, 333–334. For Arendt's intellectual connections with New York intellectuals, especially David Riesman, see George Cotkin, "Illuminating Evil: Hannah Arendt and Moral History," *Modern Intellectual History* 4, no. 3 (2007), 463–490.

26. Orlando Figes, *The Whisperers: Private Life in Stalin's Russia* (New York: Metropolitan Books, 2007), is particularly brilliant at recording how Soviet totalitarianism ruined the lives of many, usually without rhyme or reason.

27. Levi, *Survival in Auschwitz* trans. Stuart Woolf (New York: Touchstone, 1996), 90.

28. Milton, *Paradise Lost,* ed. Christopher Ricks (New York: Signet, 1968), Book I, 54.

29. Jeffrey Burton Russell, *Mephistopheles: The Devil in the Modern World* (Ithaca, N.Y.: Cornell University Press, 1986), 249, 275.

30. Excellent for analysis of the problem of evil in philosophical literature is Susan Neiman, *Evil in Modern Thought: An Alternative History of Philosophy* (Princeton, N.J.: Princeton University Press, 2002). Also, Russell, *Mephistopheles: The Devil in the Modern World.* For a view that bemoans a presumed absence of discussions of evil in American society, see Andrew Delbanco, *The Death of Satan: How Americans Have Lost the Sense of Evil* (New York: Farrar, Straus and Giroux, 1995). Delbanco examines the ubiquity of evil in the Puritan worldview; he devotes only the briefest mention to Arendt. For an analysis of how the reality of evil entered into the work of post–World War II political scientists, see Katznelson, *Desolation and Enlightenment.* Also, Jeffrey C. Isaac, *Arendt, Camus, and Modern Rebellion* (New Haven: Yale University Press, 1992).

31. Arendt, "What Remains? The Language Remains," in *Essays in Understanding*, 13–14.

32. Arendt, "Nightmare and Flight" (originally in *Partisan Review,* 1945) in *Essays in Understanding,* (hereafter cited as *EU*), 134.

33. Denis de Rougemont, *The Devil's Snare,* trans. Hakkon Chevalier (Wash-

ington, D.C.: Bollingen, 1944), 60, 86. Also, Arendt's "Organized Guilt and Universal Responsibility" (1945) in *Essays in Understanding*, 128–131.

34. Rougemont, *Devil's Snare*, 116.

35. Arendt, "Nightmare and Flight," in *Essays in Understanding*, 133–135.

36. Rougemont, *Devil's Snare*, 83–84.

37. Here lies Arendt's affinity with some of the emphases found in Adi Ophir, *The Order of Evils: Toward an Ontology of Morals*, trans. Rela Mazali and Havi Carel (New York: Zone Books, 2005), 11–14, on the particular appearances and contexts of evil, and of its preventability.

38. On Arendt's refusal to examine the depths of evil in Hitler and Stalin, see George Kateb, *Hannah Arendt: Politics, Conscience, Evil* (Totowa, N.J.: Rowman and Allanheld, 1984), 80.

39. Frank is quoted in G. M. Gilbert, *Nuremberg Diary* (1947; New York: Signet, 1961), 136; Redlich, *Hitler: Diagnosis of a Destructive Prophet* (New York: Oxford University Press, 1999), 339.

40. The notion of "industrial killing" is central to Omer Bartov, *Murder in Our Midst: The Holocaust, Industrial Killing and Representation* (New York: Oxford University Press, 1996).

41. Hannah Fenichel Pitkin, *Attack of the Blob: Hannah Arendt's Concept of the Social* (Chicago: University of Chicago Press, 1998), 212; Bauer, *History of the Holocaust*, 31.

42. Himmelfarb, "No Hitler, No Holocaust," *Commentary* 77 (March 1984), 37–43. For a strong rejection of Arendt's refusal to deal with Hitler and Stalin, see Kateb, *Hannah Arendt*, 54–55.

43. Young-Bruehl, *Why Arendt Matters*, 107.

44. Arendt to Jaspers, 17 Aug. 1946, in *Hannah Arendt/Karl Jaspers Correspondence, 1926–1969*, trans. Robert and Rita Kimber (New York: Harcourt Brace Jovanovich, 1992), 54.

45. Jaspers to Arendt, 19 Oct. 1946, in *Correspondence*, 62.

46. Arendt to Jaspers, 17 Dec. 1946, in *Correspondence*, 69.

47. For the influence of Kant on Arendt, see Jerome Kohn, "Evil and Plurality: Hannah Arendt's Way to *The Life of the Mind*," in *Hannah Arendt: Twenty Years Later*, ed. Larry May and Jerome Kohn (Cambridge, Mass.: MIT Press, 1997), 150–151.

48. On Kant's notion of evil, see Neiman, *Evil in Modern Thought*, 64f; Richard Bernstein, "Radical Evil: Kant at War with Himself," in *Radical Evil: A Philosophical Interrogation* (Cambridge, England: Polity Press, 2002), 11–45

49. Kant, *Religion Within the Limits of Reason Alone*, trans. Theodore M. Greene and Hoyt H. Hudson, 2nd ed. (La Salle, Ill.: Open Court Publishing, 1960), 32; original emphasis.

50. Bernstein, "Radical Evil," 43.

51. See Bettelheim's influential "Individual and Mass Behavior in Extreme Situations" (1943) in Bettelheim, *Surviving and Other Essays* (New York: Alfred A. Knopf, 1979), 48–83; David Rousset, *The Other Kingdom*, trans. Ramon Guthrie (New York: Reynal and Hitchcock, 1947); Eugene Kogon, *The Theory and Practice of Hell: The German Concentration Camps and the System Behind Them*, trans. Heinz

Norden (1946, New York: Farrar, Straus & Co., n.d.). Hereafter, page citations for Rousset appear in the text.

52. Arendt, "Social Science and the Concentration Camps," in Arendt, *Essays in Understanding*, 243. On Arendt's style, see Lisa Jane Disch, *Hannah Arendt and the Limits of Philosophy* (Ithaca, N.Y.: Cornell University Press, 1994), 112–121.

53. Jeremy D. Popkin, "Holocaust Memories, Historians' Memoirs," *History and Memory* 15 (Spring–Summer, 2003), 53.

54. Arendt, "Appearance," in *The Life of the Mind: One Volume Edition* (New York: Harcourt Brace Jovanovich, 1978), 19. Also, Arendt, *The Human Condition* (Chicago: University of Chicago Press, 1958).

55. Elaine Scarry, *The Body in Pain: The Making and the Unmaking of the World* (New York: Oxford University Press, 1985), 5. On the contextualization of images as a method of communication, see Susan Sontag, *Regarding the Pain of Others* (New York: Farrar, Straus and Giroux, 2003), 29f.

56. Arendt, *On Revolution* (New York: Viking, 1963), 86.

57. On the attempt to make humans superfluous, see Margaret Canovan, *Hannah Arendt: A Reinterpretation of Her Political Thought* (Cambridge: Cambridge University Press, 1992), 12f. A powerful account of these various rules and regulations regarding Jews, and "Aryans" married to Jews, is Victor Klemperer, *I Will Bear Witness, 1942–1945: A Diary of the Nazi Years,* trans. Martin Chalmers (New York: Modern Library, 2001).

58. Arendt to McCarthy, 20 Sept. 1963, in *Between Friends*, 147–148. The moral implications of this are examined in Susan Neiman, "Theodicy in Jerusalem," *Hannah Arendt in Jerusalem*, 87f.

59. Des Pres holds that acts of morality, humanity, and comradeship are possible, even in these conditions. Des Pres, *The Survivor: An Anatomy of Life in the Death Camps* (New York: Oxford University Press, 1976). In the same vein, see Tzvetan Todorov, *Facing the Extreme: Moral Life in the Concentration Camps,* trans. Arthur Denner and Abigail Pollak (New York: Metropolitan Books, 1996).

60. *Origins* (new ed.), 473.

61. For Bettelheim's famous analysis of the concentration camp, often revised and reprinted, see "Individual and Mass Behavior in Extreme Situations," (1943) in *Surviving and Other Essays*, 48–83. For a devastating picking apart of his argument and its foundations in observation and experience, see Richard Pollak, *The Creation of Dr. B: A Biography of Bruno Bettelheim* (New York: Touchstone, 1997), 116–126, 362–367.

62. Levi and Ferdinando Camon, in *Conversations with Primo Levi,* trans. John Shepley (Marlboro, Vt.: Marlboro Press, 1989), 68.

63. "The Burden of Our Time" was the original title intended for *Origins*. That title was used for the edition of *Origins* published in the United Kingdom.

64. Arendt to Jaspers, 4 March 1951, in *Correspondence*, 166.

65. Arendt, *The Origins of Totalitarianism* (New York: Harcourt, Brace, 1951). Hereafter, citations to this edition will appear in the text.

66. Excellent on Arendt's sense of a community and polis is Canovan, *Hannah Arendt*, 162–163. A strong assertion of this point of view is in Arendt, "On the Nature of Totalitarianism," (1954) in *EU*, 357–359.

67. Arendt to McCarthy, 20 June, 1960, in *Between Friends*, 81–82. For a fascinating account of the impact of this trial on the American conscience, see Marianna Torgovnick, *The War Complex: World War II in Our Time* (Chicago: University of Chicago Press, 2005), 45–69.

68. Arendt to Jaspers, 1 April 1961, in *Correspondence*, 432.

69. Peter Novick, *The Holocaust in American Life* (Boston: Houghton Mifflin, 1999).

70. Marie Syrkin, "Hannah Arendt: The Clothes of the Empress," *Partisan Review* 30 (1963), 347. One historian refers to the "sometimes reckless argumentation" that marred *Eichmann in Jerusalem*. See Michael R. Marrus, "Eichmann in Jerusalem: Justice and History," in *Hannah Arendt in Jerusalem*, 205.

71. J. Baron to Arendt, 25 May 1963, in Hannah Arendt Papers, Library of Congress, Misc. Correspondence.

72. Podhoretz, "Hannah Arendt on Eichmann: A Study in the Perversity of Brilliance," in Podhoretz, *Doings and Undoings: The Fifties and After in American Writing* (New York: Farrar, Straus & Giroux, 1964), 337. A very vociferous attack on problems in Arendt's research is Jacob Robinson, *And the Crooked Shall Be Made Straight: A New Look at the Eichmann Trial* (Philadelphia: Jewish Publication Society of America, 1965).

73. Arendt, *Eichmann in Jerusalem* (rev. ed.). Hereafter, citations to this work will appear in the text.

74. Quoted in Jerome Kohn, "Evil and Plurality," in *Twenty Years Later*, 174.

75. After meeting with Winston Churchill in September 1944 and discussing atomic bomb issues, Roosevelt stated, "When a bomb is finally available, it might perhaps, after mature consideration, be used against the Japanese, who should be warned that this bombardment will be repeated until they surrender." Quoted in Martin J. Sherwin, *A World Destroyed: Hiroshima and Its Legacies*, 3rd ed. (Stanford, Calif.: Stanford University Press, 2003), 111.

76. Arendt to McCarthy, 20 June 1960, in *Between Friends*, 81.

77. Arendt, "What Remains? The Language Remains," in *EU*, 17.

78. The strongest presentation of this view is Thomas W. Laqueur, "The Arendt Cult," in *Hannah Arendt in Jerusalem*, 63–64. For a more subtle view, see Robert B. Pippen, "Hannah Arendt and the Bourgeois Origins of Totalitarian Evil," in *Modernity and the Problem of Evil*, ed. Alan D. Schrift (Bloomington: Indiana University Press, 2005), 148–160.

79. Abel, "The Aesthetics of Evil: Hannah Arendt on Eichmann and the Jews," *Partisan Review* 30 (1963), 211.

80. Abel, "The Aesthetics of Evil," 221.

81. Nora Levin, *The Holocaust: The Destruction of European Jewry, 1933–1945* (New York: Thomas Y. Crowell, 1968), esp. chapter 6, "Eichmann in Austria," 95–112.

82. Yaacov Lozowick, *Hitler's Bureaucracies: The Nazi Security Police and the Banality of Evil*, trans. Haim Watzman (London: Continuum, 2000); David Cesarani, *Becoming Eichmann: Rethinking the Life, Crimes, and Trial of a "Desk Murderer"* (New York: DaCapo Press, 2006), 6. Also, Richard Overy, *Interrogations: The Nazi Elite in Allied Hands, 1945* (New York: Viking, 2001), 360, where Dieter

Wisliceny recalls being told by Eichmann not to be "sentimental" about orders to kill Jews.

83. Breton and Wintrobe, "The Bureaucracy of Murder Revisited," *Journal of Political Economy* 94, no. 5 (1986), 905–926.

84. Scholem, "'Eichmann in Jerusalem': An Exchange of Letters between Gershom Scholem and Hannah Arendt," *Encounter* (Jan. 1964), 56. For the placement of this debate in the context of Jewish history, see David Suchoff, "Gershom Scholem, Hannah Arendt, and the Scandal of Jewish Particularity," *Germanic Review* 72, no. 3 (1997), 57–76; Dan Diner, "Hannah Arendt Reconsidered: On the Banal and the Evil in Her Holocaust Narrative," trans. Rita Bradshaw, *New German Critique* 71 (Spring–Summer 1997), 177–190.

85. Novick, *The Holocaust in American Life*, 136–137.

86. The most famous, although complex, expression of this view is in Daniel Bell, *The End of Ideology: On the Exhaustion of Political Ideas in the Fifties* (New York: Free Press, 1962). For a critique of Arendt's work in light of the Cold War context, see Alan Wald, "Radical Evil," *Reviews in American History* 9, no. 2 (June 1981), 260–265.

87. Arendt, "Introduction," *The Life of the Mind*, 4. Very good on the connections between evil and thoughtlessness are two chapters in Richard Bernstein, *Hannah Arendt and the Jewish Question* (Cambridge, Mass.: MIT Press, 1996).

88. Arendt, "Introduction," *Life of the Mind*, 5. On her views, see Canovan, *Hannah Arendt: A Reinterpretation*, 178f. For a similar position, see Stanley Hauerwas with David B. Burrell, "Self-Deception and Autobiography: Reflections on Speer's *Inside the Third Reich*," in Hauerwas, Richard Bondi, and Burrell, *Truthfulness and Tragedy: Further Investigations in Christian Ethics* (Notre Dame, Ind.: University of Notre Dame Press, 1977), 95.

89. Friedlander, "The 'Final Solution': On the Unease in Historical Interpretation," in *Lessons and Legacies: The Meaning of the Holocaust in a Changing World*, ed. Peter Hayes (Evanston, Ill.: Northwestern University Press, 1991), 24–25.

90. Arendt, *Responsibility and Judgment* (New York: Schocken Books, 2003), 176. Hereafter, citations appear in the text.

91. On openness to plurality in Arendt, see Young-Bruehl, *Why Arendt Matters*, 166.

92. Hoess, *Commandant of Auschwitz: The Autobiography of Rudolf Hoess*, trans. Constantine FitzGibbon (Cleveland: World Publishing, 1959), 198.

93. Robert Jay Lifton, *The Nazi Doctors: Medical Killing and the Psychology of Genocide* (1986; New York: Basic Books, 2000), 175–176.

94. On the essential elements of Nazi ideology, see Claudia Koonz, *The Nazi Conscience* (Cambridge, Mass.: Harvard University Press, 2003), 6.

95. Gitta Sereny, *Into That Darkness: An Examination of Conscience* (New York: Vintage, 1983), 201.

96. Gitta Sereny, *Albert Speer: His Battle with Truth* (New York: Alfred A. Knopf, 1995), 222, 208.

97. Sereny, *Into That Darkness*, 164.

98. On the Heidegger connection to thinking, see the passing reference in Stephen Miller, "A Note on the Banality of Evil," *Wilson Quarterly* 22, no. 4 (1998),

54. On thinking in Arendt's hierarchy, see Steve Buckler, "Coming Out of Hiding: Hannah Arendt on Thinking in Dark Times," *European Legacy* 6, no. 5 (2001), 615–631.

Chapter 2. A Sky That Never Cared Less

1. David A. Bell, *The First Total War: Napoleon's Europe and the Birth of Warfare as We Know It* (Boston: Houghton Mifflin, 2007).

2. Michael Walzer, *Just and Unjust Wars: A Moral Argument with Historical Illustrations* (1977; 2nd ed., New York: Basic Books, 1992), 247, 251f. On how the illusion of Just War may, ironically, sanction killing, see Andrew Fiala, *The Just War Myth: The Moral Illusions of War* (Lanham, Md.: Rowman and Littlefield, 2008). For the argument that Just War has been, unfortunately, irrelevant to the conduct of warfare, see Hugo Slim, *Killing Civilians: Method, Madness, and Morality in War* (New York: Columbia University Press, 2008).

3. As quoted in David M. Kennedy, *Freedom from Fear: The American People in Depression and War, 1939–1945* (New York: Oxford University Press, 1999), 425; Frank Freidel, *Franklin D. Roosevelt: A Rendezvous with Destiny* (New York: Backbay Books, 1990), 324.

4. Ian Patterson, *Guernica and Total War* (Cambridge, Mass.: Harvard University Press, 2007), 29.

5. Auden, "New Year Letter (January 1, 1940)," in W. H. Auden, *Collected Poems*, ed. Edward Mendelson (New York: Modern Library, 2007), 220.

6. The most compelling account of the Nanking massacre is Iris Chang, *The Rape of Nanking: The Forgotten Holocaust of World War II* (New York: Basic Books, 1977). For a fuller accounting of the atrocity, see Joshua Fogel, ed. *The Nanjing Massacre in History and Historiography* (Berkeley: University of California Press, 2000).

7. Douhet, *The Command of the Air*, trans. Dino Ferrari (New York: Coward-McCann, 1942).

8. Quoted in Kennedy, *Freedom from Fear*, 131.

9. For the text of Roosevelt's message, "Appeal of President Franklin D. Roosevelt on Aerial Bombardment of Civilian Populations," 1 Sept. 1939, http://dannen.com/decision/int-law.html. For renewed expressions of this position, see "President Renews Plea on Bombings," *New York Times* (19 Sept. 1939), 1.

10. "Hitler Promises Limited Bombing," *New York Times* (1 Sept. 1939), 16; "Halifax Text on Bombing of Civilians," *New York Times* (14 Sept. 1939), 8.

11. "21 Civilians Killed in Raid on Warsaw," *New York Times* (3 Sept. 1939), 1; "Poles Charge Aerial Gas Attacks on Cities As Germany Agrees to 'Humanize' the War," *New York Times* (4 Sept. 1939), 1.

12. Davies, *No Simple Victory: World War II in Europe, 1939–1945* (New York: Viking, 2006), 79.

13. Essential to understanding the role of air power in this period is Michael S. Sherry, *The Rise of American Air Power: The Creation of Armageddon* (New Haven: Yale University Press, 1987). Also, Robert A. Pape, *Bombing to Win: Air Power and*

Coercion in War (Ithaca, N.Y.: Cornell University Press, 1996), 254–313. Pape argues that air power directed against civilian centers is less important for securing victory than the ability to render an enemy's army ineffective. Also, John Buckley, *Air Power in the Age of Total War* (Bloomington: Indiana University Press, 1999), 4–6; R. J. Overy, *The Air War: 1939–1945* (New York: Stein and Day, 1981).

14. Ronald Schaffer, *Wings of Judgment: American Bombing in World War II* (New York: Oxford University Press, 1985), 36. Also Schaffer, "American Military Ethics in World War II: The Bombing of German Civilians," *Journal of American History* 67 (Sept. 1980), 318–334; Kenneth P. Werrell, "The Strategic Bombing of Germany in World War II: Costs and Accomplishments," *Journal of American History* 73 (Dec. 1986).

15. Gerhard L. Weinberg, *A World at Arms: A Global History of World War II* (Cambridge: Cambridge University Press, 1994), 48f.

16. Russell F. Weigley, *The American Way of War: A History of United States Military Strategy and Policy* (New York: Macmillan, 1973), 354; Rhodes, *Making*, 469; Richard B. Frank, *Downfall: The End of the Imperial Japanese Empire* (New York: Penguin Books, 1999), 41.

17. "Bombing of Cities Poll" (13 Dec. 1941), in George H. Gallup, *The Gallup Poll: Public Opinion, 1935–1971* (New York: Random House, 1971), I, 311.

18. Ronald H. Spector, *Eagle Against the Sun: The American War with Japan* (New York: Vintage Books, 1985), 154; Robert Dallek, *Franklin D. Roosevelt and American Foreign Policy, 1932–1945* (New York: Oxford University Press, 1979), 334.

19. Capt. Ted W. Lawson, *Thirty Seconds Over Tokyo* (New York: Pocket Star Books, 2004), 65; Paolo E. Coletta, "Launching the Doolittle Raid on Japan, April 18, 1942," *Pacific Historical Review* 62 (Fall 1993), 73–86.

20. Lawson, *Thirty Seconds*, 82.

21. Joanna Doolittle Hoppes, *Calculated Risk: The Extraordinary Life of Jimmy Doolittle—Aviation Pioneer and World War II Hero* (Santa Monica, Calif.: Santa Monica Press, 2005), 212.

22. Craig Nelson, *The First Heroes: The Extraordinary Story of the Doolittle Raid—America's First World War II Victory* (New York: Penguin Books, 2003), 142, 145, 148.

23. Gen. James H. "Jimmy" Doolittle, with Carroll V. Glines, *I Could Never Be So Lucky Again* (New York: Bantam Books, 1992) 246. For the view that the raid was less benign and a harbinger of immoral bombing, especially since it was originally intended to occur at night, when accuracy would be lessened, see Sherry, *Rise*, 122–124. One analyst claims that fifty Japanese were killed in the raid, and that "over one hundred houses damaged." See Conrad Black, *Franklin Delano Roosevelt: Champion of Freedom* (New York: Public Affairs, 2003), 726–727.

24. Doolittle, with Glines, *Never Be So Lucky Again*, 246.

25. For Walzer's brilliant analysis, see *Just and Unjust Wars*, 251–262. James Turner Johnson remarks, contra Walzer, that all nations feel at some point that they may be under an ultimate threat and that their cause is just. If so, then should the rights of civilians have a hardier immunity? Johnson, "The Significance of History for the Restraint of War: Two Perspectives," in Johnson, *Just War and the Restraint*

of War: A Moral and Historical Inquiry (Princeton, N.J.: Princeton University Press, 1981), 20–25. On "dirty hands," see Walzer, "Political Action: The Problem of Dirty Hands," *Philosophy and Public Affairs* 2 (Winter 1973), 160–180. Other questions for Walzer are the degree to which all nations see their wars as justified by the highest ideals, and how nations at war will recognize that their actions cross the line of justified war actions.

26. Doolittle, with Glines, *Never Be So Lucky Again*, 259.

27. Roosevelt, "Radio Address Following Declaration of War with Japan," 9 Dec. 1941, http://ibiblio.org/pha/7-2-188/188-32.html.

28. John W. Dower, *War Without Mercy: Race and Power in the Pacific War* (New York: Pantheon, 1986), 36.

29. "Stimson Warns West Coast to Expect Jap Reprisal Raid," *Los Angeles Times* (29 May 1942), 1; Max Hill, "Tokyo Face-Saving Trick After Raid Backfires," *Los Angeles Times* (27 July 1942), 2; "Raids on Japanese Cities Urged," *Los Angeles Times* (14 June 1942), 8. American lives were lost in the raid, in large part, because the pilots had to take off farther than intended from the targets. This meant that they would lack sufficient fuel to make it to preplanned landing zones in China.

30. "Gas at Midnight," *Time* (3 May 1943), http://www.time.com/time/printout/0,8816,774485,00 html; W. H. Lawrence, "President Solemn," *New York Times* (9 June 1943), 1. Roosevelt had also issued a warning against employing poison gas in a White House News Release (5 June 1942), http://www.ibiblio.org/pha/policy/1942/42060b.html.

31. Greg Goebel, "A History of Chemical and Biological Warfare," http://greyfalcon.us/A%20History%of%20Chemical.htm; Barton J. Bernstein, "America's Biological Warfare Program in the Second World War," *Journal of Strategic Studies* 11 (Sept. 1998), 300–301; Robert Harris and Jeremy Paxman, *A Higher Form of Killing: The Secret Story of Gas and Germ Warfare* (London: Chatto and Windus, 1983), 62–64; Tim Cook, "'Against God-Inspired Conscience': The Reception of Gas Warfare as a Weapon of Mass Destruction, 1915–1939," *War and Society* 18 (May 2000), 47–69.

32. "Winston Churchill's Secret Poison Gas Memo" (7 June 1944), http://globalresearch.ca/articles/CHU407A.html. On the memo, see Harris and Paxman, *Higher Form*, 128–132.

33. "Memorandum of Conversation with General Marshall," 29 May 1945, Record 107, Stimson Safe File, National Security Archives. During the war, on a visit to an army installation, Stimson was impressed by the ability of forces to employ poison gas in test scenarios. Stimson Diary, 10 Feb. 1943, Stimson Papers, Yale University, Reel 8, microfilm edition. General Douglas MacArthur, American commander in the Pacific, and John J. McCloy, assistant secretary of war, agreed with Marshall.

34. John Toland, *The Rising Sun: The Decline and Fall of the Japanese Empire, 1936–1945* (New York: Random House, 1940), 648; Max Hastings, *Retribution: The Battle for Japan, 1944–45* (New York: Alfred A. Knopf, 2008), 247–265.

35. Bill D. Ross, *Iwo Jima: The Legacy of Valor* (New York: Vanguard Press, 1985), 80.

36. Matthews, *The Assault* (New York: Venture Press, 1947), 37.

37. For the higher casualty figures, see Robert P. Newman, *Truman and the*

Hiroshima Cult (East Lansing: Michigan State University Press, 1995), 3. For the lower figures, see Toland, *The Rising Sun*, 669. For overall figures on this campaign, see Frank, *Downfall*, 140.

38. Ross, *Iwo Jima*, 80.

39. Richard Wheeler, *Iwo* (New York: Lippincott and Crowell, 1980), 13.

40. Black, *Roosevelt*, 996.

41. Gallup, *The Gallup Poll*, I, 469, 483, 521–522.

42. Bernstein, "Truman and the A-Bomb: Targeting Noncombatants, Using the Bomb, and Defending the 'Decision,'" *Journal of Military History* 62 (July 1998), 563; Bernstein, "Why We Didn't Use Poison Gas in World War II," *American Heritage* (Aug.–Sept. 1985), online, www.americanheritage.com/articles/magazine/ah/1985/5/1985_5_40.shtml. On biological and chemical weapons, see Bernstein, "America's Biological Warfare Program in the Second World War," *Journal of Strategic Studies* 11 (Sept. 1998), 292–317.

43. After the war, Truman wrote that he considered atomic weapons "far worse" than "gas and biological weapons because it affects the civilian population and murders them wholesale." See Barton J. Bernstein, "Truman and the A-Bomb," 562.

44. On German nerve gas programs, see Harris and Paxman, *Higher Form of Killing*, 53f. On Speer's role in deciding against Himmler and others on nerve gas use, see Seymour M. Hersh, *Chemical and Biological Warfare: America's Hidden Arsenal* (Indianapolis: Bobbs-Merrill, 1968), 7–12.

45. Pape, *Bombing to Win*, 103.

46. *The Diaries of Sir Alexander Cadogan, 1938–1945*, ed. David Dilks (London: Cassell, 1971), 283.

47. Quoted in Richard Rhodes, *The Making of the Atomic Bomb* (New York: Simon and Schuster, 1986), 466.

48. Ronald Schaffer, "American Military Ethics in World War II: The Bombing of German Civilians," *Journal of American History* 67 (Sept. 1980), 319–320. On American bombing in Europe, A. C. Grayling's highly critical account, *Among the Dead Cities: The History and Moral Legacy of the WW II Bombing of Civilians in Germany and Japan* (New York: Walker, 2006). Also critical is Sherry, *Rise*, 117. Excellent on American strategy, its promise and limits, is Conrad C. Crane, *Bombs, Cities, and Civilians: American Airpower Strategy in World War II* (Lawrence: University of Kansas Press, 1993). A compelling narrative account is in Geoffrey Perret, *Winged Victory: The Army Air Forces in World War II* (New York: Random House, 1993).

49. Quoted in Sherry, *Rise*, 291.

50. Weigley, *American Way of War*, 359.

51. Thomas Childers, "'*Facilis descensus averni est*': The Allied Bombing of Germany and the Issue of German Suffering," *Central European History* 38, no. 1 (2005), 102–104. Stafford, "At the Bombing Site," www.poetryfoundation.org/archive/poem.html?id=171499.

52. Maj. Gen. Haywood S. Hansell, *Strategic Air War Against Japan* (Washington, D.C.: U.S. Government Printing Office, 1980), 60.

53. Curtis E. LeMay, with MacKinlay Kantor, *Mission with LeMay: My Story*

(Garden City, N.Y.: Doubleday, 1965), 355. On the fire raids as part and parcel of total war, see Crane, *Bombs*, 133–134.

54. "Special Fire Bomb Used to Set Blazes in Japan," *New York Times* (11 March 1945), 13.

55. Martin Sheridan, "Giant Tokyo Fires Blackened B-29s," *New York Times* (11 March 1945), 14.

56. LeMay, *Mission*, 352.

57. Warren Moscow, "City's Heart Gone," *New York Times* (11 March 1945), 1.

58. Sahr Conway-Lanz, *Collateral Damage: Americans, Noncombatant Immunity, and Atrocity After World War II* (New York: Routledge, 2006), 1.

59. LeMay, *Mission*, 384.

60. *Fire and the Air War*, ed. Horatio Bond, Chief Engineer, National Fire Protection Association (Boston: National Fire Protection Association, 1946), 193.

61. "Tokyo in Flames," *New York Times* (12 March 1945), 18.

62. Moscow, "City's Heart Gone."

63. James Turner Johnson, *Can Modern War Be Just?* (New Haven: Yale University Press, 1984); Johnson, *Just War and the Restraint of War.*

64. A. C. Grayling, *Among the Dead Cities*, 272; Glover, *Humanity: A Moral History of the Twentieth Century* (New Haven: Yale University Press, 1999).

65. Robert P. Newman, *Truman and the Hiroshima Cult*, 115f. LeMay, *Mission*, 384.

66. Nozick, *Anarchy, State, and Utopia* (New York: Basic Books, 1974), 99, 341, n.7. Against Nozick's views, as earlier expressed on this issue, see Thomas Nagel, "War and Massacre," *Philosophy and Public Affairs* 1 (Winter 1972), 139–140.

67. Walzer, *Just and Unjust Wars*, 251–262.

68. The fires of contention continue to burn. See *History Wars: The Enola Gay and Other Battles for the American Past*, ed. Edward T. Linenthal and Tom Engelhardt (New York: Henry Holt, 1996).

69. Quoted in Rhodes, *Making*, 742.

70. Memorandum from Groves to the Chief of Staff, 6 Aug. 1945, RG 77, MED Records, Top Secret Documents, File 56. National Security Archive On-Line. "The Atomic Bomb and the End of World War II: A Collection of Primary Sources," http://www.gwu.edu/~nsarchiv/NSAEBB/NSAEBB162/index2.htm.

71. Rhodes, *Making*, 734.

72. Ronald Takaki, *Hiroshima: Why America Dropped the Atomic Bomb* (Boston: Little, Brown, 1995), 46–47.

73. Bernstein, "Correspondence," 220; Bernstein, "Roosevelt, Truman and the Atomic Bomb, 1941–1945: A Reinterpretation," *Political Science Quarterly* 90, no. 1 (Spring 1975), 62; Bernstein, "Understanding the Atomic Bomb and the Japanese Surrender: Missed Opportunities, Little-Known Disasters, and Modern Memory," *Diplomatic History* 19 (Spring 1995), 235; Sherwin, *A World Destroyed: Hiroshima and Its Legacy*, 3d ed., (Stanford, Calif.: Stanford University Press, 2003), 5. Marshall quoted in Leonard Mosley, *Marshall: Hero for Our Times* (New York: Hearst Books, 1982), 338. For support of Marshall's view, see Herbert Feis, *The Atomic Bomb and the End of World War II* (Princeton, N.J.: Princeton University Press, 1966), 189.

74. Stimson and McGeorge Bundy, *On Active Service in Peace and War* (New

York: Harper and Brothers, 1948), 621; Stimson Papers, 11 Jan. 1945, Yale University, Reel 9, microfilm edition.

75. Hastings, *Retribution*, 513.

76. Gregg Herken, *Brotherhood of the Bomb: The Tangled Lives and Loyalties of Robert Oppenheimer, Ernest Lawrence, and Edward Teller* (New York: Henry Holt, 2002), 132; Rhodes, *Making*, 639–640. On Stimson, see Sean L. Molloy, *Atomic Tragedy: Henry L. Stimson and the Decision to Use the Bomb Against Japan* (Ithaca, N.Y.: Cornell University Press, 2008).

77. Stimson Diary (15 Oct. 1943), Stimson Papers, Yale University, Reel 8, microfilm edition.

78. Stimson and Bundy, *Active Service*, 632–633.

79. Barton J. Bernstein, "Eclipsed by Hiroshima and Nagasaki: Early Thinking About Tactical Nuclear Weapons," *International Security* 15 (Spring 1991), 156; Conrad C. Crane, "'Contrary to Our National Ideals': American Strategic Bombing of Civilians in World War II," in *Civilians in the Path of War*, ed. Mark C. Grimsley and Clifford J. Rogers (Lincoln: University of Nebraska Press, 2002), 226. On Stimson's failure to control area bombing and to push moral issues concerning the atomic bomb, see Geoffrey Hodgson, *The Colonel: The Life and Wars of Henry Stimson, 1867–1950* (New York: Alfred A. Knopf, 1990), 325, 341; Robert C. Batchelder, *The Irreversible Decision, 1932–1950* (Boston: Houghton Mifflin, 1961), 186–187. For Stimson's problem with details, as regards the atomic bomb, see Molloy, *Atomic Tragedy*, 186. For a brilliant critique of historical approaches to the bomb, from a tragic and postmodern perspective, see Walter A. Davis, *Deracination: Historicity, Hiroshima, and the Tragic Imperative* (Albany: State University of New York Press, 2001).

80. Rhodes, *Making*, 640.

81. Stimson and Bundy, *Active Service*, 333, 376 passim. On Stimson's limited control over military operations, see Rhodes, *Making*, 639–640. Also, Bernstein, "Eclipsed by Hiroshima and Nagasaki," 152–156.

82. "Memorandum of Conference with the President," 6 June 1945, Stimson Papers, Yale University, Reel 9, microfilm edition.

83. On the concept of the "Cold Joke," see Glover, *Humanity*, 36–37.

84. Frank, *Downfall*, 271, 277.

85. Truman, "Diary," Harry S. Truman Presidential Library, online version. http://www.trumanlibrary.org/whistlestop/study_collections/bomb/small/mb.htm. A transcript of the diary entry may be found in *Off the Record: The Private Papers of Harry S. Truman*, ed. Robert H. Ferrell (New York: Harper and Row, 1980), 52–53. Also, Barton J. Bernstein, "Truman at Potsdam: His Secret Diary," *Foreign Service Journal* (July–Aug. 1980), 30–31.

86. A few years earlier, Stimson was in London surveying the damage caused to civilian areas by German bombs. He considered the attacks heinous and marveled at the resiliency of the British populace. He did not, later, show this same type of concern about the negative aspects of bombing civilian centers, at least to a significant degree. Stimson Diary, 19 July 1943, Yale University, Reel 8, microfilm edition.

87. Stimson Diary, 17 July 1945, Yale University, Reel 9, microfilm edition.

88. Stimson, Diary, 30 May 1945, Yale University, microfilm edition.

89. LeMay, *Mission*, 383.

90. Luis W. Alvarez, *Alvarez: Adventures of a Physicist* (New York: Basic Books, 1987), 7–8, 3.

91. Compton, *Atomic Quest: A Personal Narrative* (New York: Oxford University Press, 1956), 309.

92. For a thoughtful discussion that decides the use of the bomb was necessary, see McGeorge Bundy, *Choices About the Bomb in the First Fifty Years* (New York: Random House, 1988), 58–97. For the view that there was vigorous ethical debate in the government, see Batchelder, *Irreversible*, 107.

93. Bernstein, "Truman and the A-Bomb," 558–559. On Stimson as the major player on atomic policy, see Richard G. Hewlett and Oscar Anderson, Jr., *A History of the United States Atomic Energy Commission: The New World, 1939–1946* (University Park: Pennsylvania State University Press, 1962), I, 406f.

94. Stimson Diary, 24 July 1945, Stimson Papers, Yale University, Reel 9, microform edition. On Stimson's discussion with Groves, see Leslie R. Groves, *Now It Can Be Told: The Story of the Manhattan Project* (New York: Harper and Brothers, 1962), 274. Groves admitted that Stimson had been correct in his judgment. Also, on the confrontation over Kyoto, see Rhodes, *Making*, 640.

95. Stimson Diary, 15 May 1945, Stimson Papers, Yale University, Reel 9, microfilm edition.

96. "Memorandum for Mr. Harrison," Notes of the Interim Committee Meetings, for 6 June and 21 June 1945. MED Records, H-B Files, National Security Administration. Hodgson, *The Colonel*, 313.

97. *Talking with Harry: Candid Conversations with President Harry S. Truman*, ed. Ralph E. Weber (Wilmington, Del.: Scholarly Resources, 2001), 5.

98. Barton J. Bernstein, "Reconsidering the 'Atomic General': Leslie R. Groves," *Journal of Military History* 67 (July 2003), 896.

99. Batchelder, *Irreversible Decision*, 186–187. Truman could show insight and ask proper questions. At a meeting with the Joint Chiefs of Staff and others, he discussed aspects of the planned invasion of the Japanese islands. Might the invasion of Japan "by white men" threaten to unify the Japanese? Stimson admitted that this was possible. But the point was forgotten, and plans for the invasion went ahead. Complications appear to not be the main diet for government officials. "Minutes of Meeting Held at the White House," 18 June 1945, Record Group 218, Records of the Joint Chiefs of Staff, Central Decimal Files, 1942–1945, Box 198, National Security Documents, online edition.

100. *Off the Record*, 55.

101. Truman, *Memoirs by Harry S. Truman: Year of Decisions* (Garden City, N.Y.: Doubleday, 1955), I, 420.

102. A few government officials did raise concerns, but they were practical rather than moral. Bombs were acceptable as a last resort, after additional diplomacy, such as dropping the demand for unconditional surrender, or by setting up a demonstration. Ralph A. Bard, "Memorandum on the Use of S-1 Bomb," 27 June 1945, Rg-77, MED, H-B files. National Security Administration. George Harrison, an assistant to Henry Stimson, had a few conversations with Bard about his proposal. He sent it

along to Secretary Stimson, noting that it represented a shift in Bard's perspective and was now at odds with the recommendations of the Interim Committee that no warning be issued. Nor was there any desire on the part of Truman and Stimson to change the conditions for surrender. The memo, suffice it to say, went nowhere. Harrison, "Memorandum for the Secretary of War," 28 June 1945, Rg77, MED, H-B Files. National Security Administration. On Bard, see Batchelder, *Irreversible Decision*, 58–59. Also recommending a shift in the government's position on unconditional surrender was Joseph C. Grew, who had been ambassador to Japan. Grew, *Turbulent Era: A Diplomatic Record of Forty Years, 1904–1945*, ed. Walter Johnson (Boston: Houghton Mifflin, 1952), II, 1429.

103. On the radio broadcasts in response to Hiroshima, see the John Hersey Files in *New Yorker* Magazine Archive, New York Public Library, Box, 966. On the reception of Hersey's book, see Paul S. Boyer, *By the Bomb's Early Light: American Thought and Culture at the Dawn of the Atomic Age* (New York: Pantheon, 1985), 203–210; Boyer, "Exotic Resonances: Hiroshima in American Memory," *Diplomatic History* 19 (Spring 1995), 299. Also, Michael J. Yavenditti, "John Hersey and the American Conscience: The Reception of *Hiroshima*," in *Hiroshima's Shadow*, ed. Kai Bird and Lawrence Lifschultz (Stony Creek, Conn.: Pamphleteer's Press, 1998), 288–302. Originally published in *Pacific Historical Review* 43 (Feb. 1974); Spencer R. Weart, *Nuclear Fear: A History of Images* (Cambridge, Mass.: Harvard University Press, 1988), 107–109.

104. Martin J. Sherwin, "Hiroshima as Politics and History," *Journal of American History* 82, no. 3 (Dec. 1995), 1085. For a defense of what Stimson wrote, see Robert P. Newman, "Hiroshima and the Trashing of Henry Stimson," *New England Quarterly* 71 (March 1998), 5–32. For a long, but not too helpful, analysis of Stimson's moral quandaries and claims, see John Bonnett, "Jekyll and Hyde: Henry L. Stimson, *Mentalite*, and the Decision to Use the Atomic Bomb on Japan," *War in History* 4, no. 2 (1997), 174–212. On the genesis of Stimson's response, see Barton J. Bernstein, "Seizing the Contested Terrain of Early Nuclear History: Stimson, Conant, and Their Allies Explain the Decision to Use the Atomic Bomb," *Diplomatic History* 17 (Winter 1993), 35–72.

105. Stimson, "The Decision to Use the Bomb," reprinted in *The Atomic Bomb: The Great Decision*, ed. Paul R. Baker (New York: Holt, Rinehart and Winston, 1968), 12. Hereafter, page references appear in the text.

106. Stimson Diary, 4 Aug. 1943, Yale University, Reel 8, microfilm edition.

107. Some argue that it was Japanese military vulnerability rather than conventional or atomic bombing that brought about surrender. See Robert A. Pape, "Why Japan Surrendered," *International Security* 18 (Fall 1993), 154–201.

108. On the numbers dispute over the invasion toll, see Barton J. Bernstein, "Reconsidering Truman's Claim," 54–95. Suffice it to say, Bernstein finds Truman's and Stimson's figure of high losses to be grossly inflated. However, even if the numbers of Americans killed and wounded were lower, the question remains whether Truman would have been willing to sanction the loss of perhaps 10,000 Americans in lieu of using the bomb. Unlikely.

109. Alperovitz, *Atomic Diplomacy: Hiroshima and Potsdam* (New York: Simon and Schuster, 1965), 14, 237–242; Alperovitz, *The Decision to Use the Atomic Bomb*

(New York: HarperCollins, 1995). Contra Alperovitz, for example, see Robert James Maddox, "Atomic Diplomacy: A Study in Creative Writing," *Journal of American History* 59 (March 1973), 925–939. For a middle-ground position, Barton J. Bernstein, "Correspondence: Marshall, Truman, and the Decision to Drop the Bomb," *International Security* 16 (Winter 1991–92), 204–221; J. Samuel Walker, *Prompt and Utter Destruction: Truman and the Use of Atomic Bombs Against Japan* (1997; rev. ed., Chapel Hill: University of North Carolina Press, 2004). A good historiographical overview is J. Samuel Walker, "Recent Literature on Truman's Atomic Bomb Decision: A Search for a Middle Ground," *Diplomatic History* 29 (April 2005), 311–334.

110. "Report of Protestant Church Leaders on Atomic Warfare," *New York Times*, 6 March 1946, 15.

111. James F. Childress, "Reinhold Niebuhr's Critique of Pacifism," *Review of Politics* 36 (Oct. 1974), 467–491.

112. James B. Hershberg, "A Footnote on Hiroshima and Atomic Morality: Conant, Niebuhr, and an 'Emotional Clergyman,'" 1945–1946," *Society for Historians of American Foreign Relations* (Dec. 2002), online edition: www.shafr.org/newsletter/2002.dec/hiroshima.htm.

113. Harvey Bundy conversation with Stimson, quoted in Hodgson, *The Colonel*, 333.

114. Sherry, *Rise*, 219f. Sherry sees such "technological fanaticism" in the steady increase in bombing power against civilian and military targets in general.

115. Conant to Bradford Young, 7 Dec. 1945, Conant Presidential Papers, Box 273, Pusey Library, Harvard University. Another factor in the use of the bomb was retribution and revenge against Japan. This is not to say that had the bombs been available earlier, they might not have been used against the Germans. All that can be said with certainty is that moral luck came into play for the Germans—they had bowed out of the war just prior to the successful experiment with the atomic bomb; Japan, in contrast, had not. But certainly, as John Dower and others have suggested, the particular enmity against Japan after Pearl Harbor, given her inhumane treatment of prisoners of war and the peculiar ferocity of the battles waged at Iwo Jima and Okinawa, combined with a racist view that increasingly saw the Japanese as subhuman, all contributed to making the use of the atomic bomb against Japan more pressing and unexamined. See John W. Dower, *War Without Mercy*; Takaki, *Hiroshima*, 93–100.

116. Interestingly, American scientists and strategists seemed unaware, or unconcerned, about Japanese efforts to develop a nuclear arms program. See Newman, *Truman*, 131–133; Rhodes, *Making*, 458; Frank, *Downfall*, 253f. On intelligence concerning the German effort, see William L. Laurence, *Man and Atoms: The Discovery, the Uses and the Future of Atomic Energy* (New York: Simon and Schuster, 1959), 88.

117. Quoted in William Lanouette, with Bela Szilard, *Genius in the Shadows: A Biography of Leo Szilard* (New York: Charles Scribner's Sons, 1992), 259. Once convinced that German atomic possibilities were a fantasy, Szilard led the opposition against use of atomic weapons. He later wrote an essay wondering whether he and other scientists might be justly charged as war criminals. See Szilard, "My Trial as

a War Criminal," in *The Voice of the Dolphins and Other Stories* (Stanford: Stanford University Press, 1989), 103–116.

118. Davis, *Lawrence and Oppenheimer*, 224.

119. Bethe quoted in Batchelder, *Irreversible Decision*, 43.

120. Quotes are in Charles Thorpe, *Oppenheimer: The Tragic Intellect* (Chicago: University of Chicago Press, 2006), 152–153, 157.

121. R. R. Wilson, "Hiroshima: The Scientists' Social and Political Reaction," *Proceedings of the American Philosophical Society* 140, no. 3 (Sept. 1996), 350–351.

122. Leo Szilard, *His Version of the Facts: Selected Recollections and Correspondence*, ed. Spencer R. Weart and Gertrude Weiss Szilard (Cambridge, Mass.: MIT Press, 1978), 186; Lanouette, *Genius*, 272–273.

123. Rotblat, "Leaving the Bomb Project," in *Assessing the Nuclear Age: Selections from the "Bulletin of Atomic Scientists,"* ed. Len Ackland and Steven McGuire (Chicago: Educational Foundation for Nuclear Science, 1986), 19–21.

124. "Recommendations on the Immediate Use of Nuclear Weapons," RG77, MED Records, H-B Files, Folder 17, National Security Administration, Microfilm edition.

125. Quoted in David C. Cassidy, *J. Robert Oppenheimer and the American Century* (New York: Pi Press, 2005), 241.

126. Alice Kimball Smith, *A Peril and a Hope: The Scientists' Movement in America, 1945–47* (Cambridge, Mass.: MIT Press, 1970), 377.

127. The full text of the Franck report is contained as an appendix to Smith, *Peril*, 378–379.

128. Kershaw, *Fateful Choices: Ten Decisions That Changed the World, 1940–1941* (New York: Penguin Press, 2007).

129. Janis, "Groupthink Among Policy Makers," in *Sanctions for Evil: Sources of Social Destructiveness* (Boston: Beacon Press, 1972), 71–89.

130. Bruce Kuklick, *Blind Oracles: Intellectuals and War from Kennan to Kissinger* (Princeton, N.J.: Princeton University Press, 2006); Richard E. Neustadt and Ernest R. May, *Thinking in Time: The Uses of History for Decision Makers* (New York: Free Press, 1986), 1–16.

131. Quoted in Rhodes, *Making*, 596.

132. R. B. Brandt, "Utilitarianism and the Rules of War," *Philosophy and Public Affairs* 1 (Winter 1972), 161.

133. Margalit, *The Ethics of Memory* (Cambridge, Mass.: Harvard University Press, 2002), 8–9, 32–40.

134. Barton J. Bernstein on the "as if" scenarios, in "Truman and the Atomic Bomb," 565f; "Understanding the Atomic Bomb," 227–273. On civilian losses, see Kenneth P. Worrell, *Blankets of Fire: U.S. Bombers over Japan During World War II* (Washington, D.C.: Smithsonian Institution Press, 1996), 163–166.

135. Some contend that the atomic bombs had little or no effect on bringing about Japanese surrender. See Tsuyoshi Hasegawa, *Racing the Enemy: Stalin, Truman, and the Surrender of Japan* (Cambridge, Mass.: Belknap Press, 2005); Richard Minear, "Atomic Holocaust: Some Reflections," *Diplomatic History* 19 (Spring 1995), 347–365. In contrast, see Newman, *Truman and the Hiroshima Cult*, 49, 185–197; Robert James Maddox, "Atomic Diplomacy," 925–934. On how Hirohito sought to

delay surrender and Truman's desire to hasten it, see Herbert P. Bix, "Japan's Delayed Surrender: A Reinterpretation," *Diplomatic History* 49 (Spring 1995), 223.

136. For an excellent discussion of the logic of the atomic bombs without skirting the moral problems, see Michael Bess, *Choices Under Fire: Moral Dimensions of World War II* (New York: Alfred A. Knopf, 2006), 198–253. Bess is surely correct when he notes that "World War Two was a morally complicated event" (340).

137. *The Price of Vision: The Diary of Henry A. Wallace, 1942–1946*, ed. John Morton Blum (Boston: Houghton Mifflin, 1973), 496.

138. *Washington Post* (25 Oct. 1946), 12; (26 Oct. 1946), 14, 18.

139. Kai Bird and Martin J. Sherwin, *American Prometheus: The Triumph and Tragedy of J. Robert Oppenheimer* (New York: Vintage, 2006), 416–417.

140. This account is drawn from Peter Michelmore, *The Swift Years: The Robert Oppenheimer Story* (New York: Dodd, Mead, 1969), 121. Michelmore places Acheson at the meeting, which is incorrect. The best chronicle of the various accounts will be found in Bird and Sherwin, *American Prometheus*, 323–335. Barton J. Bernstein, citing Oppenheimer's wish to get along with those in power, doubts that such an outburst occurred. See Bernstein, "The Puzzles of Interpreting J. Robert Oppenheimer, His Politics, and the Issues of His Possible Communist Party Membership," in *Reappraising Oppenheimer: Centennial Studies and Reflections*, ed. Cathryn Carson and David A. Hollinger (Berkeley, Calif.: Berkeley Papers in History of Science), vol. 21, 80.

141. As quoted in Nuel Pharr Davis, *Lawrence and Oppenheimer* (New York: Simon and Schuster, 1968), 258.

142. Quoted in Janet Landman, *Regret: The Persistence of the Possible* (New York: Oxford University Press, 1993), 9.

143. "Expiation," *Time* 51 (23 Feb. 1948), 94.

144. Bird and Sherwin, *American Prometheus*, 324.

145. Bernstein, "The Puzzles," 78, 81, 88. On the regret issue, see David Holloway, "Parallel Lives? Oppenheimer and Khariton," in *Reappraising*, 124. Michael D. Gordin finds Oppenheimer's remarks about regret immediately after the dropping of the bombs unusual "rare equivocations." Gordin, *Five Days in August: How World War II Became a Nuclear War* (Princeton, N.J.: Princeton University Press, 2007), 113.

146. Charles Thorpe, *Oppenheimer*, 88.

147. On the "organic necessity" as central, see Cassidy, *Oppenheimer and the American Century*, 211f.

148. For a very involved examination of issues of how an individual may or may not be held responsible in moral terms, see Richard Mason, *Oppenheimer's Choice: Reflections from Moral Philosophy* (Albany: State University of New York Press, 2006).

149. The "cry-baby" characterization comes from Merle Miller, *Plain Speaking: An Oral Biography of Harry S. Truman* (New York: G. P. Putnam's Sons, 1974), 228.

150. Gaita, *A Common Humanity: Thinking About Love and Truth and Justice* (London: Routledge, 2000), 4–5.

151. In 1960, Oppenheimer visited Japan, and in a typically obtuse pronouncement, he stated: "I do not regret that I had something to do with the technical success of the atomic bomb. It isn't that I don't feel bad; it is that I don't feel worse

tonight than I did last night." Bird and Sherwin, *American Prometheus*, photo caption, n.p.

152. "Notes of the Interim Committee Meeting, 31 May 1945," RG77, MED Records, folder n.100, National Security Archives, online edition.

153. Slim, *Killing Civilians*, 3. Slim is not celebrating this sad fact. He intends to demonstrate how widespread and traditional such killing is in order to foster a degree of empathy for civilians that might mitigate somewhat their suffering.

Chapter 3. The Moral Mystery of My Lai

1. On the massacre, see the following accounts: Michael R. Belknap, *The Vietnam War on Trial: The My Lai Massacre and the Court-Martial of Lieutenant Calley* (Lawrence: University Press of Kansas, 2002); Michael Bilton and Kevin Sim, *Four Hours in My Lai* (New York: Viking, 1992); Martin Gershen, *Destroy or Die: The True Story of Mylai* (New Rochelle, N.Y.: Arlington House, 1971); Seymour M. Hersh, *My Lai 4: A Report on the Massacre and Its Aftermath* (New York: Random House, 1970); Richard Hammer, *One Morning in the War: The Tragedy at Son My* (New York: Coward-McCann, 1970); W. R. Peers, Lt. General, *Report of the Department of Army Review of the Preliminary Investigations into the My Lai Incident* (Washington, D.C.: Department of the Army, 1970), I. On the complexities of the hamlet/village distinction and the names of the places, see Hammer, *One Morning*, 31–32. For the sake of simplicity, I will use the term My Lai to encompass the entire killing zone of that day. On the Vietnam War in general, see James William Gibson, *The Perfect War: The War We Couldn't Lose and How We Did* (New York: Vintage, 1988); Stanley Karnow, *Vietnam: A History* (New York: Viking Press, 1983); Guenter Lewy, *America in Vietnam* (New York: Oxford University Press, 1978); George Herring, *America's Longest War: The United States and Vietnam, 1950–1975* (New York: Wiley, 1979). Useful for an overview and relevant documents is James S. Olson and Randy Roberts, *My Lai: A Brief History with Documents* (Boston: Bedford/St. Martins, 1998).

2. Charles A. West, "Testimony," *Department of Army Review* (hereafter, *DOA Review*) v.3, book 28, 1. Pagination for the many books of testimony is confusing. Pages are numbered the same for the summary and for the testimony.

3. Bergthold, "Testimony," *DOA Review*, vol. 3, book 24, 16.

4. Carter, "Testimony, " *DOA Review*, vol. 2, book 24, 29.

5. Stanley, "Testimony," *DOA Review*, vol. 2, book 25, 44.

6. Bunning, "Testimony," *DOA Review*, vol. 2, book 26, 16–17.

7. Stanley, 14; Carter, 32.

8. Bunning, 26.

9. Richard Pendleton, "Testimony," *DOA Review*, vol. 3, book 27, 20.

10. Meadlo, "Transcript of Interview," *New York Times* (25 Nov. 1969), 16; Olson and Roberts, *My Lai*, 36; Stanley, 21; Elmer G. Haywood, *DOA Review*, vol. 3, book 28, 19.

11. Pendleton, 15.

12. The term was applied earlier to Vietnam in general by Jack P. Smith, "Men All Around Me Were Screaming," (Nov. 1965), in *Reporting Vietnam: American Journalism, 1959–1975* (New York: Library of America, 2000), 130.

13. Robert Jay Lifton, *Home from the War: Vietnam Veterans, Neither Victims nor Executioners* (New York: Simon and Schuster, 1973), 37.

14. An excellent summary of reasons offered for the massacre can be found in David L. Anderson, ed., *Facing My Lai: Moving Beyond the Massacre* (Lawrence: University Press of Kansas, 1998), 6.

15. For the case that the soldiers had a moral responsibility that was beyond their legal responsibility to follow orders, see Haskell Fain, "Some Moral Infirmities of Justice," in *Individual and Collective Responsibility: The Massacre at My Lai*, ed. Peter A. French (Cambridge, Mass.: Schenkman, 1972), 32–33.

16. Tim O'Brien, "The Mystery of My Lai," in *Facing My Lai: Moving Beyond the Massacre*, ed. David L. Anderson (Lawrence: University Press of Kansas, 1998), 173–175.

17. Capps, *The Unfinished War: Vietnam and the American Conscience* (Boston: Beacon Press, 1982), 107.

18. Koestler quoted in Viola W. Bernard, Perry Ottenberg, Fritz Redl, "Dehumanization," in *Sanctions for Evil: Sources of Social Destructiveness* (Boston: Beacon Press, 1972), 111.

19. Christopher Lehmann-Haupt, "The Calley Case Not Resolved," *New York Times* (7 Sept. 1971), 37.

20. Katz, *Ordinary People and Extraordinary Evil: A Report on the Beginnings of Evil* (Albany: State University of New York Press, 1993), 102.

21. On how the war was framed, by government officials and newspapers, to focus on issues of individual responsibility below, rather than on institutional and Cold War powers above, see Kendrick Oliver, "Atrocity, Authenticity and American Exceptionalism: (Ir)rationalising the Massacre at My Lai," *Journal of American Studies* 37 (2003); Oliver, *The My Lai Massacre in American History and Memory* (Manchester: Manchester University Press, 2006), 25–26, 55, 59. Focus on the My Lai veterans and the general trauma of Vietnam veterans, in general, can undermine focus on the victims. In this vein, see Jonathan Shay, *Achilles in Vietnam: Combat Trauma and the Undoing of Character* (New York: Scribner, 1994).

22. Peers, *Report*, 7; Bilton and Sim, *Four Hours*, 120–121; Hersh, *My Lai 4*, 62f.

23. Peers, *Report*, 253, xii.

24. The best account of the trial is Belknap, *Vietnam War on Trial*. Also, Seymour M. Hersh, *Cover-Up* (New York: Random House, 1972); William L. Calley, *Lieutenant Calley: His Own Story*, with John Sack (New York: Viking, 1971).

25. "High Court Denies Appeal by Calley," *New York Times* (6 April 1976), 73; Seymour M. Hersh, "Army's Secret Inquiry Charges 43 Mylai Failures to Top Officers," *New York Times* (4 June 1972), 1.

26. Hammer, *The Court-Martial of Lt. Calley* (New York: Coward, McCann & Geoghegan, 1971), 263.

27. "Appeals Court Reinstates Calley Court-Martial Convictions in My Lai Killings," *New York Times* (11 Sept. 1975), 26.

28. "Calley Backs Full Amnesty for Vietnam Evaders" *New York Times* (9 Sept. 1976), 24.

29. Niebuhr, quoted in Robert D. McFadden, "Calley Verdict Brings Home the Anguish of War to Public," *New York Times* (4 April 1971), 56. On the presumed "national trauma" and how it destroyed innocence, see Capps, *The Unfinished War,* 2; Loren Baritz, *Backfire: A History of How American Culture Led Us into Vietnam and Made Us Fight the Way We Did* (New York: William Morrow, 1985), 19f.

30. Quoted in Seymour Hersh, "Hamlet Attack Called 'Point-Blank Murder'" (20 Nov. 1969), in *Reporting Vietnam*, 420.

31. Fred Turner, *Echoes of Combat: The Vietnam War in American Memory* (New York: Anchor Books, 1996), 29. If, after all, Calley and a handful of men were involved in 128 murders, then the rest of the three platoons killed fewer than four hundred civilians. Compare this with the best estimate that about 10 percent of American combat soldiers in Vietnam committed atrocities against Vietnamese civilians and prisoners.

32. The metaphor comes from Tim O'Brien, *The Things They Carried* (New York: Broadway Books, 1990), 1–27.

33. Christian G. Appy, *Working-Class War: American Combat Soldiers and Vietnam* (Chapel Hill: University of North Carolina Press, 1993), 12, 26, 48.

34. Keniston, *The Uncommitted: Alienated Youth in American Society* (New York: Harcourt Brace, and World, 1965), 61, 102–103, 193.

35. Gershen, *Destroy or Die*, 72; Bilton and Sim, *Four Hours*, 329.

36. "Experiencing the Darkness: An Oral History: William G. Eckhardt, Ron Ridenhour, Hugh C. Thompson, Jr.," in *Facing My Lai: Moving Beyond the Massacre*, 37.

37. Mother quoted in Hersh, *My Lai 4*, 181.

38. Hammer, *The Court-Martial*, 54.

39. *Miami Herald* (28 Nov. 1969), 22a; Linda Greenhouse, "The Only Man Convicted for My Lai," *New York Times* (26 Sept. 1974), 17.

40. Will Herberg, *Protestant-Catholic-Jew: An Essay in American Religious Sociology* (New York: Doubleday, 1956), 71f.

41. *Miami Herald* (28 Nov. 1969), 22.

42. Appiah, *Experiments in Ethics* (Cambridge, Mass.: Harvard University Press, 2008), 33–72.

43. Milgram, *Obedience to Authority* (1974, New York: Perennial Classics, 2004), 5–9.

44. Milgram, *Obedience*, 54.

45. For a rejection of the validity of Milgram and his views about Eichmann in all of us, see Daniel Bell, "Is Eichmann in All of Us?" *New York Times* (26 May 1974), 101. Responses to Bell in *New York Times* (30 June 1974), 100. For an overview, see Herbert C. Kelman and V. Lee Hamilton, *Crimes of Obedience: Toward a Social Psychology of Authority and Responsibility* (New Haven: Yale University Press, 1989).

46. Zimbardo, *The Lucifer Effect: Understanding How Good People Turn Evil* (New York: Random House, 2007), 187.

47. Zimbardo, *Lucifer*, 211.

48. Copies of the cards are in *Report of the Department of the Army Review of the*

Preliminary Investigations into the My Lai Incident (Washington, D.C.: U.S. Government Printing Office, 1974), vol. 3, book 4, 9–13.

49. Bergthold, 25.

50. Kinch, "Testimony," *DOA Review*, vol. 2, book 28, 26.

51. Roy Trevino, "Testimony," *DOA Review*, vol. 2, book 27, 25.

52. Trevino, 33, 29.

53. Trevino, 37–38.

54. Hersh, *My Lai 4*, 41–42.

55. Medina, "Testimony," *DOA Review*, vol. 2 book 23, 8.

56. James J. Dursi, "Testimony," *DOA Review*, vol. 2, book 24, 5.

57. Medina, 4, 19.

58. Kinch, 4, 5.

59. James H. Flynn, "Testimony," *DOA Review*, vol. 2, book 28, 2.

60. Abel Flores, "Testimony," *DOA Review*, vol. 2, book 27, 26; George A. Garza, "Testimony," *DOA Review*, vol. 2, book 26, 19.

61. Leo Maroney, "Testimony," *DOA Review*, vol. 2, book 28, 49–50.

62. Pendleton, 32.

63. Bernhardt, 28.

64. Quoted in Hersh, *My Lai 4*, 42.

65. Lifton, *Home*, 65.

66. Appy, *Working-Class War*, 199.

67. Dursi, 26.

68. Quoted in "Calley Backs Full Amnesty for Vietnam Evaders," *New York Times* (9 Sept. 1976), 24.

69. James Reston, "The Massacre of Songmy: Who Is to Blame?" *New York Times* (26 Nov. 1969), 44.

70. Linda Greenhouse, "The Only Man Convicted for My Lai," *New York Times* (26 Sept. 1974), 17; David Nelson, "Rusty Calley: The Man Remains a Mystery," *Miami Herald* (28 Nov. 1969), 1, 22A.

71. Neil Sheehan, "Should We Have War Crime Trials?" *New York Times* (28 May 1971), 5.

72. Hersh, "The My Lai Massacre" (13 Nov. 1969), in *Reporting Vietnam*, 417.

73. Hersh, *My Lai 4*, 21.

74. Bernhardt quoted in Susan Faludi, *Stiffed: The Betrayal of the American Man* (New York: Harper Perennial, 2000), 334.

75. Hersh, *My Lai 4*, 19–25.

76. Hersh, *My Lai 4*, 134.

77. Jay Buchanon, "Testimony," *DOA Review*, vol. 2, book 25, 41.

78. Fall, "'Unrepentant, Unyielding': An Interview with Vietcong Prisoners" (Jan. 1967), in *Reporting Vietnam*, 192.

79. Hersh, *My Lai 4*, 8; Hammer, *One Morning*, 202–203.

80. Quoted in Hammer, *Court-Martial*, 263.

81. Hammer, *Court-Martial*, 263, 240.

82. Meadlo Interview, *New York Times*, 16.

83. Charles Sledge, "Testimony," *DOA Review*, vol. 2, book 25, 43.

84. Dennis I. Conti, "Testimony," *DOA Review*, vol. 2, book 24, 32.

85. Joseph W. Konwinski, *DOA Review*, vol. 2, book 24, 6.

86. Bunning, 16.

87. Thomas R. Partsch, "Testimony," *DOA Review*, vol. 2, book 26, 27.

88. Buchanon, 40.

89. Moss, "Testimony," *DOA Review*, vol. 2, book 26, 17.

90. Bunning, 48, 33.

91. Trevino, 25.

92. Garza, 19–20.

93. Stanley, 19, 37.

94. West, 13.

95. Dursi, 11.

96. Partsch, "Testimony," 38; Dursi, 12; Leonard R. Gonzalez, "Testimony," *DOA Review*, vol. 2, book 26, 13.

97. Tim O'Brien, "The Mystery of My Lai," in *Facing My Lai*, 174.

98. Quoted in Myra MacPherson, *Long Time Passing: Vietnam and the Haunted Generation* (Garden City, N.Y.: Doubleday, 1984), 484. Other examples, see Fred Turner, *Echoes of Combat: The Vietnam War in American Memory* (New York: Anchor Books, 1996), 29.

99. For the argument that many soldiers in combat initially do not fire their weapons and have to be acclimated to killing, see Lt. Col. Dave Grossman, *On Killing: The Psychological Cost of Learning to Kill in War and Society* (Boston: Little, Brown, 1995).

100. Lifton, *Home*, 44.

101. Bourke, *An Intimate History of Killing: Face to Face in Twentieth-Century Warfare* (New York: Basic Books, 1999).

102. Gray, *The Warriors: Reflections on Men in Battle* (1959; Lincoln: University of Nebraska Press, 1998), 51, 52.

103. Hammer, *Court-Martial*, 333.

104. Fagan, 37; Carter, 39: Sledge, 14.

105. Gonzalez, 14.

106. Transcript from *Frontline*, "Remember My Lai," broadcast 23 May 1989. http:www.pbs.org/wgbh/pages/frontline/programs/transcripts/714.htm. Also, Simpson, quoted in Bilton and Sim, *Four Hours*, 130–131; Floyd D. Wright, "Testimony," *DOA Review*, vol. 2, book 28, 14.

107. Bunning, 23; Charles E. Hutto, "Testimony," *DOA Review*, vol. 2, book 26.

108. Stanley, "Testimony," 14.

109. Herbert L. Carter, "Testimony," *DOA Review*, vol. 2, book 24, 37.

110. Partsch, 38.

111. Konwinski, 5.

112. Moss, 10, 22.

113. *Life* 67 (5 Dec. 1969), 37; Hersh, *My Lai 4*, 68.

114. Gladwell, *The Tipping Point: How Little Things Can Make a Big Difference* (Boston: Little, Brown, 2000).

115. Browning, *Ordinary Men: Reserve Police Battalion 101 and the Final Solution in Poland* (New York: HarperCollins, 1992).

116. Martin E. Fagan, "Testimony," *DOA Review*, vol. 2, book 28, 36–37.

117. Carter, 47.

118. Garza, 19.

119. Bunning, 46.

120. Transcript from *Frontline*, "Remember My Lai."

121. Appy, *Working-Class War*, 252.

122. Lifton, "Looking into the Abyss: Bearing Witness to My Lai and Vietnam," in *Facing My Lai*, 21. Also, Lifton, "Existential Evil," in *Sanctions for Evil*, 38–41.

123. Lifton, "Looking into the Abyss," 22. Also, Lifton, "The American as Blind Giant Unable to See What It Kills," *New York Times Book Review* (14 June 1970), 250f.

124. MacPherson, *Long Time Passing*, 501.

125. Belknap, *The Vietnam War on Trial*, 56.

126. Philip D. Beidler, *Late Thoughts on an Old War: The Legacy of Vietnam* (Athens: University of Georgia Press, 2004), 157–159.

127. Bernhardt quoted in Susan Faludi, *Stiffed*, 318–319.

128. Calley, under questioning by his counsel at his court-martial, in Hammer, *Court-Martial*, 240.

129. Robert S. Rivkin, "Is Discipline Bad for the Army?" *New York Times* (21 Dec. 1970), 35.

130. Arendt, *Eichmann in Jerusalem: A Report on the Banality of Evil* (New York: Viking, 1963), 120–122.

131. Aristotle, *The Nichomachean Ethics*, trans. J. A. K. Thomson (Middlesex.: Penguin Books, 1985), 110.

132. McWilliams, *Military Honor, After My Lai* (New York: Council on Religion and International Affairs, 1972), 26.

133. Baritz, *Backfire*, 310.

134. Appy, *Working-Class War*, 89.

135. Terrence Des Pres, *The Survivor: An Anatomy of Life in the Death Camps* (New York: Oxford University Press, 1976); Tzvetan Todorov, *Facing the Extreme: Moral Life in the Concentration Camps* (New York: Metropolitan Books, 1996).

136. On the death of a world view, see the powerful analysis by Jonathan Lear, *Radical Hope: Ethics in the Face of Cultural Devastation* (Cambridge, Mass.: Harvard University Press, 2006), 50.

137. Lifton, "Looking into the Abyss," 20.

Chapter 4. The Hate Stare

1. On Griffin, Robert Bonazzi, *Man in the Mirror: John Howard Griffin and the Story of* Black Like Me (Maryknoll, N.Y.: Orbis Books, 1997). Excellent on the "visual dynamics" of seeing is Georgina Kleege, "The Strange Life and Times of John Howard Griffin," *Raritan* 26 (Spring 2007), 96–112; Griffin, *Black Like Me* (San Antonio: Wings Press, 2004), 164–171. A few days before the hanging of the effigy, an account of Griffin's journey into the South and his condemnation of his

fellow Southerners had appeared in *Time* (28 March 1960) http://www.time.com/time/magazine/article/0,9171,826167,00.html.

2. John Howard Griffin, *Journals*, John Howard Griffin Papers, Butler Library, Columbia University (hereafter, Griffin, *Journals*), (9 Dec. 1962), 1263.

3. Griffin, *Journals* 7 (9 Aug. 1960), 1050; 7 (12 March 1960), 7 (19 June 1960), 1041; 7 (5 and 7 April 1960), 1031–1032.

4. Noel Thomas Cash, a.ms. "Account of the Hanging of John Howard Griffin's Effigy," n.d., John Howard Griffin Papers, Butler Library, Columbia University. Box 6, Folder 203.

5. On Arendt, see George Cotkin, "Illuminating Evil: Hannah Arendt and Moral History," *Modern Intellectual History* 4 (Aug. 2007), 463–490.

6. Bonazzi, "Man in the Mirror," 114.

7. Griffin, *Black Like Me*, 170.

8. Taylor, *The Ethics of Authenticity* (Cambridge, Mass.: Harvard University Press, 1991), 49–51.

9. Griffin had intended to title his book *Journey into Fear*, but found that title already in use. Griffin to Sallie Gillespie (30 Sept. 1959), Griffin Papers, Box 5, Folder 188.

10. Here he could be seen as anticipating whiteness studies, with his emphasis on the constructed nature of identity. On the construction of race, especially for immigrants to America, see *Race Traitor*, ed. Noel Ignatiev and John Garvey (New York: Routledge, 1996). Also, Ignatiev, *How the Irish Became White* (New York: Routledge, 1995); David R. Roediger, *Working Towards Whiteness: How America's Immigrants Became White* (New York: Basic Books, 2005); Matthew Frye Jacobson, *Whiteness of a Different Color: European Immigrants and the Alchemy of Race* (Cambridge, Mass.: Harvard University Press, 1998); Peter Kolchin, "Whiteness Studies: The New History of Race in America," *Journal of American History* 89, no. 1 (2002), 154–173.

11. Griffin, *Black Like Me*, 11. Hereafter, all citation to *Black Like Me* will appear in the text.

12. Griffin, *Journals* 7 (31 Oct. 1959), 982.

13. Griffin, *Journals* 5 (27 March, 5 Aug. 1956).

14. On this Catholic imperative, see Paul Elie, *The Life You Save May Be Your Own: An American Pilgrimage* (New York: Farrar, Straus and Giroux, 2003).

15. Jacques Maritain, *Scholasticism and Politics*, trans. Mortimer J. Adler (Garden City, N.Y.: Image Books, 1960), 163f; Josef Goldbrunner, *Holiness Is Wholeness* (New York: Pantheon, 1955), 45.

16. Griffin, *Journals* 7 (7 Feb. 1960), 1023.

17. Lawrence Blum, *"I'm Not a Racist, But . . .": The Moral Quandary of Race* (Ithaca, N.Y.: Cornell University Press, 2002), 27.

18. Wickberg, "What Is the History of Sensibilities? On Cultural Histories, Old and New," *American Historical Review* 112 (June 2007), 661–684. On the emotions and history, see Peter N. Stearns and Carol Z. Stearns, "Emotionology: Clarifying the History of Emotions and Emotional Standards," *American Historical Review* 90 (Oct. 1985), 813–836; Barbara H. Rosenwein, "Worrying About Emotions in History," *American Historical Review* 107 (June 2002), 821–845; Joanna Bourke, "Fear

and Anxiety: Writing About Emotion in Modern History," *History Workshop Journal* no. 55 (2003), 111–133.

19. Malcolm X, as told to Alex Haley, *The Autobiography of Malcolm X* (1964; reprint New York: Random House, 1992), 399.

20. Griffin to Sallie Gillespie, Griffin Papers (30 Sept. 1959), box 5, folder 188.

21. Griffin is unmentioned, for example, in such fine works as Taylor Branch, *Parting the Waters: America in the King Years, 1954–1963* (New York: Simon and Schuster, 1988); David L. Chappell, *Inside Agitators: White Southerners in the Civil Rights Movement* (Baltimore: Johns Hopkins University Press, 1994); Adam Fairclough, *Better Day Coming: Blacks and Equality, 1890–2000* (New York: Viking, 2001); Carol Polsgrove, *Divided Minds: Intellectuals and the Civil Rights Movement* (New York: W. W. Norton, 2001); Juan Williams, *Eyes on the Prize: America's Civil Rights Years, 1954–1965* (New York: Viking, 1987); *The Eyes on the Prize: Civil Rights Reader*, ed. Clayborne Carson et al., (New York: Viking, 1991); Harvard Sitkoff, *The Struggle for Black Equality, 1954–1980* (New York: Hill and Wang, 1981); Jason Sokol, *There Goes My Everything: White Southerners in the Age of Civil Rights, 1945–1975* (New York: Alfred A. Knopf, 2006).

22. On the Freedom Riders, see Raymond Arsenault, *Freedom Riders: 1961 and the Struggle for Racial Justice* (New York: Oxford University Press, 2006).

23. Gayle Wald, "'A Most Disagreeable Mirror': Reflections on White Identity in *Black Like Me*," in *Passing and the Fictions of Identity*, ed. Elaine K. Ginsberg (Durham, N.C.: Duke University Press, 1996), 151–177; Nelson Hathcock, "'A Spy in the Enemy's Country': *Black Like Me* as Cold War Narrative," *American Studies* 44 (Fall 2003), 99–120; Kate Baldwin, "Black Like Who? Cross-Testing the 'Real' Lines of John Howard Griffin's *Black Like Me*," *Cultural Critique* no. 40 (Autumn, 1998), 103–143; Eric Lott, "White Like Me: Racial Cross-Dressing and the Construction of American Whiteness," in *Cultures of United States Imperialism* ed. Amy Kaplan and Donald R. Pease (Durham, N.C.: Duke University Press, 1993), 474–494; Laura Browder, *Slippery Characters: Ethnic Impersonations and American Identities* (Chapel Hill: University of North Carolina Press, 2000), 203–230; Susan Gubar, *Race Changes: White Skin, Black Face in American Culture* (New York: Oxford University Press, 1997), 27–30, passim.

To a degree, these criticisms are correct. Griffin did bolster Cold War liberalism by presenting the problem of race as a simple case of expanding American democracy in the South; and he did understand the challenge of Southern racism within a Cold War context. He was always aghast at how, unwittingly, super-patriot types failed to see how their racism undermined democratic ideals and undermined America's place in the world. Griffin, in *Black Like Me*, spent almost no time presenting African Americans as agents in their own liberation; rather, his attention was fixated on how they are victimized. Yet he avoided presenting a pathology of black life, showing himself to be well aware of black religious institutions. His concern, instead, was in demonstrating the pathology of white racism. Griffin was on his own spiritual quest, couched in his devout Catholicism, to experience the pain of African Americans, to testify to the absurdity of their condition, and to convince white Americans that racism was an affront to American ideals, both religious and secular. If this makes him an idealist, then Griffin would certainly plead guilty to the charge.

24. Nussbaum, *The Fragility of Goodness: Luck and Ethics in Greek Tragedy and Philosophy* (Cambridge: Cambridge University Press, 1986); Nagel, "Moral Luck," in *Mortal Questions*, 24–38; Williams, "Moral Luck," in *Moral Luck: Philosophical Papers, 1973–1980* (Cambridge: Cambridge University Press, 1981), 20–39; Williams, *Ethics and the Limits of Philosophy* (Cambridge, Mass.: Harvard University Press, 1985), 174–196; Williams, *Problems of the Self* (Cambridge: Cambridge University Press, 1973), esp. chapters 11, 13.

25. Stampp, *The Peculiar Institution: Slavery in the Antebellum South* (New York: Alfred A. Knopf, 1956), vii.

26. Stanley M. Elkins, *Slavery: A Problem in American Institutional and Intellectual Life* (Chicago: University of Chicago Press, 1959). George Cotkin, phone interview with Stanley M. Elkins, 8 March 2006. On the controversial aspects of Elkins's presentation of slaves as Sambo personalities, see *The Debate over Slavery: Stanley Elkins and His Critics*, ed. Ann J. Lane (Urbana: University of Illinois Press, 1971); Richard H. King, *Race, Culture, and the Intellectuals, 1940–1970* (Washington, D.C.: Woodrow Wilson Center Press, 2004), 155ff.; Kirsten Fermaglich, *American Dreams and Nazi Nightmares: Early Holocaust Consciousness and Liberal America, 1957–1965* (Waltham, Mass.: Brandeis University Press, 2006), 24–57. Eric J. Sundquist, *Strangers in the Land: Blacks, Jews, Post-Holocaust America* (Cambridge, Mass.: Belknap Press, 2005), is excellent for an overview of the issues.

27. "Justice as Fairness," for example, appeared in 1958, and other parts of his later work came out in the early 1960s. See John Rawls, *A Theory of Justice* (rev. ed., Cambridge, Mass.: Belknap Press, 1999), 11. On Rawls and his historical context in relation to issues of authenticity and individualism, see Mary Esteve, "Shipwreck and Autonomy: Rawls, Riesman, and Oppen in the 1960s," *Yale Journal of Criticism* 18, no. 2 (2005), 323–349.

28. On Griffin's Catholic imperatives, see Kleege, "Strange Life," 108.

29. Lott, *Love and Theft: Blackface Minstrelsy and the American Working Class* (New York: Oxford University Press, 1993).

30. Mark Pittenger, "A World of Difference: Constructing the 'Underclass' in Progressive America," *American Quarterly* 49, no. 1. (1997), 26–65. On the need for vitality among the upper and middle classes, see George Cotkin, *William James: Public Philosopher* (Baltimore: Johns Hopkins University Press, 1990), 73–94; Cotkin, *Reluctant Modernism: American Thought and Culture, 1880–1900* (New York: Twayne, 1992); T. J. Jackson Lears, *No Place of Grace: Antimodernism and the Transformation of American Culture, 1880–1920* (New York: Pantheon Books, 1981). Also, Hutchins Hapgood, *The Spirit of the Ghetto* (1902; reprint Cambridge, Mass.: Belknap Press, 1967).

31. Mailer, "The White Negro," *Dissent* 4 (Summer 1957), 276–297; reprinted in Mailer, *Advertisements for Myself* (1959; reprint Cambridge, Mass.: Harvard University Press, 1992), 331–358. On Mailer's piece, see Cotkin, *Existential America* (Baltimore: Johns Hopkins University Press, 2003), 192–198.

32. Styron, *The Confessions of Nat Turner* (New York: Random House, 1967), n.p. Of course, Styron would later jump into controversy again with his novel about

the horrible choice confronted by a Holocaust survivor in *Sophie's Choice* (New York: Random House, 1979). On the moral dilemma faced by the main character of this work, see Suzanne Dovi, "*Sophie's Choice*: Letting Chance Decide," *Philosophy and Literature* 30 (2006), 174–189.

33. See the essays in *William Styron's Nat Turner: Ten Black Writers Respond* (Boston: Beacon Press, 1968). Also on the controversy, Albert E. Stone, *The Return of Nat Turner: History, Literature, and Cultural Politics in Sixties America* (Athens: University of Georgia Press, 1992), 38–100.

34. "Interview with Alvin F. Poussaint, M.D.," in *Nat Turner: A Slave Rebellion in History and Memory*, ed. Kenneth S. Greenberg (Oxford: Oxford University Press, 2003), 236.

35. Faulkner, quoted in Greenberg, *Nat Turner*, 213.

36. Myrdal, *An American Dilemma* (New York: Harper & Row, 1962), lxxv, lxxi, 658. On Myrdal, see Walter A. Jackson, *Gunnar Myrdal and America's Conscience: Social Engineering and Racial Liberalism, 1938–1987* (Chapel Hill: University of North Carolina Press, 1990); David W. Southern, *Gunnar Myrdal and Black and White Relations: The Use and Abuse of "An American Dilemma," 1944–1969* (Baton Rouge: Louisiana State University Press, 1987), 171–183. Another influential work that attacked racist assumptions from a universalist perspective was Gordon W. Allport, *The Nature of Prejudice* (1954; reprint Cambridge, Mass.: Perseus Books, 1979).

37. Wright, *Black Boy* (New York: Harper and Brothers, 1945), 65.

38. Wright, *Native Son* (New York: Harper and Brothers, 1940).

39. Nussbaum, *Poetic Justice*, 94–95.

40. On the need for context in empathy, see Susan Sontag, *On Photography* (New York: Dell, 1978). For a revision of her original views, see Sontag, *Regarding the Pain of Others* (New York: Farrar, Straus and Giroux, 2003). Also, Susan D. Moeller, *Compassion Fatigue: How the Media Sell Disease, Famine, War, and Death* (New York: Routledge, 1999), 35f.

41. Randall A. Lake, "The Metaethical Framework of Anti-Abortion Rhetoric," *Signs* 11, no. 3 (1986), 478–499.

42. Karen Halttunen, "Humanitarianism and the Pornography of Pain in Anglo-Christian Culture," *American Historical Review* 100 (April 1995), 303–334.

43. On the challenges of empathy as applied to fictional characters, see Colin Radford, "Tears and Fiction," *Philosophy* 52 (April 1977), 208–213; Barrie Paskins, "On Being Moved by Anna Karenina and *Anna Karenina*," *Philosophy* 52 (July 1977), 344–347.

44. Aristotle, *Rhetoric*, trans. W. Rhys Roberts (New York: Modern Library, 1984), 113–114. On empathy and tragedy, also see Martha C. Nussbaum, *Upheavals of Thought: The Intelligence of Emotions* (Cambridge: Cambridge University Press, 2001); Bernard Williams, *Shame and Necessity* (Berkeley: University of California Press, 1993). For a highly critical view of pity and empathy, see Nietzsche's critiques in Nietzsche, *Beyond Good and Evil*, trans. R. J. Hollingdale (Middlesex: Penguin Books, 1979), 136 passim; *The Will to Power*, trans. Walter Kaufmann and R. J. Hollingdale (New York: Vintage, 1968), 199.

45. Quoted in Martha C. Nussbaum, *Poetic Justice: The Literary Imagination and Public Life* (Boston: Beacon Press, 1995), 66.

46. Margalit, *The Ethics of Memory* (Cambridge, Mass.: Harvard University Press, 2002), 6–9, 33; Rorty, *Contingency, Irony, and Solidarity* (Cambridge: Cambridge University Press, 1989). On cruelty as the problem liberals must confront, see Judith N. Shklar, *Ordinary Vices* (Cambridge, Mass.: Belknap Press, 1984), 7–14.

47. Smith, *The Theory of Moral Sentiments* (1759; reprint Oxford: Clarendon Press, 1976), 39–44.

48. Rousseau, *Emile: Julie and Other Writings* (Woodbury, N.Y.: Barron's Educational Series, 1964), 73–78.

49. Arendt, *On Revolution* (New York: Viking, 1963), 85.

50. Andre Comte-Sponville, *A Small Treatise on the Great Virtues: The Uses of Philosophy in Everyday Life*, trans. Catherine Temerson (New York: Metropolitan Books, 2001), 112–113.

51. Robert L. Katz, *Empathy: Its Nature and Uses* (New York: Free Press, 1963), 33. On empathy as a form of imaginative projection, see Alvin I. Goldman, "Empathy, Mind, and Morals," *Proceedings and Addresses of the American Philosophical Society* 66 (Nov. 1963), 17–41. On the need for empathy within historical literature, see Eve Kornfeld, "The Power of Empathy: A Feminist, Multicultural Approach to Historical Pedagogy," *History Teacher* 26 (Nov. 1992), 23–31.

52. Halttunen, "Humanitarianism and the Pornography of Pain in Anglo-Christian Culture," 303–334; Lynn Hunt, *Inventing Human Rights: A History* (New York: W. W. Norton, 2007), 35–69; Thomas W. Laqueur, "Bodies, Details, and the Humanitarian Narrative," in *The New Cultural History*, ed. Lynn Hunt (Berkeley: University of California Press, 1989), 176–204. Also, on the challenges of empathy, see Carolyn J. Dean, *The Fragility of Empathy: After the Holocaust* (Ithaca, N.Y.: Cornell University Press, 2004).

53. On the notion of widening the circle in terms of plurality and postmodernity, see David A. Hollinger, *Postethnic America: Beyond Multiculturalism* (New York: Basic Books, 1995).

54. Nagel, "What Is It Like to Be a Bat?" in *Mortal Questions* (Cambridge: Cambridge University Press, 1979), 169. For a brief overview on the question of other minds, see Nagel, *The View from Nowhere* (Oxford: Oxford University Press, 1986), 19–22.

55. On the range of racial conceptions, see Sokol, *There Goes My Everything*, 56f. Also, Grace Elizabeth Hale, *Making Whiteness: The Culture of Segregation in the South, 1890–1940* (New York: Vintage, 1999).

56. Griffin, *Journals* 6 (1 Nov. 1959), 988.

57. Griffin, *A Time to Be Human* (New York: Macmillan, 1977), 9.

58. Myrdal, *American Dilemma*, 102.

59. Griffin, "The Intrinsic Other," in *The John Howard Griffin Reader*, ed. Bradford Daniel (Boston: Houghton Mifflin, 1968), 465–466.

60. Griffin, *Journals*, 6 (Nov. 1959), 988.

61. Griffin, *Journals* 6 (1 Nov. 1959), 985.

62. Griffin, *Journals* (15 Dec. 1959), 997.

63. Even whites sympathetic to blacks were willing to inscribe racial license onto blacks. See Margaret Halsey, *Color Blind: A White Woman Looks at the Negro* (New York: Simon and Schuster, 1946), 117.

64. On how the presumed pathology of African Americans came to dominate white sociological approaches to the problems of race in America, see Daryl Michael Scott, *Contempt and Pity: Social Policy and the Image of the Damaged Black Psyche, 1880–1996* (Chapel Hill: University of North Carolina Press, 1997); Ellison, "An American Dilemma: A Review" (1944), in *Shadow and Act* (New York: Random House, 1964), 303–317.

65. Griffin, *Journals* 9 (April 1962), 1182.

66. Griffin to Gillespie Sisters (12 Jan. 1960), Griffin Papers, box 5, folder 188.

67. Griffin, "What Happened Since," in *Black Like Me*, 196.

68. Griffin to Gillespie Sisters (15 Sept. 1963), Griffin Papers, Box 5, folder 191.

69. Smith, *Killers of the Dream* (New York: W. W. Norton, 1949).

70. George Lipsitz, *The Possessive Investment in Whiteness: How White People Profit from Identity Politics* (Philadelphia: Temple University Press, 1998), 1–23.

71. Copied into his journal as a "strange letter . . . from a lady in Michigan," *Journals* 9 (5 Jan. 1962), 1159.

72. Griffin, *Journals* 7 (8 June 1960), 1038.

73. Griffin, *A Time to Be Human*, 33.

74. Jay Copp, "Still Walking in Another's Shoes," *Christian Science Monitor* 93 (15 Feb. 2001), 17. Also, Adam Kirsch, "A Spy in the Gender Wars," *New York Sun* (4 Jan. 2006), 1. Kirsch praised Griffin's "ultimate experiment in immersion journalism . . . as a sacrificial victim, suffering the pain that most whites refused to acknowledge, much less share." In 1977, Griffin thought that if he were to repeat his masquerade as a black man in cities such as "Boston or Louisville or Detroit," the hatred over school busing or integration would be withering. Griffin, *A Time to Be Human*, 101.

Chapter 5. Just Rewards?

1. Material on Gilmore and his crimes is from Mikal Gilmore, *Shot in the Heart* (New York: Anchor Books, 1995), and Norman Mailer, *The Executioner's Song* (New York: Vintage Books, 1998).

2. Gilmore, *Shot in the Heart*, 287.

3. Gilmore, *Shot in the Heart*, 326.

4. William O. Hochkammer, Jr., "The Capital Punishment Controversy," *Criminal Law Comments and Case Notes* 60 (Sept. 1969), 364; Joseph H. Rankin, "Changing Attitudes Toward Capital Punishment," *Social Forces* 58 (Sept. 1979), 195.

5. Richard A. Berk, Robert Weiss, and Jack Boger, "Chance and the Death Penalty," *Law and Society Review* 27, no. 1 (1993), 91.

6. Lewis F. Powell, Jr., "Capital Punishment," *Harvard Law Review* 102 (March 1989), 1035–1046.

7. Hugo Adam Bedau, "The Right to Die by Firing Squad," *Hastings Center Report* 7 (Feb. 1977), 6.

8. Jon Nordheimer, "Gilmore Wins Plea for Execution," *New York Times* (1 Dec. 1976), 24.

9. "An American Punishment Again," *New York Times* (18 Jan. 1977), 25.

10. Nordheimer, "Plane Scatters Gilmore's Ashes as Utah Returns to Normal," *New York Times* (19 Jan. 1977), 14.

11. Nordheimer, "Plane Scatters Gilmore's Ashes," 14.

12. Fuhrman, "Letter to the Editor," *Los Angeles Times* (23 Jan. 1977), D4.

13. Hazel Erskine, "The Polls: Capital Punishment," *Public Opinion Quarterly* 34 (Summer 1970), 290. While support for the death penalty moved into the 60 percent range in the 1970s and 1980s, some analysts argued that it was stronger as a symbolic gesture than as a reality. See Franklin E. Zimring and Gordon Hawkins, *Capital Punishment and the American Agenda* (Cambridge: Cambridge University Press, 1986), 15. On the figures for this period, see Stuart Banner, *The Death Penalty: An American History* (Cambridge, Mass.: Harvard University Press, 2002), 275–279.

14. GMM, "The Executioner's Song: Is There a Right to Listen?" *Virginia Law Review* 69 (March 1983), 373.

15. Joseph M. Giarratano, "'To the Best of Our Knowledge, We Have Never Been Wrong': Fallibility vs. Finality in Capital Punishment," *Yale Law Journal* 100 (Jan. 1991), 1005.

16. Powell, Jr., "Capital Punishment," 1037.

17. Anna Quindlen, "The Failed Experiment," *Newsweek* (26 June 2006), 64.

18. Foucault, "What Is Called 'Punishing'?" in *Power: Essential Works of Foucault, 1954–1984*, ed. James D. Faubion, trans. Robert Hurley and others (New York: New Press, 1994), III, 387. The foundations for differences in sentences can be perplexing. Why, after all, should a successful murderer, someone whose bullet hits his victim's heart, be punished more severely than someone whose bullet goes astray and hits the shoulder of the intended victim? One could argue that the "wholeheartedness" of the former may have been stronger than that of the latter, but it is more a case of simple ability to aim or pure luck. How can intentions here be discerned as different? For a brilliant discussion that also tries to fix a response to why it is correct (at least theoretically) to have different penalties imposed, see David Lewis, "The Punishment that Leaves Something to Chance," *Philosophy and Public Affairs* 18, no. 1 (Winter 1989), 53–67.

19. Andreas Killen, *1973, Nervous Breakdown: Watergate, Warhol, and the Birth of Post-Sixties America* (New York: Bloomsbury, 2006); Philip Jenkins, *Moral Panic: Changing Concepts of the Child Molester in Modern America* (New Haven: Yale University Press, 1998); Jenkins, *Decade of Nightmares: The End of the Sixties and the Making of Eighties America* (New York: Oxford University Press, 2006); Jonathan Mahler, *Ladies and Gentlemen, The Bronx Is Burning: 1977, Baseball, Politics, and the Battle for the Soul of a City* (New York: Picador, 2005).

20. James T. Patterson, *Grand Expectations: The United States, 1945–1974* (Oxford: Oxford University Press, 1996), 776. Material that follows on the 1970s is from Patterson, *Restless Giant: The United States from Watergate to Bush v. Gore* (Oxford: Oxford University Press, 2005), chapters 1–3. Also, Bruce J. Schulman, *The Seventies: The Great Shift in American Culture, Society, and Politics* (New York: Free Press, 2001), 78–101.

21. Mahler, *Ladies and Gentlemen*, 224.

22. Selwyn Raab, "Violent Crimes Drop 0.4%," *New York Times* (24 April 1976),

44. Crime in New York City, it had been reported in the previous year, had increased by 13 percent. What made this statistic less significant was that crime in the United States had gone up 18 percent. Raab, "Sharp Rise Noted in City Crime," *New York Times* (3 Aug. 1975), 1, 19.

23. Mahler, *Ladies and Gentlemen*, 186–223.

24. Mahler, *Ladies and Gentlemen*, 245–257.

25. Van den Haag, *Punishing Criminals: Concerning a Very Old and Painful Question* (New York: Basic Books, 1975), 5.

26. "Crime Boom," *Time* (14 April 1975), www.time.com.time/magazine/article/0,9171.917297,00.html.

27. Wilson, *Thinking About Crime* (New York: Basic Books, 1975), 83, 163, 173.

28. Obituary, "E. van den Haag," *New York Times* (27 March 2002), A21.

29. Banner, *The Death Penalty*, 283–284.

30. Van den Haag, *Punishing Criminals*, 211. Also, in even stronger terms, see Van den Haag, "For the Death Penalty," Editorial, *New York Times* (17 Oct. 1983), A1.

31. Van den Haag, "On Deterrence and the Death Penalty," *Ethics* 78, no. 4 (July 1968), 280–288. The essay appeared also in slightly different form in *Journal of Criminal Law, Criminology and Police Science* 60, no. 2 (June 1969), 141–147. For a response, see Hugo Adam Bedau, "The Death Penalty as a Deterrent: Argument and Evidence," *Ethics* 80, no. 3 (April 1970), 205–217. Also Van den Haag, "Deterrence and the Death Penalty: A Rejoinder," *Ethics* 81, no. 1 (Oct. 1970), 74–75.

32. Ehrlich, "The Deterrent Effect of Capital Punishment: A Question of Life and Death," *American Economic Review* 65, no. 3 (June 1975), 398; Ehrlich, "Capital Punishment and Deterrence: Some Further Thoughts and Additional Evidence," *Journal of Political Economy* 85, no. 4 (Aug. 1977), 741–788.

33. Zeisel, "The Deterrent Effect of the Death Penalty: Facts v. Faiths," *Supreme Court Review* (1976), 317–343. For a summing-up of the evidence as presented in the *Yale Law Journal* symposium on Ehrlich's findings, see Jon K. Peck, "The Deterrent Effect of Capital Punishment: Ehrlich and His Critics," *Yale Law Journal* 85, no. 3 (Jan. 1976), 359–367.

34. Van den Haag, "Death Penalty *Does* Deter Murderers," *Los Angeles Times* (12 Dec. 1976), 15.

35. Van den Haag, "The Criminal Law as a Threat System," *Journal of Criminal Law and Criminology* 73, no. 2 (1982), 769–785, with comments: John Braithwaite, "Comment on 'The Criminal Law as a Threat System;" Braithwaite, "Reply to Dr. Ernest Van Den Haag;" Van den Haag, "Reply to Dr. John Braithwaite," ibid., 786–796. Also, Jeffrey H. Reiman, "Justice, Civilization, and the Death Penalty: Answering van den Haag"; Stephen Nathanson, "Does It Matter If the Death Penalty Is Arbitrarily Administered?" and Van den Haag, "Refuting Reiman and Nathanson," *Philosophy and Public Affairs* 14, no. 2 (Spring 1985), 115–176; "The Ultimate Punishment: A Defense," *Harvard Law Review* 99, no. 7 (May 1986), 1662–1669. In addition to his *Punishing Criminals*, Van den Haag published *Political Violence and Civil Disobedience* (New York: Harper and Row, 1972), which touched on some of these issues. Finally, Van den Haag and John P. Conrad, *The Death Penalty: A Debate, Pro and Con* (New York: Plenum Press, 1983), 76, 260.

36. Berns, *For Capital Punishment: Crime and the Morality of the Death Penalty* (New York: Basic Books, 1979), 83.

37. On Berns, see Andrew Hacker, "On Original Sin and Conservatives," *New York Times Magazine* (25 Feb. 1973), 67; "Interview with Walter Berns," (4 Aug. 2004), www.renewamerica.us/columns/evans/040804.

38. Herbert Fingarette, "Punishment and Suffering," *Proceedings and Addresses of the American Philosophical Association* 50, no. 6 (Aug. 1977), 500–501.

39. Christopher Lehmann-Haupt, "Review," *New York Times* (16 July 1979), C14.

40. Norval Morris, *The Future of Imprisonment* (Chicago: University of Chicago Press, 1974), 75.

41. Jacoby, *Wild Justice: The Evolution of Revenge* (New York: Harper & Row, 1983), 309. Also, William Ian Miller, *Eye for an Eye* (Cambridge: Cambridge University Press, 2006), is excellent on the literary history of the notion of *lex talionis* and "settling accounts." For an appreciation of retribution without acceptance of the death penalty, see Wendy Kaminer, *It's All the Rage: Crime and Culture* (Reading, Mass.: Addison-Wesley, 1995), 3, 266.

42. A particularly strong argument against capital punishment and the justice system is Austin Sarat, *When the State Kills: Capital Punishment and the American Condition* (Princeton, N.J.: Princeton University Press, 2001).

43. Van den Haag, "On Deterrence," *Journal of Criminal Law*, 141.

44. Van den Haag, "Refuting Reiman and Nathanson," *Philosophy and Public Affairs*, 172.

45. Joe Soss et al., "Why Do White Americans Support the Death Penalty?" *Journal of Politics* 65, no. 2 (May 2003), 398.

46. William Martin, *With God on Our Side: The Rise of the Religious Right in America* (New York: Broadway Books, 1986), 117–143; James Davison Hunter, *Culture Wars: The Struggle to Define America* (New York: Basic Books, 1992).

47. Frances FitzGerald, *Cities on a Hill: A Journey Through Contemporary American Cultures* (New York: Simon and Schuster, 1986), 125; David Bebbington, "Evangelicism in Its Setting: The British and American Movements Since 1940," in *Evangelicalism: Comparative Studies of Popular Protestantism in North America, the British Isles, and Beyond, 1700–1990*, ed. Mark A. Noll et al. (New York: Oxford University Press, 1994), 377. On postwar religion, Patrick Allitt, *Religion in America Since 1946: A History* (New York: Columbia University Press, 2003), 148–169.

48. For the view that fundamentalists' positions on capital punishment were complex, see James D. Unnever and Francis T. Cullen, "Christian Fundamentalism and Support for Capital Punishment," *Journal of Research in Crime and Delinquency* 43, no. 2 (May 2006), 169–197. However, another study suggests that fundamentalists were more supportive of corporal punishment than other Americans. See Christopher G. Ellison and Darren E. Sherkat, "Conservative Protestantism and Support for Corporal Punishment," *American Sociological Review* 58 (Feb. 1993), 131–144.

49. Quoted in Steve Bruce, *The Rise and Fall of the New Christian Right: Conservative Protestant Politics in America, 1978–1988* (Oxford: Clarendon Press, 1988), 77.

50. Falwell, "An Agenda for the 1980s," in *Piety and Politics: Evangelicals Confront the World*, ed. Richard John Neuhaus and Michael Cromartie (Washington, D.C.: Ethics and Public Policy Center, 1987), 109, 111. On Falwell, see Mark Silk, *Spiritual Politics: Religion and America Since World War II* (New York: Simon and Schuster, 1988), 164ff.

51. Wuthnow, "The Future of the Religious Right," in *No Longer Exiles: The Religious Right in American Politics*, ed. Michael Cromartie (Washington, D.C.: Ethics and Public Policy Center, 1992), 32.

52. Quoted in Sara Diamond, *Not by Politics Alone: The Enduring Influence of the Christian Right* (New York: Guilford Press, 1998), 146, 149.

53. Balmer, *Mine Eyes Have Seen the Glory: A Journey into the Evangelical Subculture in America* (New York: Oxford University Press, 1993), 161.

54. Hacker, "On Original Sin," 13.

55. Menninger, *The Crime of Punishment* (New York: Viking, 1968). Hereafter, references to this book appear in the text. While popular author Jessica Mitford agreed with much in Menninger's critique of the criminal justice system and the causes of crime, she rejected the value of medicalizing prisoners. Drugs, in her view, were used as a means of punishment and control rather than as a means to the end of therapy. From the point of view of the convict, she stated, "'treatment' is a humiliating game." Mitford, *Kind and Unusual Punishment: The Prison Business* (New York: Alfred A. Knopf, 1973), 99–103.

56. Absolute antagonism to the death penalty continues. In the view of Wendy Lesser, "execution is murder." Lesser, *Pictures at an Exhibition: An Inquiry into the Subject of Murder* (Cambridge, Mass.: Harvard University Press, 1993), 5. Also, Robert Jay Lifton and Greg Mitchell, *Who Owns Death? Capital Punishment, the American Conscience, and the End of Executions* (New York: William Morrow, 2000).

57. Bedau, "Survey of the Death Penalty Today," in *Debating the Death Penalty: Should America Have Capital Punishment?* ed. Hugo Adam Bedau and Paul G. Cassell (Oxford: Oxford University Press, 2004), 41. Bedau's book, *The Death Penalty in America*, went through three editions, in 1964, 1967, and 1997. Important early essays by Bedau are "The Death Penalty as a Deterrent: Argument and Evidence," *Ethics* 80, no. 3 (April 1970), 205–217; "Retribution and the Theory of Punishment," *Journal of Philosophy* 75, no. 11 (Nov. 1978), 601–620. Useful for biographical background on Bedau is "Resolution on the Retirement of Hugo Adam Bedau," (17 May 1999), at http://ase.tufts.edu/philosophy/people/hugo/htm. An excellent philosophical analysis marked by openness to contending viewpoints is Stephen Nathanson, *An Eye for an Eye? The Morality of Punishing by Death* (Totowa, N.J.: Rowman and Littlefield, 1987).

58. Bedau, "Thinking of the Death Penalty as a Cruel and Unusual Punishment," *University of California, Davis Law Review* 18, no. 4 (1984–1985), 915. Hereafter, citations to this article appear in the text.

59. Philip P. Hallie, *Cruelty*, rev. ed. (Middletown, Conn.: Wesleyan University Press, 1982).

60. Sister Helen Prejean, *Dead Man Walking: An Eyewitness Account of the Death Penalty in the United States* (New York: Vintage, 1994), 40. Hereafter, citations to this work appear in the text.

61. Lifton and Mitchell, *Who Owns Death?*, 203. For the view that closure is more complex, see Lynn Waddell and Arian Campo-Flores, "Execution: What Happens After?" *Newsweek* (6 Nov. 2006), 8.

62. Kaminer, *It's All the Rage*, 74ff.

63. For two very thoughtful works on the role of the emotions in justice, see Thane Rosenbaum, *The Myth of Moral Justice: Why Our Legal System Fails to Do What's Right* (New York: HarperCollins, 2004); Robert C. Solomon, *A Passion for Justice: Emotions and the Origins of the Social Contract* (Reading, Mass..: Addison-Wesley, 1990).

64. Jeffrie G. Murphy and Jean Hampton, *Forgiveness and Mercy* (Cambridge: Cambridge University Press, 1988), 6, 16, 93. Excellent on these issues is Martha Minow, *Between Vengeance and Forgiveness: Facing History After Genocide and Mass Violence* (Boston: Beacon Press, 1998), 4, 10–14.

65. D. D. Devinci, *Dead Family Walking: The Bourque Family Story of Dead Man Walking* (New Iberia, La.: Goldlamp, 2005).

66. Austin Sarat reads the film as conservative, in that it does not focus on the "legal and political issues" of capital punishment. Sarat, *When the State Kills*, 225–227.

67. Prejean, *The Death of Innocence: An Eyewitness Account of Wrongful Executions* (New York: Random House, 2005), 225.

68. Zimring and Hawkins, *Capital Punishment and the American Agenda* (Cambridge: Cambridge University Press, 1986), 157. Zimring, *The Contradictions of American Capital Punishment* (Oxford: Oxford University Press, 2003), x.

69. Richard Moran, "The Presence of Malice," *New York Times* (2 Aug. 2007), A21. On reversals, see Jack Greenberg, "Against the American System of Capital Punishment," *Harvard Law Review* 99, no. 7 (May 1986), 1670–1680. A well-known work on this subject is Charles Black, *Capital Punishment: The Inevitability of Caprice and Mistake* (New York: W. W. Norton, 1974). For Black, the system was more arbitrary than corrupt.

70. Giarratano, " 'To the Best of Our Knowledge,' " 1009.

71. Tucker, *May God Have Mercy: A True Story of Crime and Punishment* (New York: Delta, 1997); Grisham, *The Innocent Man: Murder and Injustice in a Small Town* (New York: Doubleday, 2006).

72. Jodi Wilgoren, "Citing Issue of Fairness, Governor Clears Out Death Row in Illinois," *New York Times* (12 Jan. 2003), L1.

73. Wilgoren, "Panel in Illinois Seeks to Reform Death Sentence," *New York Times* (15 April 2002), A1, A21. Among the reforms suggested by the commission, which did not have the charge to make a statement about keeping or jettisoning the death penalty, were mandatory DNA tests by independent laboratories, reduction in the number of offenses that would warrant the death penalty, and videotaping of all confessions.

74. For the full text of Ryan's speech at Northwestern College of Law, see "I Will Not Stand for It," 11 Jan. 2003, http://www.worldpolicy.org/projects/globalrights/dp/2002-0111-Ryan%20speech%20on%20capital%20punishment.html.

75. Wilgoren, "Illinois Prosecutors Assess Death Penalty's New Era," *New York Times* (14 Jan. 2003), A18.

76. Pam Belluck, "Push in Massachusetts for a Death Penalty," *New York Times* (23 Sept. 2003), A14.

77. Al Baker, "Effort to Reinstate Death Penalty Law Stalled in Albany," *New York Times* (18 Nov. 2004), A1, B6.

78. Bush's successor, Rick Perry, has since surpassed his predecessor's record for number of prisoners executed in the state.

79. Sister Helen Prejean, "Death in Texas," *New York Review of Books* (13 Jan. 2005), http://www.nybooks.com/articles/17670.

80. Berlow, "The Texas Clemency Memos," *Atlantic Monthly* (July–Aug. 2003), http://www.theatlantic.com/doc/print/200307/berlow. Also online are copies of the memos prepared by Gonzales.

81. Gonzales no doubt gave Bush precisely the type of memos he desired. On Gonzales and Bush in Texas, see Bill Minutaglio, *The President's Counselor: The Rise to Power of Alberto Gonzales* (New York: HarperCollins, 2006), 123–154.

82. Bush, *A Charge to Keep* (New York: William Morrow, 1999), 147.

83. Erika Casriel, "Bush and the Texas Death Machine," *Rolling Stone* (6 July 2000), htpp://www.rollingstone.com/artists/georgewbush/articles/story/592.

84. Jim Yardley, "Texas' Busy Death Chamber Helps Define Bush's Tenure," *New York Times* (7 Jan. 2000).

85. On the Tucker decision, see Bush, "Karla Faye Tucker and Henry Lee Lucas," chapter 11 in *A Charge to Keep*, 150–166. The bulk of the chapter deals with Tucker.

86. Bush, *A Charge to Keep*, 140.

Chapter 6. Muddiness and Moral Clarity

1. The best account of this meeting is in George Packer, *The Assassin's Gate: America in Iraq* (New York: Farrar, Straus and Giroux, 2005), 96–97. See also Bob Woodward, *Plan of Attack* (New York: Simon and Schuster, 2004), 258–260. On Makiya, see Lawrence Weschler, *Calamities of Exile: Three Nonfiction Novellas* (Chicago: University of Chicago Press, 1996), 1–61. Also, Robert Draper, *Dead Certain: The Presidency of George W. Bush* (New York: Free Press, 2007), 187–189; Dexter Filkins, "Regrets Only?" *New York Times* (7 Oct. 2007), 52–57.

2. Al-Khalil [Makiya], *Republic of Fear: The Politics of Modern Iraq* (Berkeley: University of California Press, 1989).

3. Al-Khalil [Makiya], *The Monument: Art, Vulgarity and Responsibility in Iraq* (Berkeley: University of California Press, 1991).

4. Makiya was accompanied by two other Iraqi exiles—Hatem Mukhlis, a Sunni Muslim surgeon and founder of the Iraqi National Congress, and Rend al-Rahim, director of the Iraq Foundation. Packer, *Assassin's Gate*, 96–97.

5. "Transcript of Iraq Seminar with Richard Perle and Kanan Makiya" (17 March 2003): http://www.benadorassociates.com/pf.php?id+664.

6. Makiya interview with Bill Moyers, *Now,* 17 March 2003, http://www.pbs.org/now/031703.

7. As employed in this chapter, *moral clarity* is similar to Susan Neiman's usage. For her, in search of a heroic moral figure, moral clarity is the ability to uphold principles *with* recognition of the complexities of life and its attendant tragedy. But I am more concerned with the inherent elusiveness of moral clarity while recognizing the imperative for moral action. See Neiman, *Moral Clarity: A Guide for Grown-Up Idealists* (Orlando, Fla.: Harcourt, 2008).

8. "Three Years, Few Regrets," Interview with Kanan Makiya by Michael Young, *Reasononline* (6 April 2006): http://www.reason.com/news/show/117383.html.

9. Dexter Filkins, "Regrets Only?" 56.

10. Sharansky, *Fear No Evil*, trans. Stefani Hoffman (New York: Random House, 1988), 374–375. His spirits were buoyed somewhat by an excerpt from Albert Camus' essay "The Myth of Sisyphus," surreptitiously given to him by a fellow prisoner. The story is about how the demi-god Sisyphus—because of his desire for earthly love and existence and consequent refusal to heed Zeus's orders—was condemned to roll a rock up a mountain, only to find at the top that the rock rolled down each time. It was an endless labor and absurd endeavor. The sorrow of Sisyphus's fate is tempered by the fact that he is alive. As Camus' famous gloss on the story puts it, "One must imagine Sisyphus happy." Albert Camus, *The Myth of Sisyphus and Other Essays*, trans. Justin O'Brien (New York: Vintage Books, 1955), 91.

11. The best accounts of the meeting are in Fred Kaplan, *Daydream Believers: How a Few Grand Ideas Wrecked American Power* (New York: John Wiley and Sons, 2008), 141–150, and Natan Sharansky with Ron Dermer, "Preface to the Paperbound Edition," *The Case for Democracy: The Power of Freedom to Overcome Tyranny and Terror* (New York: Public Affairs, 2006). Hereafter, citations to the Sharansky volume appear in the text.

12. Kaplan, *Daydream*, 146.

13. Elisabeth Bumiller, "White House Letter: Bush Borrows a Page from Natan Sharansky," *International Herald Tribune* (31 Jan. 2005): http://iht.com/articles/2005/01/31/letter_ed3_.php.

14. Gladwell, *Blink: The Power of Thinking Without Thinking* (New York: Little, Brown, 2005).

15. Gigerenzer, *Gut Feelings: The Intelligence of the Unconscious* (New York: Viking, 2007), 3–7.

16. Bumiller, "White House Letter."

17. Bumiller, "White House Letter."

18. Sharansky, *Case for Democracy*, xxxiii.

19. John F. Burns, "How Many People Has Saddam Hussein Killed?" *New York Times* (26 Jan. 2003), WK4.

20. Middle East Watch, *Human Rights in Iraq* (New Haven: Yale University Press, 1990), 11. Hereafter, citations appear in the text.

21. Burns, "How Many," WK4.

22. *Saddam's Killing Fields*, film by Michael Wood, directed by Chris Jeans, October 1993.

23. Kanan Makiya, *Cruelty and Silence: War, Tyranny, Uprising and the Arab World* (New York: W. W. Norton, 1993), 135–140. Central for understanding the nature of the Baath party and the Iraqi regime is Samir al-Khalil [Kanan Makiya],

Republic of Fear. Also helpful are some of the essays collected in *The Saddam Hussein Reader: Selections from Leading Writers on Iraq*, ed. Turi Munthe (New York: Thunder's Mouth Press, 2002).

24. Various reports can be found throughout September 1988 in the *New York Times.* For the picture, see Alan Cowell, "This Spring Iraq and Iran Take Their War to the People," *New York Times* (10 April 1988), 172.

25. Makiya, *Cruelty and Silence*, 178–199.

26. *Saddam's Killing Fields*, October 1993.

27. Falk, Contribution to Symposium, "Humanitarian Intervention," *Nation* (14 July 2003), 12. Falk, however, found the role the White House had been playing in this area to be counterproductive and accidental.

28. On the sweep of the Atlantic Charter and its relation to United States ideals and the United Nations, see Elizabeth Borgwardt, *A New Deal for the World: America's Vision for Human Rights* (Cambridge, Mass.: Harvard University Press, 2005). A far-reaching and inspired examination of American humanitarian interventions is Gary J. Bass, *Freedom's Battle: The Origins of Humanitarian Intervention* (New York: Alfred A. Knopf, 2008).

29. For a brilliant critique of these NGOs and the moment of humanitarian intervention, see David Rieff, *A Bed for the Night: Humanitarianism in Crisis* (New York: Simon and Schuster, 2002), and *At the Point of a Gun: Democratic Dreams and Armed Intervention* (New York: Simon & Schuster, 2005). In a similar vein, David Kennedy, *The Dark Sides of Virtue: Reassessing International Humanitarianism* (Princeton, N.J.: Princeton University Press, 2004). On the inadequacy of America's response to humanitarian crises, see the classic by Samantha Power, *"A Problem from Hell": America and the Age of Genocide* (New York: Basic Books, 2002). Also, John Shattuck, *Freedom on Fire: Human Rights Wars and America's Response* (Cambridge, Mass.: Harvard University Press, 2003).

30. Ignatieff, "The Burden," *New York Times* (5 Jan. 2003), 22.

31. Ignatieff, *Human Rights as Politics and Idolatry* (Princeton, N.J.: Princeton University Press, 2001); *The Rights Revolution* (Toronto: Anansi Press, 2000), 43.

32. Samantha Power, "*Problem from Hell*," 511. Power's enthusiasm for humanitarian intervention has remained strong, although it has been tempered somewhat by her recognition of the complexities that afflict many nations and the general difficulties in any intervention. For a deeper sense of this challenge, see her *Chasing the Flame: Sergio Vieira de Mello and the Fight to Save the World* (New York: Penguin, 2008).

33. In this vein, see Rieff, "Dangerous Pity," *Prospect* (23 June 2005): http://lexisnexis.com/us/Inacademic/fraqme.do?tokenKey+rsh-2; "Long After We Withdraw," *New York Times* (26 Nov. 2006), pp. E17–18.

34. David Chandler, "The Road to Military Humanism: How the Human Rights NGOs Shaped a New Humanitarian Agenda," *Human Rights Quarterly* 23 (2001), 678–700. Extremely critical of NGOs and other interventions are David Rieff, *A Bed for the Night*, and *At the Point of a Gun*.

35. Rieff, "Moral Blindness: The Case for Darfur," *New Republic* (5 and 15 June 2006), 13-16.

36. The contradictions and problems of this intervention are immense. Some

argue that the Kosovars were guilty of war crimes against Serbs, especially after Milosevic retreated. See Diane Johnstone, *Fool's Crusade: Yugoslavia, NATO and Western Delusions* (New York: Monthly Review Press, 2002); David Rieff, "Lost Kosovo," in *At the Point of a Gun*, 123–139.

37. Wolfowitz, "Statesmanship in the New Century," in *Present Dangers: Crisis and Opportunity in American Foreign Policy*, ed. Robert Kagan and William Kristol (San Francisco: Encounter Books, 2000), 99–110.

38. Kate Zernike, "Some of Intellectual Left's Longtime Doves Taking on Role of Hawks," *New York Times* (14 March 2003), A16.

39. Berman, "Thirteen Observations on a Very Unlucky Predicament," in *The Fight Is for Democracy: Winning the War of Ideas in America and the World*, ed. George Packer (New York: HarperCollins, 2003), 275.

40. Berman, "Resolved: What Lincoln Knew About War," *New Republic* (3 March 2003), 27.

41. On Berman's background, see Stephen Malone, Interview with Berman, "The Real Oppression of Our Time," *New York Press* (11 Jan. 2006): http://nypress.com/print.cfm?content_id+14511; Packer, *Assassin's Gate*, 47–50; Alan Johnson, "An Interview with Paul Berman," *Democratiya* (24 May 2006): http://www.democratiya.com/interview.asp?issueid=5.

42. Berman, *A Tale of Two Utopias: The Political Journey of the Generation of 1968* (New York: W. W. Norton, 1996).

43. Berman, *Power and the Idealists, or the Passion of Joschka Fischer and Its Aftermath* (Brooklyn, N.Y.: Soft Skull Press, 2005).

44. Berman, *Terror and Liberalism* (New York: W. W. Norton, 2003), 24–32, on Camus; *Power and the Idealists*, 169–171, on Arendt and Makiya. Hereafter, citations to *Terror and Liberalism* appear in the text. On Hayden, see George Cotkin, *Existential America* (Baltimore: Johns Hopkins University Press, 2003), 225–251.

45. "Dialogue: Liberal Hawks Reconsider the Iraq War," *Slate* (12 Jan. 2004): http://www.slate.com/id/2093620/entry/2093641/.

46. Berman, "Totalitarianism and the Role of Intellectuals," *Chronicle Review* 49 (9 May 2003), B11.

47. Hitchens, "Taking Sides," reprinted in *Christopher Hitchens and His Critics: Terror, Iraq, and the Left*, ed. Simon Cottee and Thomas Cushman (New York: New York University Press, 2008), 101–104. This volume is excellent for its selection of pieces by Hitchens and for central works by his critics, as well as a reply from Hitchens that demonstrates that he has no doubts that most of his reasons for going to war in Iraq remain valid.

48. Berman, "Totalitarianism and the Role of Intellectuals," B11.

49. Berman, "Commentary: Iraq Was Bungled, but the United States Should Promote Democracy," *Daily Star* (9 May 2008): http://www.dailystar.com.lb/printable.asp?art_ID=91837&cat_ID=5.

50. Berman, "'His Toughness Problem—And Ours': An Exchange," with Ian Buruma, *New York Review of Books* (8 Nov. 2007): http://www.nybooks.com/articles/20801; James Atlas, "What It Takes to Be a Neo-Neoconservative," *New York Times* (19 Oct. 2003), WK12.

51. Especially insightful on the war are Packer, *Assassin's Gate*; Michael R. Gordon and General Bernard E. Trainor, *Cobra II: The Inside Story of the Invasion and Occupation of Iraq* (New York: Pantheon, 2006); Seymour M. Hersh, *Chain of Command: The Road from 9/11 to Abu Ghraib* (New York: HarperCollins, 2004). Also, James Bamford, *A Pretext for War: 9/11, Iraq, and the Abuse of America's Intelligence Agencies* (New York: Doubleday, 2004). Very helpful on how Bremer's dissolution of the Iraqi armed forces and civil service crippled the nation is Ali A. Allawi, *The Occupation of Iraq: Winning the War, Losing the Peace* (New Haven: Yale University Press, 2007), 147–162.

52. These figures come from the Iraqi Body Count Website. http://www.iraqbodycount.org/

53. Thomas Cushman and Adam Michnik, "An Interview with Adam Michnik: Authoritarianism as a Vocation," in *A Matter of Principle: Humanitarian Arguments for War in Iraq*, ed. Thomas Cushman (Berkeley: University of California Press, 2005), 273.

54. Paul Berman and Anatol Lieven, "Anti-Fascist War or Gift to the Terrorists," *Micromega* (Oct., 2004): http://www.carnegieendowment.org/publications/index.cfm?fa=princ. Not all felt comfortable with Berman's regular use of "fascism" as a designation for Saddam and Bin Laden. See Alexander Stille, "The Latest Obscenity Has Seven Letters," *New York Times* (13 Sept. 2003), B9.

55. For a spirited if somewhat disjointed critique of the war hawks, see Stephen Marshall, *Wolves in Sheep's Clothing: The New Liberal Menace in America* (New York: Disinformation, 2007). Also, Anatol Lieven and John Hulsman, *Ethical Realism: A Vision for America's Role in the World* (New York: Pantheon, 2006).

56. Tilly, *Credit and Blame* (Princeton, N.J.: Princeton University Press, 2008). For a strong argument on the importance of blame to moral philosophy, see George Sher, *In Praise of Blame* (Oxford: Oxford University Press, 2006), 93–122. In a similar manner, see P. F. Strawson, "Freedom and Resentment," in *Free Will*, ed. Gary Watson (Oxford: Oxford University Press, 1982).

57. Peter Beinart, *The Good Fight : Why Liberals—and Only Liberals—Can Win the War on Terror and Make America Great Again* (New York : HarperCollins, 2006), xiii. On Beinart, see Kevin Mattson, "Age of Anxiety: The Old Ideas Won't Work in the War on Terror," *Boston Review* (July–Aug. 2006): http://bostonreview.net/BR31.4mattson.html.

58. Beinart, "Partisan Review," *New Republic* (28 June 2004), 6. "The Fighting Democrats: Interview with Peter Beinart," examiner.com: http://www.examiner.com/printa- 124265~The_fighting_Democrats.htm.

59. Dexter Filkins, "Regrets Only," 56; "Overthrowing Iraq Was Right: Interview with Kanan Makiya" (11 Oct. 2006), *Radio Free Europe*: http://rferl.org/featuresarticleprint/2006/10/48fe le5b-f460-4a7.

60. Packer, *Assassin's Gate*, 384. At the outset of hostilities, Packer stated that he had been "barely for the war." David Glenn, "Unfinished Wars," *Columbia Journalism Review* (Sept.–Oct. 2005): http://cjarchives.org/issues/2005/5glenn.asp?

61. Antonio R. Damasio, *Descartes' Error: Emotion, Reason, and the Human Brain* (New York: Grosset/Putnam, 1994).

62. Ignatieff, "The Year of Living Dangerously," *New York Times* (14 March 2004), 13; "Getting Iraq Wrong," *New York Times* (5 Aug. 2007): http://www.nytimes.com2007/08/05/magazine/05iraq-t.html.

63. Editors, "Were We Wrong?" *New Republic* (28 June 2004), 8–9.

64. Friedman, "Why I Still Have Hope: People Power," *New Republic* (28 June 2004), 27.

65. Editors, "Were We Wrong?" 9; Wieseltier, "What Remains: Disillusion and Its Limits," *New Republic* (28 June 2004), 12.

66. Some argue that such was not the case—that the liberal war hawks' position was influenced by their concerns about Israeli security in the Middle East. See Tony Judt, "Bush's Useful Idiots," *London Review of Books* (21 Sept. 2006): http://www.lrb.co.uk/v28/n18/judt01_.html.

67. Filkins, "Regrets Only?" 55.

68. Rieff, *At the Point of a Gun* , 8–9; "Blueprint for a Mess," *New York Times* (2 Nov. 2003), 28.

69. The strongest case for counterfactual thinking is in Niall Ferguson, ed., *Virtual History: Alternatives and Counterfactuals* (New York: Basic Books, 1999). Also, *What Ifs? of American History*, ed. Robert Cowley (New York: G. P. Putnam's Sons, 2003).

70. The situational aspects of ethical actions, based on examples from experimental psychology, are discussed in Kwame Anthony Appiah, *Experiments in Ethics* (Cambridge, Mass.: Harvard University Press, 2008), 33f; Richard H. Thaler and Cass R. Sunstein, *Nudge: Improving Decisions About Health, Wealth, and Happiness* (New Haven: Yale University Press, 2008).

71. Walzer, "Five on Iraq," in *Arguing About War* (New Haven: Yale University Press, 2004), 149.

72. Kant, *Groundwork of the Metaphysics of Morals*, trans. Mary Gregor (Cambridge: Cambridge University Press, 1997), 37.

Conclusion
Torture and the Tortured

1. "The United States in the World—Just Wars and Just Societies: An Interview with Michael Walzer," *Imprints: A Journal of Analytical Socialism* (2003): http://eis.bris.ac.uk/~plcdib/imprints/michaelwalzerinterview.html.

2. Back cover comment, Niebuhr, *The Irony of American History* (Chicago: University of Chicago Press, 2008). Also, on Niebuhr's return to prominence, see Brian Urquhart, "What You Can Learn from Reinhold Niebuhr," *New York Review of Books* (26 March 2009), 22–24. Also, John Patrick Diggins, "The Decline of Presidential Ethics," *Chronicle Review* (7 Nov. 2008), B8–11.

3. Hugo Slim, *Killing Civilians: Method, Madness, and Morality in War* (New York: Columbia University Press, 2008).

4. Dershowitz, *Why Terrorism Works: Understanding the Threat, Responding to the Challenge* (New Haven, Conn.: Yale University Press, 2002), 131–164; Der-

showitz, "Tortured Reasoning," in *Torture: A Collection,* ed. Sanford Levinson (New York: Oxford University Press, 2004), esp. 266–267. Elaine Scarry offers a strong critique of Dershowitz in Levinson's edited volume, in "Five Errors in the Reasoning of Alan Dershowitz," 281–290. For Scarry's powerful argument against torture in general, see *The Body in Pain: The Making and the Unmaking of the World* (New York: Oxford University Press, 1985). For another excellent refutation of Dershowitz, along with a history of American torture practices since World War II, see Alfred W. McCoy, *A Question of Torture: CIA Interrogation, from the Cold War to the War on Terror* (New York: Metropolitan Books, 2006), esp. 110–113. On the torture at Abu Ghraib, see Philippe Sands, *Torture Team: Rumsfeld's Memo and the Betrayal of American Values* (New York: Palgrave Macmillan, 2008); Philip Gourevitch and Errol Morris, *Standard Operating Procedure* (New York: Penguin, 2008).

5. A recent paper addresses in a useful fashion the value of "moral principles," in contrast to moral laws, as a way of clarifying issues; see Luke Robinson, "Moral Principles Are Not Moral Laws," *Journal of Ethics and Social Philosophy* 2 (Nov. 2008), 1–22.

6. The South African Truth and Reconciliation Commission appears as a valuable way of approaching such concerns. See Martha Minow, *Between Vengeance and Forgiveness: Facing History After Genocide and Mass Violence* (Boston: Beacon Press, 1998).

Index

Acknowledgments

I could not have written this book without the support of many friends and colleagues. Casey Nelson Blake, Ray Haberski, James Hoopes, Nelson Lichtenstein, Kevin Mattson, and Ann Schofield read many chapters and drafts. They exulted in my highs and commiserated with me in my lows. I cherish their emails and friendship. Many others have helped me with their observations, good cheer, and asides. I am indebted to the late Hazel E. Barnes, Tim Becher, Lloyd Beecher, Thomas Bender, Kendra Boileau, Eileen Boris, Paul S. Boyer, Howard Brick, Ron Bush, Charles Capper, Simon Evnine, Mary Kay Harrington, Melody Herr, Larry Inchausti, Neil Jumonville, Bruce Kuklick, Ralph Leck, Steven Marx, Michael McCormick, Paul Miklowitz, Lewis Perry, Giovanna Pompele, Maria Quintana, Jennifer Ratner-Rosenhagen, Joan Shelley Rubin, Robert Rydell, David Stiegerwald, Stephen Tootle, Jeffrey Ward Larsen, Daniel Wickberg, and Martin Woessner. Comments from my fine colleagues in the Department of History at Cal Poly, insights from audiences at lectures at the Ohio State University and Cal Poly, and from discussions with my students in History 304 and 505 have helped greatly. My appreciation to Linda Halisky, Dean of the College of Liberal Arts at Cal Poly, for a one-course teaching reduction at an opportune moment. Some of the initial ideas for this book were presented in *Journal of the History of Ideas;* I thank Martin Burke for his comments, and I am grateful for the insights from the symposium on my piece. A portion of Chapter 2 appeared in *Modern Intellectual History,* and I thank Charles Capper for all his help with it.

I have benefited from the assistance of archivists at the Butler Library at Columbia University (for the John Howard Griffin Papers), the New York Public Library (the New Yorker Magazine Archive), and Pusey Library at Harvard University (the James Conant Presidential Papers). Online access to the Hannah Arendt Papers, the National Security Administration Archive, and collections relating to the My Lai Massacre has been invaluable. So, too, was the microfilm edition of the Henry L. Stimson Papers at Yale University. Cal Poly's interlibrary loan has been critical to my research; thank you Janice Stone and Linda Hauck.

I thank my agent, John Thornton, for his encouragement and efforts on behalf of this project. Robert Lockhart, my editor, has been consistently enthusiastic and helpful. My copyeditor Mindy Brown and Penn Press project editor Noreen O'Connor-Abel have been superlative, helping my manuscript in a multitude of ways.

This book deals with many sobering and perplexing events. I often found myself lost in a fog of sadness and uncertainty. That fog was dissipated by my friends and my wife, Marta Peluso, and my father, Morris Cotkin. Marta has been with me through all of my books, and she has supported me with her enthusiasm and good cheer. My ninety-five-year-old father has been the longest presence in my life. I bask in his good humor, good will, and engagement with life.